AEROFILMS GUIDE

FOOTBALL GROUNDS

TWELFTH REVISED EDITION

AEROFILMS GUIDE

FOOTBALL GROUNDS

TWELFTH REVISED EDITION

CONTENTS

CONTENTS

Front cover: **The largest new club ground to be constructed in recent years was the City of Manchester Stadium, the new home of Manchester City. Even its capacity will soon be overtaken as further new grounds — such as Arsenal's new stadium — are developed.**

Preceding pages: **After years of controversy, Wimbledon — now known as Milton Keynes Dons — have finally relocated to the National Hockey Stadium, where temporary stands have been constructed. This, however, is only a short-term measure whilst the club looks to construct a new stadium in the city. One of the grounds to have witnessed a major change over the past season is Carrow Road, home of the Premiership new boys Norwich City. Such is the pace, however, of modern developments — and the potential increase in gates as a result of promotion — that further expansion is already in hand.**

First published in 1993;

Reprinted 1993 (twice); Second edition 1994; Third edition 1995; Fourth edition 1996; Fifth edition 1997; Sixth edition 1998; Seventh edition 1999; Eighth edition 2000; Ninth edition 2001; tenth edition 2002; 11th edition 2003, reprinted 2003.
12th edition 2004.

ISBN 0 7110 3011 1

Published by Ian Allan Publishing
an imprint of Ian Allan Publishing Ltd, Hersham, Surrey KT12 4RG.
Printed and bound in Scotland

Code: 0408/E2

Aerofilms Limited have been specialists in aerial photography since 1919. Their library of aerial photographs, both new and old, is in excess of 1.5 million images. Aerofilms undertake to commission oblique and vertical survey aerial photography, which is processed and printed in their specialised photographic laboratory. Digital photomaps are prepared using precision scanners.

Free photostatic proofs are available on request for any site held within the collection and price lists will be forwarded detailing the size of photographic enlargement available without any obligation to purchase.

Introduction

Welcome to the 12th edition of *Aerofilms Guide: Football Grounds*. Since the book was first published more than a decade ago, the face of football in England and Wales has been transformed. Almost a quarter of the clubs in the Premiership or Football League have either moved to new grounds or are actively pursuing relocation over the next few seasons and, of the clubs that have remained in their traditional homes, the vast majority have undertaken significant upgrades since the early 1990s.

Unusually, for the start of the 2004/05 season there are no wholly new grounds to record, although there are a number of clubs — such as Coventry City — for which, if all goes according to plan, the new season will be their last in the current homes. In terms of promotion from the Conference, we welcome back two old League teams — Chester City and Shrewsbury Town — the former already playing at a relatively new ground, whilst the latter is actively seeking to relocate.

The interest in football as a spectator sport seems to show no sign of abating, with crowds continuing to grow at all levels of the game. However, the financial status of a number of clubs remains parlous. Bradford City, for example, came within hours of closing during the close season whilst neighbours Leeds United are now selling the freehold of Elland Road as part of a strategy to restore the club's battered finances. Whilst no League team has succumbed since the loss of Maidstone United in the early 1990s, sooner or later a League team will probably succumb. The demise of Conference outfit Telford United during the close season comes as a stark warning to all 92 teams in the Premiership and Football League.

As always, the start of the season brings great optimism: relegated teams, for example, hope that their fortunes will improve and promoted teams that they can prosper at a higher level. Unfortunately, there will always be winners and losers; we hope that your team, whatever it is, falls into the former category.

Aerofilms

Aerofilms was founded in 1919 and has specialised in the acquisition of aerial photography within the United Kingdom throughout its history. The company has a record of being innovative in the uses and applications of aerial photography.

Photographs looking at the environment in perspective are called oblique aerial photographs. These are taken with Hasselblad cameras by professional photographers experienced in the difficult conditions encountered in aerial work.

Photographs taken straight down at the landscape are termed vertical aerial photographs. These photographs are obtained using Leica survey cameras, the products from which are normally used in the making of maps.

Aerofilms has a unique library of oblique and vertical photographs in excess of one and a half million in number covering the United Kingdom. This library of photographs dates from 1919 to the present day and is being continually updated.

Oblique and vertical photography can be taken to customers' specification by Aerofilms' professional photographers.

To discover more of the wealth of past or present photographs held in the library at Aerofilms or to commission new aerial photographs, please contact:

Simmons Aerofilms, 32-34 Station Close, Potters Bar, Herts EN6 1TL.
Telephone: 01707 648390 Fax: 01707 648399
Web-site: www.simmonsaerofilms.com E-mail: info@aerofilms.com

Disabled Facilities

We endeavour to list the facilities for disabled spectators at each ground. Readers will appreciate that these facilities can vary in number and quality and that, for most clubs, pre-booking is essential. Some clubs also have dedicated parking for disabled spectators; this again should be pre-booked if available.

MILLENNIUM STADIUM

Westgate Street, Cardiff CF10 1JA

Tel No: 0870 013 8600
Fax: 029 2023 2678
Stadium Tours: 02920 822228
Web Site: www.millenniumstadium-sportcentric.com
E-Mail: info@cardiff-stadium.co.uk
Brief History: The stadium, built upon the site of the much-loved and historic Cardiff Arms Park, was opened in 2000 and cost in excess of £100 million (a tiny sum in comparison with the current forecast spend — if it happens — of over £600 million on the redevelopment of Wembley). As the national stadium for Wales, the ground will be primarily used in sporting terms by Rugby Union, but will be used by the FA to host major fixtures (such as FA Cup and Carling Cup finals) until, in theory, 2006 when the new Wembley is scheduled for completion.
(Total) Current Capacity: 72,500
Nearest Railway Station: Cardiff Central
Parking (Car): Street parking only.
Parking (Coach/Bus): As directed by the police
Police Force and Tel No: South Wales (029 2022 2111)
Disabled Visitors' Facilities:
Wheelchairs: c250 designated seats. The whole stadium has been designed for ease of disabled access with lifts, etc.
Blind: Commentary available.
Anticipated Development(s): None planned

KEY
Office address:
Millennium Stadium plc,
First Floor, Golate House,
101 St Mary Street,
Cardiff CF10 1GE

⬆ North direction (approx)

❶ Cardiff Central station
❷ Bus station
❸ River Taff
❹ Castle Street
❺ Westgate Street
❻ Wood Street
❼ Tudor Street
❽ High Street
❾ St Mary Street
❿ To Cardiff Queen Street station

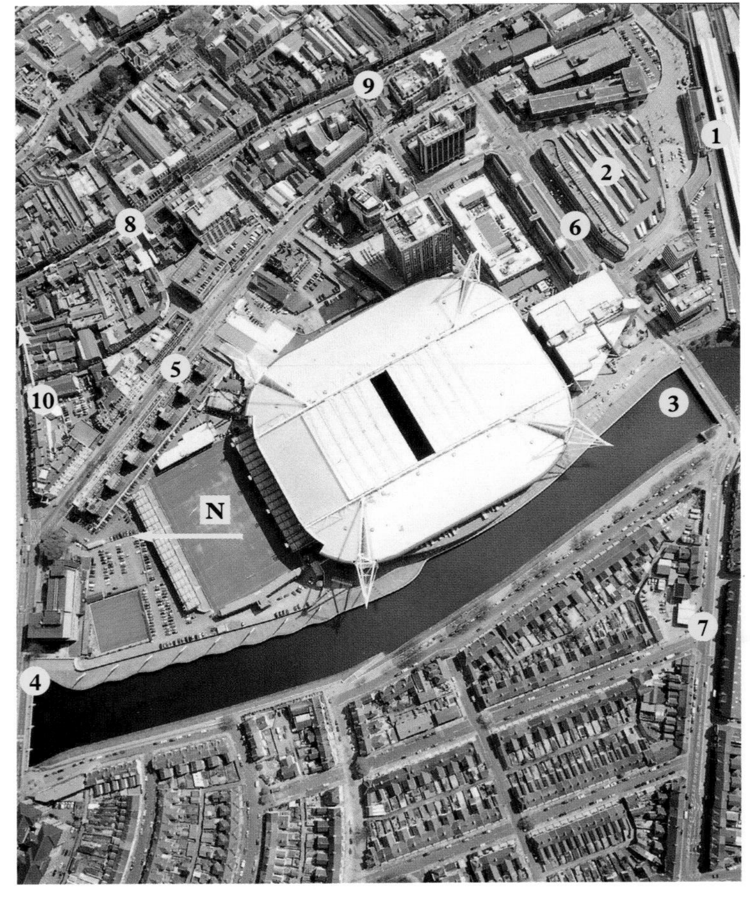

Above: 688019; *Right:* 687998

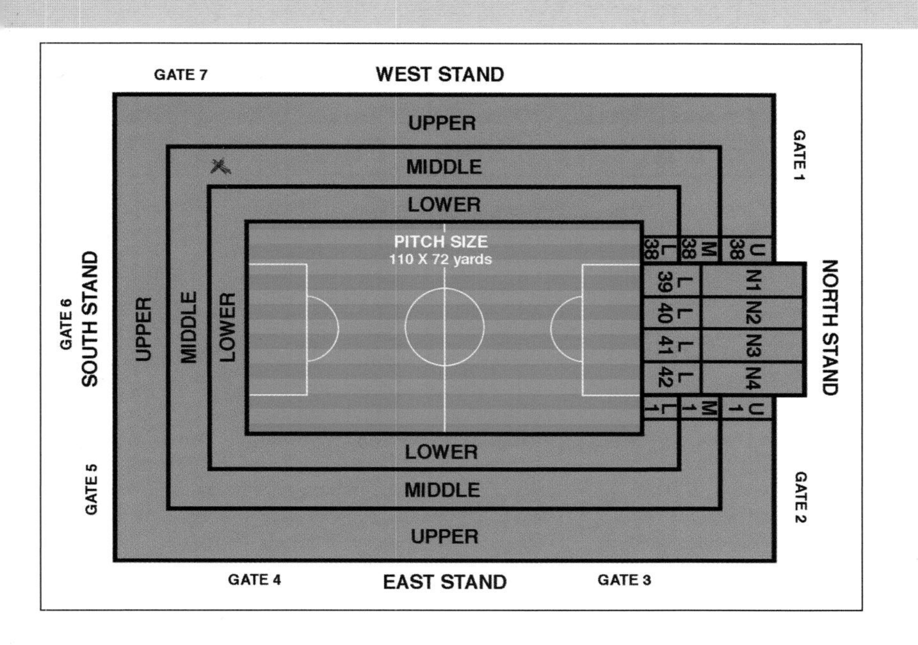
GATE 7
WEST STAND
UPPER
MIDDLE
LOWER
PITCH SIZE
110 X 72 yards
GATE 1
U 38
M 38
L 38
L 39
L 40
L 41
L 42
N1
N2
N3
N4
L 1
M 1
U 1
NORTH STAND
GATE 6
SOUTH STAND
UPPER
MIDDLE
LOWER
LOWER
MIDDLE
UPPER
GATE 5
GATE 2
GATE 4
EAST STAND
GATE 3

ARSENAL

Arsenal Stadium, Avenell Road, Highbury, London, N5 1BU

Tel No: 020 7704 4000
Advance Tickets Tel No: 020 7704 4040
Fax: 020 7704 4001
Web Site: www.arsenal.com
E-Mail: info@arsenal.co.uk
League: F.A. Premier
Brief History: Founded 1886 as Royal Arsenal, changed to Woolwich Arsenal in 1891, and Arsenal in 1914. Former grounds: Plumstead Common, Sportsman Ground, Manor Ground (twice), moved to Arsenal Stadium (Highbury) in 1913. Record attendance 73,295
(Total) Current Capacity: 38,548 (all seated)
Visiting Supporters' Allocation: 2,900 (all seated Clock End and Lower Tier West Stand)
Club Colours: Red shirts with white sleeves, white shorts
Nearest Railway Station: Drayton Park or Finsbury Park (main line). Arsenal (tube)
Parking (Car): Street Parking
Parking (Coach/Bus): Drayton Park
Police Force and Tel No: Metropolitan (020 7263 9090)
Disabled Visitors' Facilities:
Wheelchairs: Lower tier East Stand
Blind: Commentary available
Anticipated Development(s): The club is moving forward with the development of the new 60,000-seat £350 million stadium at Ashburton Grove and plans to start the 2006/07 season at the new ground. Once the team moves from Highbury the existing ground will be redeveloped, although this work will incorporate the listed East and West stands.

KEY

- **C** Club Offices
- **S** Club Shop
- **E** Entrance(s) for visiting supporters

⬆ North direction (approx)

1. Avenell Road
2. Highbury Hill
3. Gillespie Road
4. To Drayton Park BR Station (1/4 mile)
5. Arsenal Tube Station
6. Clock End
7. St Thomas's Road (to Finsbury Park station)
8. North Bank
9. West Stand
10. East Stand

Above: 688318; *Right:* 688311

Whilst it may churlish to comment that winning the Premiership title again could be considered a disappointment, given that Arsenal were chasing both the FA Cup and Champions League until the Semi-Finals of the former and the Quarter-Finals of the latter, Arsene Wenger's team dominated the championship from start to finish and wrapped up their second title in three years at Easter, without losing a game. However, the continuing lack of European success means that comparisons between the Gunners and other great English-based teams are not favourable. Nonetheless, whilst Arsenal can call on players with the talent of Henry, Vieira and Pires, then the club will continue to be a major threat in all competitions. Ironically, for a team that boasted David Seaman as keeper for many years, it is only in the goalkeeping area, where Lehrmann's temperament seems suspect, that Arsenal appear to have a significant weakness. With Wenger tied to the club until the completion of the new stadium and with the solid basis of the championship-winning team of 2004 still in place, it is hard to see Arsenal failing to retain their title considering that Man Utd are in transition and Chelsea still fickle. The major challenge for the team, however, is to see their domestic dominance translated into European success. Again, one suspects, the Champions League will be an unrealistic dream.

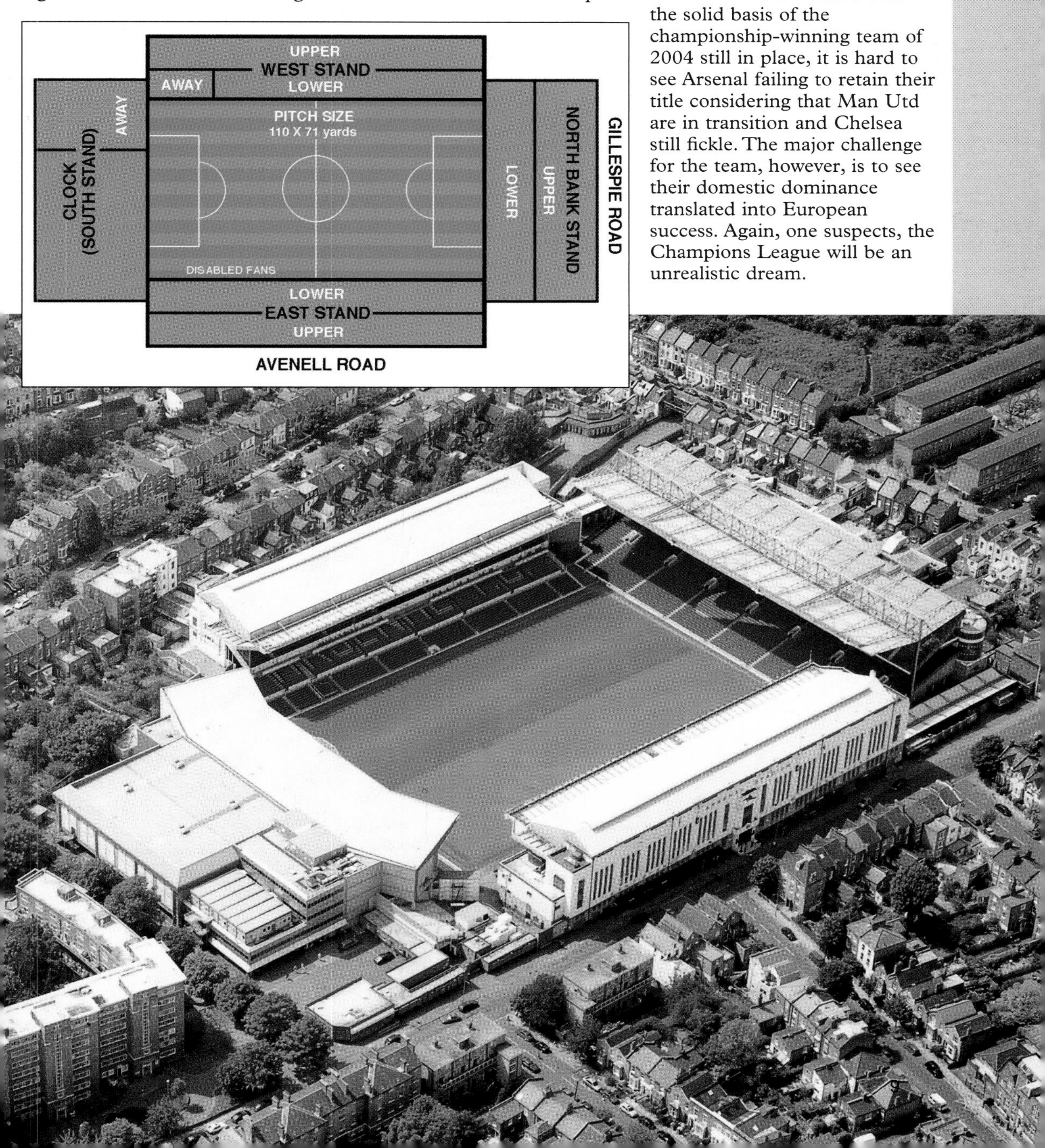

ASTON VILLA

Villa Park, Trinity Road, Birmingham, B6 6HE

Tel No: 0121 327 2299
Advance Tickets Tel No: 0121 327 5353
Fax: 0121 322 2107
Web Site: www.avfc.premiumtv.co.uk
E-Mail: commercial.dept@astonvilla-fc.co.uk
League: F.A. Premier
Brief History: Founded in 1874. Founder Members Football League (1888). Former Grounds: Aston Park and Lower Aston Grounds and Perry Barr, moved to Villa Park (a development of the Lower Aston Grounds) in 1897. Record attendance 76,588
(Total) Current Capacity: 42,584 (all seated)
Visiting Supporters' Allocation: Approx 2,983 in North Stand
Club Colours: Claret with blue stripe shirts, white shorts
Nearest Railway Station: Witton
Parking (Car): Asda car park, Aston Hall Road
Parking (Coach/Bus): Asda car park, Aston Hall Road (special coach park for visiting supporters situated in Witton Lane)
Police Force and Tel No: West Midlands (0121 322 6010)
Disabled Visitors' Facilities:
Wheelchairs: Trinity Road Stand section
Blind: Commentary by arrangement
Anticipated Development(s): In order to increase the ground's capacity to 51,000 Planning Permission has been obtained to extend the North Stand with two corner in-fills. There is, however, no confirmed timescale for the work to be completed.

KEY

- **C** Club Offices
- **S** Club Shop
- **E** Entrance(s) for visiting supporters
- **R** Refreshment bars for visiting supporters
- **T** Toilets for visiting supporters

⬆ North direction (approx)

1. B4137 Witton Lane
2. B4140 Witton Road
3. Trinity Road
4. To A4040 Aston Lane to A34 Walsall Road
5. To Aston Expressway & M6
6. Holte End
7. Visitors' Car Park
8. Witton railway station
9. North Stand
10. Trinity Road Stand

Above: 697435; *Right:* 697425

Something of a curate's egg season for Villa, with the team in the relegation zone in the autumn and then challenging for a Champions League position come May. Unfortunately, however, come the conclusion of the campaign, David O'Leary's team finished in sixth position, thereby missing out on both the Champions League and UEFA Cup. On the other hand, if you'd asked the Villa Park faithful in October whether they would have been happy with a top six finish, they would have stared at you in amazement as the team's performances up to that point had suggested that Rotherham was a more likely fixture in 2004/05. It clearly took O'Leary some time to settle in at Villa but the performances of the team – despite the end of season disappointment — during the second half of the campaign would indicate that, provided that he can keep the basis of the team together and add to it judiciously, Villa will be a force to be reckoned with in 2004/05. Whilst it's difficult to see any team threatening the Man U, Chelsea and Arsenal triumvirate at the top, Villa certainly has the potential to be the top of the chasing group. It could be an interesting year in the Midlands in 2004/05!

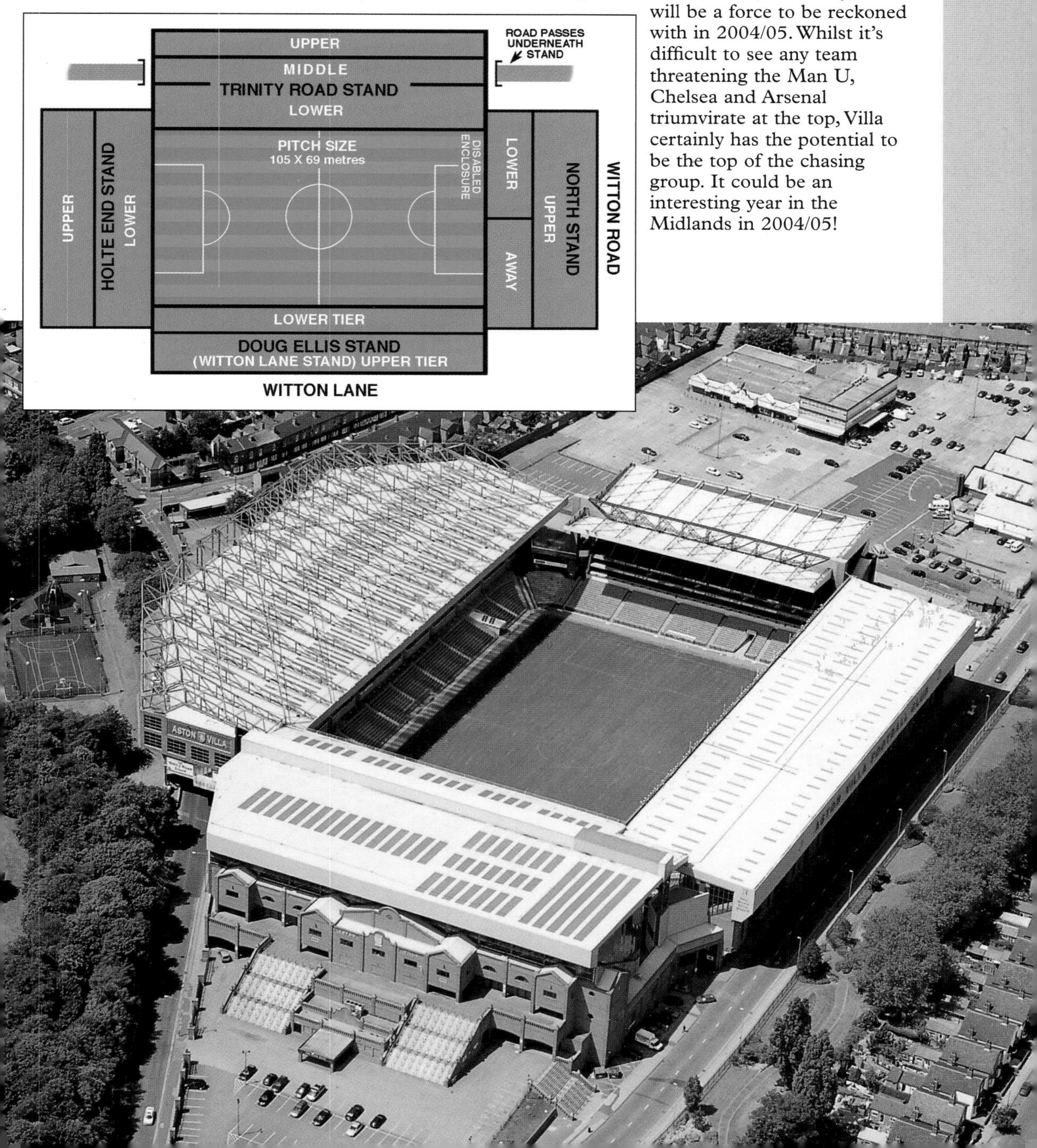

BARNSLEY

Oakwell Stadium, Grove Street, Barnsley, S71 1ET

Tel No: 01226 211211
Advance Tickets Tel No: 01226 211211
Fax: 01226 211444
Web Site: www.barnsleyfc.premiumtv.co.uk
E-mail: thereds@barnsleyfc.co.uk
League: League One
Brief History: Founded in 1887 as Barnsley St Peter's, changed name to Barnsley in 1897. Former Ground: Doncaster Road, Worsboro Bridge until 1888. Record attendance 40,255
(Total) Current Capacity: 23,186 (all seated)
Visiting Supporters' Allocation: 6,000 maximum (all seated; North Stand)
Club Colours: Red shirts, white shorts
Nearest Railway Station: Barnsley
Parking (Car): Queen's Ground car park
Parking (Coach/Bus): Queen's Ground car park
Police Force and Tel No: South Yorkshire (01266 206161)
Disabled Visitors' Facilities:
Wheelchairs: Purpose Built Disabled Stand
Blind: Commentary available
Future Development(s): With the completion of the new North Stand with its 6,000 capacity, the next phase for the redevelopment of Oakwell will feature the old West Stand with its remaining open seating. There is, however, no timescale for this work.

KEY

C Club Offices
S Club Shop
E Entrance(s) for visiting supporters

⬆ North direction (approx)

❶ A628 Pontefract Road
❷ To Barnsley Exchange BR station and M1 Junction 37 (two miles)
❸ Queen's Ground Car Park
❹ North Stand
❺ Grove Street
❻ To Town Centre

Above: 697496; *Right:* 697497

In early March, with the team having gained only eight points from a possible 33 since Christmas, Gudjon Thordarson was sacked. The club moved quickly to appoint a new boss, with ex-Nottingham Forest manager Paul Hart quickly finding new employment. Under Hart, Barnsley achieved a position of mid-table security, in 12th place equidistant in points between the relegation zone and the Play-Offs. Now under new ownership, with ex-Leeds supreme Peter Ridsdale in the chair, Barnsley are one of a number of ex-Premiership teams in League One that aspire to higher things. Hart's experience at Forest should be able to inspire the team to greater things in 2004/05.

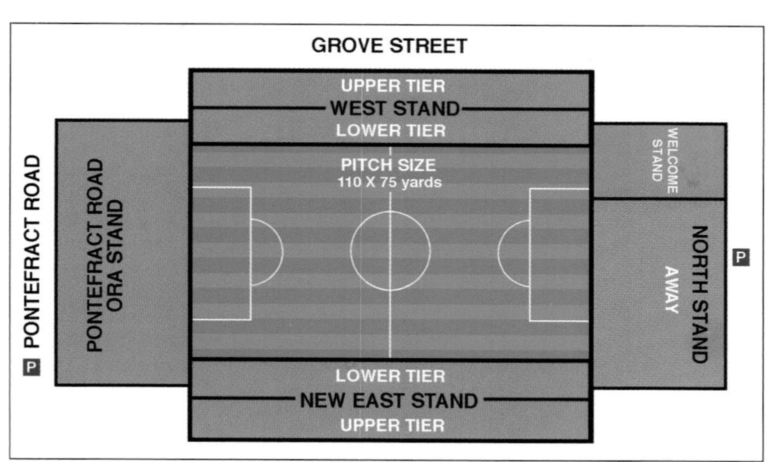

BIRMINGHAM CITY

St Andrew's Stadium, St Andrew's Street, Birmingham, B9 4NH

Tel No: 0121 772 0101
Advance Tickets Tel No: 0121 202 5333
Fax: 0121 766 7866
Web Site: www.bcfc.premiumtv.co.uk
E-Mail: reception@bcfc.com
League: FA Premiership
Brief History: Founded 1875, as Small Heath Alliance. Changed to Small Heath in 1888, Birmingham in 1905, Birmingham City in 1945. Former Grounds: Arthur Street, Ladypool Road, Muntz Street, moved to St Andrew's in 1906. Record attendance 68,844
(Total) Current Capacity: 29,796 (all seated)
Visiting Supporters' Allocation: 1-4,500 in new Railway End (Lower Tier)
Club Colours: Blue shirts, white shorts
Nearest Railway Station: Birmingham New Street
Parking (Car): Street parking
Parking (Coach/Bus): Coventry Road
Police Force and Tel No: West Midlands (0121 772 1169)
Disabled Visitors' Facilities:
Wheelchairs: 90 places; advanced notice required
Blind: Commentary available
Future Development(s): There are long term plans, in conjunction with the City Council, for the possible construction of a new 60,000-seat stadium to be shared with Warwickshire CCC at Digbeth. However, this is still at a very tentative stage and the club, in the short to medium term, intends to expand St Andrews with the next phase of the redevelopment of the ground being the rebuilding of the Main Stand, possibly in 2007, taking the ground's capacity to some 36,500.

KEY

- **C** Club Offices
- **S** Club Shop
- **E** Entrance(s) for visiting supporters
- ⬆ North direction (approx)

1. Car Park
2. B4128 Cattell Road
3. Tilton Road
4. Garrison Lane
5. To A4540 & A38 (M)
6. To City Centre and New Street BR Station (1½ miles)
7. Railway End
8. Tilton Road End
9. Main Stand
10. Kop Stand
11. Emmeline Street
12. Kingston Road
13. St Andrew's Street

Above: 679483; *Right:* 679479

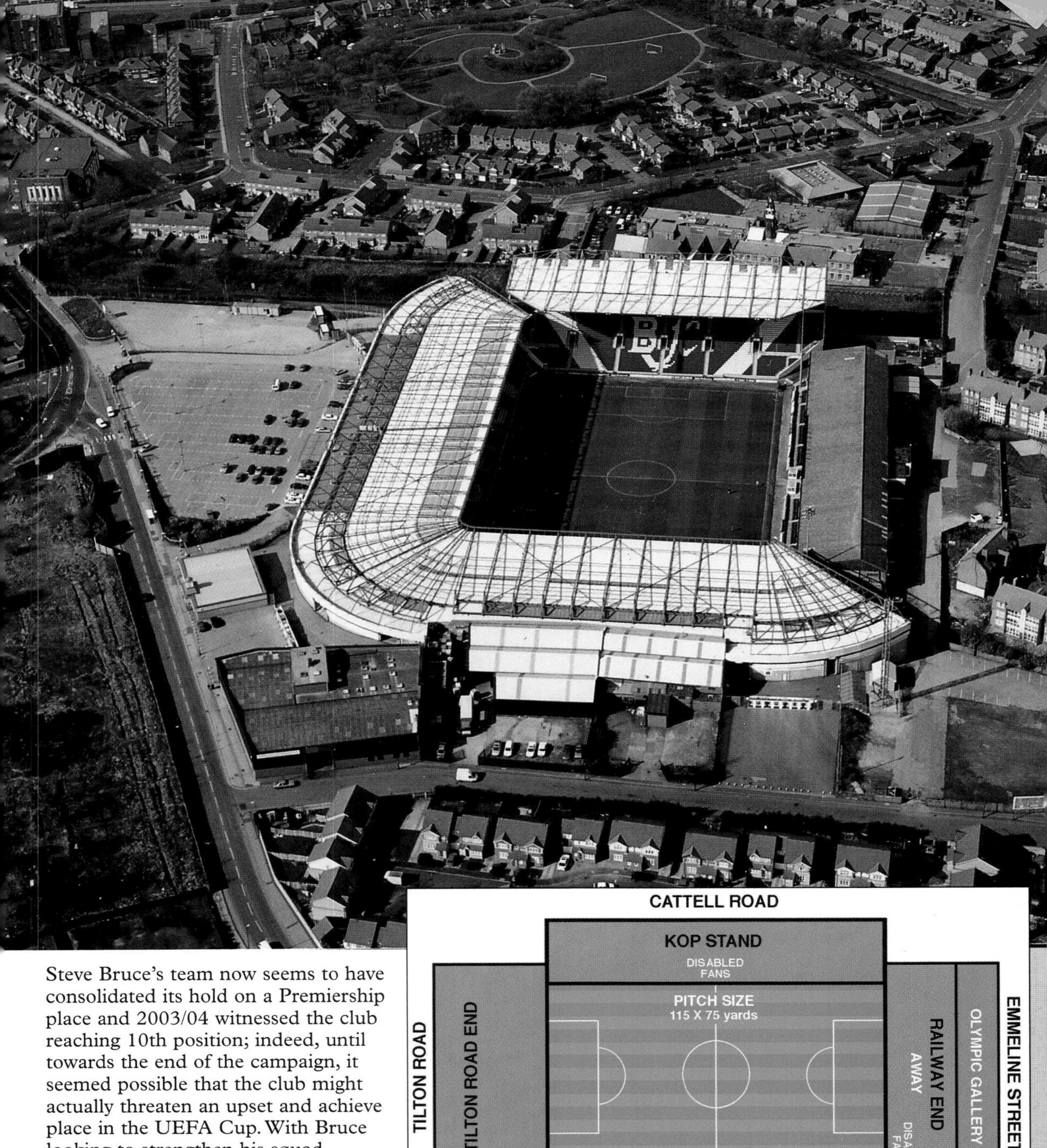

Steve Bruce's team now seems to have consolidated its hold on a Premiership place and 2003/04 witnessed the club reaching 10th position; indeed, until towards the end of the campaign, it seemed possible that the club might actually threaten an upset and achieve place in the UEFA Cup. With Bruce looking to strengthen his squad during the close season and with the three teams being promoted from the First Division looking the most likely candidates for the relegation zone, City should be capable of again consolidating in the Premiership — never good enough, perhaps, to make the top four or five teams worry about their position but certainly good enough to hold their own in the chasing pack.

BLACKBURN ROVERS

Ewood Park, Blackburn, Lancashire, BB2 4JF

Tel No: 01254 698888; 08701 113232
Advance Tickets Tel No: 01254 671666; 08701 12345
Fax: 01254 671042
Web Site: www.rovers.co.uk
E-Mail: commercial@rovers.premiumtv.co.uk
League: FA Premier
Brief History: Founded 1875. Former Grounds: Oozebooth, Pleasington Cricket Ground, Alexandra Meadows. Moved to Ewood Park in 1890. Founder members of Football League (1888). Record attendance 61,783
(Total) Current Capacity: 31,367 (all seated)
Visiting Supporters' Allocation: 3,914 at the Darwen End
Club Colours: Blue and white halved shirts, white shorts
Nearest Railway Station: Blackburn
Parking (Car): Street parking and c800 spaces at ground
Parking (Coach/Bus): As directed by Police
Police Force and Tel No: Lancashire (01254 51212)
Disabled Visitors' Facilities:
Wheelchairs: All sides of the ground
Blind: Commentary available
Anticipated Development(s): There remain plans to redevelop the Riverside (Walker Steel) Stand to take Ewood Park's capacity to c40,000, but there is no confirmation as to if and when this work will be undertaken.

KEY

- **C** Club Offices
- **S** Club Shop
- **E** Entrance(s) for visiting supporters
- **R** Refreshment bars for visiting supporters
- **T** Toilets for visiting supporters

⬆ North direction (approx)

1. A666 Bolton Road
2. Kidder Street
3. Nuttall Street
4. Town Centre & Blackburn Central BR station (1½ miles)
5. To Darwen and Bolton
6. Darwen End
7. Car Parks
8. Top O'Croft Road

Above: 692620; *Right:* 692614

From aspiring conquerors of Europe, courtesy of a UEFA Cup spot, to potential relegation candidates towards the end of the season, Graeme Souness's Rovers at one stage appeared to have only one destination — the First Division — as the team's form took an alarming dip. Seemingly incapable of winning at home, the team ultimately achieved safety largely as the result of the goal-scoring prowess of new signing Jon Stead, whose arrival from Huddersfield Town in the January transfer window was perhaps one of the inspired moves of the season. Towards the close of the campaign, a 1-0 home victory over Manchester United was a result to savour but things will need to improve significantly at Ewood Park if the club isn't to face another season towards the wrong end of the table.

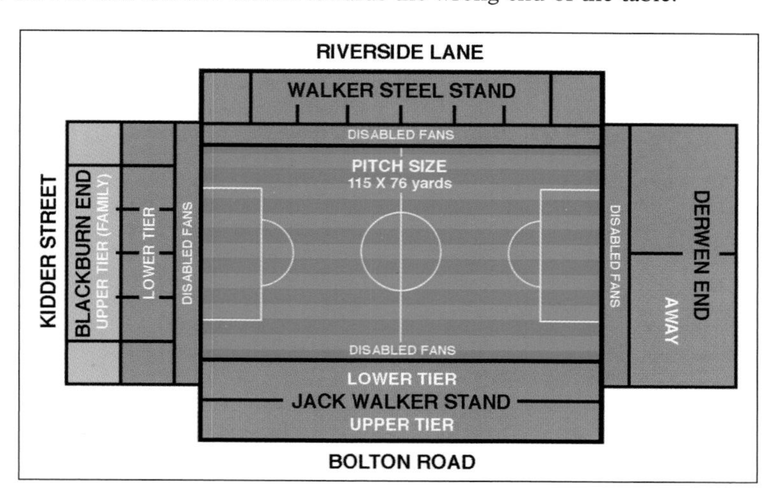

BLACKPOOL

Bloomfield Road, Blackpool, Lancashire, FY1 6JJ

Tel No: 0870 443 1953
Advance Tickets Tel No: 0870 443 1953
Fax: 01253 405011
E-Mail: info@blackpoolfc.co.uk
Web Site: www.blackpoolfcpremiumtv.co.uk
League: League One
Brief History: Founded 1887, merged with 'South Shore' (1899). Former grounds: Raikes Hall (twice) and Athletic Grounds, Stanley Park, South Shore played at Cow Cap Lane, moved to Bloomfield Road in 1899. Record attendance 38,098
(Total) Current Capacity: 11,295 (all seated)
Visiting Supporters' Allocation: 1,700 (all seated) in East Stand (open)
Club Colours: Tangerine shirts, white shorts
Nearest Railway Station: Blackpool South
Parking (Car): At Ground and street parking (also behind West Stand – from M55)
Parking (Coach/Bus): Mecca car park (behind North End (also behind West Stand – from M55)
Police Force and Tel No: Lancashire (01253 293933)
Disabled Visitors' Facilities:
Wheelchairs: North and West stands
Blind: Commentary available (limited numbers)
Anticipated Development(s): The old South Stand and East Paddock have now been demolished and the latter has been replaced by a new temporary open stand seating 1,700 and currently used by away fans. The next phase of the redevelopment of Bloomfield Road will be the construction of a new South Stand to be followed by a permanent new East Stand, ultimately taking the ground's capacity to 16,000 all-seated. There is, however, no confirmed timescale for this new work.

KEY

⬆ North direction (approx)

1. Car Park
2. To Blackpool South BR Station (1½ miles) and M55 Junction 4
3. Bloomfield Road
4. Central Drive
5. Henry Street
6. East Stand (away)
7. Site of South Stand
8. West Stand
9. North Stand

Above: 697000; *Right:* 697007

In early May, just before the final game of the season, it was announced that Steve McMahon had departed from the club by mutual agreement. Whilst the club had regained the LDV Trophy, defeating Southend United 2-0 in the final at the Millennium Stadium, it was again a season of disappointment in the League, with a mid-table position secured once more. The new manager, Colin Hendry (appointed in early June), will inherit a club that has the potential to do considerably better and, looking at the calibre of the new entrants to the League One this season, it may well be that 2004/05 represents a real opportunity for Blackpool to achieve a minimum of the Play-Offs.

P
WEST STAND
PITCH SIZE
112 X 74 yards
BLOOMFIELD ROAD
NORTH STAND
EAST STAND (OPEN)
AWAY
BACK HENRY STREET

BOLTON WANDERERS

Reebok Stadium, Burnden Way, Lostock, Bolton, BL6 6JW

Tel No: 01204 673673
Advance Tickets Tel No: 0871 871 2932
Fax: 01204 673773
E-Mail: reception@bwfc.co.uk
Web Site: www.bwfc.premiumtv.co.uk
League: FA Premiership
Brief History: Founded 1874 as Christ Church; name changed 1877. Former grounds: Several Fields, Pikes Lane (1880-95) and Burnden Park (1895-1997). Moved to Reebok Stadium for 1997/98 season. Record attendance (Burnden Park): 69,912. Record attendance of 28,353 at Reebok Stadium
(Total) Current Capacity: 27,723 (all-seater)
Visiting Supporters' Allocation: 5,200 (South Stand)
Club Colours: White shirts, blue shorts
Nearest Railway Station: Horwich Parkway
Parking (Car): 2,800 places at ground with up 3,000 others in proximity
Parking (Coach/Bus): As directed
Police Force and Tel No: Greater Manchester (01204 522466)
Disabled Visitors' Facilities:
Wheelchairs: c100 places around the ground
Blind: Commentary available
Anticipated Developments(s): The station at Horwich Parkway has now opened. There are currently no further plans for the development of the Reebok Stadium.

KEY

⬆ North direction (approx)

1. Junction 6 of M61
2. A6027 Horwich link road
3. South Stand (away)
4. North Stand
5. Nat Lofthouse Stand
6. West Stand
7. M61 northbound to M6 and Preston (at J6)
8. M61 southbound to Manchester (at J6)
9. To Horwich and Bolton
10. To Lostock Junction BR station
11. Horwich Parkway station

Above: 688307; *Right:* 688303

Something was missing from the Reebok Stadium in 2003/04 — the annual battle against relegation. Indeed, by finishing in eighth position, Wanderers have achieved their best finish in their Premiership career — in fact their best finishing position for more than four decades. Moreover, although the season ended trophy-less, the club was also to feature in the final of the Carling Cup at the Millennium Stadium, albeit defeated by Middlesbrough 2-1; less positive, however, was the 2-1 home defeat by Second Division Tranmere Rovers in the FA Cup Third Round replay. With Sam Allardyce's continuing ability to attract top class players to the stadium, Bolton seem to have established themselves in the Premiership and 2004/05 should again see the team continue as one of the teams chasing a top-half finish.

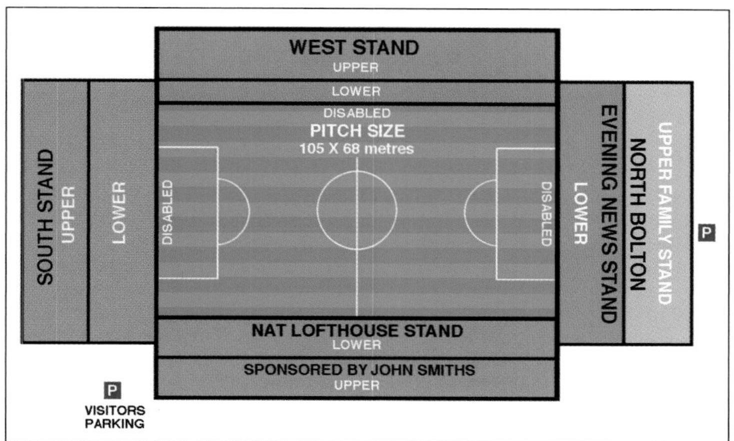

BOSTON UNITED

York Street, Boston, Lincolnshire PE21 6JN

Club Offices: 14-16 Spain Place, Boston, Lincolnshire PE21 6HN
Tel No: 01205 364406
Advance Tickets Tel No: 01205 364406
Fax: 01205 354063
Web Site: www.bostonunited.co.uk
E-mail: jan.mclucas1@playing4success.org.uk
League: League Two
Brief History: Boston Town was established in the 1880s and commenced playing at York Street. The club dropped the 'Town' suffix after World War 1 and re-formed as Boston United in 1934. The team won the Conference title in 1977 but was not allowed into the league due to the standard of the ground. The title was won again in 2002 and the club entered the Nationwide League at the start of the 2002/03 season. Record attendance 11,000
(Total) Current Capacity: 6,643 (1,769 seated)
Visiting Supporters' Allocation: 1,821 (no seated) in Town End Terrace
Club Colours: Amber and black striped shirts, black shorts
Nearest Railway Station: Boston (one mile)
Parking (Car): Limited parking at the ground; recommended car park is the John Adams NCP
Parking (Coach/Bus): As directed
Police Force and Tel No: Lincolnshire (01205 366222)
Disabled Visitors Facilities:
Wheelchairs: Finn Forest Stand
Blind: No special facility
Future Development(s): The club has been examining whether to rebuild the team's existing York Street ground or to construct a new stadium outside the town. It was reported in early May that relocation had become the favoured option, although there was no confirmed timescale.

KEY

- **E** Entrance(s) for visiting supporters
- **R** Refreshment bars for visiting supporters
- **T** Toilets for visiting supporters
- ⬆ North direction (approx)

1. John Adams Way
2. Spilsby Road
3. Haven Bridge Road
4. York Street
5. Spayne Road
6. River Witham
7. Maud Foster Drain
8. Market Place
9. To bus and railway stations
10. York Street Stand (away)
11. Spayne Road Terrace
12. Town End Terrace
13. Finnforest Stand

Above: 693105; *Right:* 693098

In early February, the club changed hands. Virtually the first action of the new owner, Jon Sotnick, was to dismiss manager Neil Thompson. As expected, ex-boss Steve Jones was appointed to replace him from 2 March following the completion of his 20-month suspension arising from accusations of financial irregularities following the Pilgrims' promotion in 2002. In terms of 'on the field' activity, the Pilgrims had a more successful season than in their first season at the league — at the very least they'd already served their points penalty — and were ultimately to finish in 11th place, 15 points off the Play-Offs. Assuming that progress continues to be positive in 2004/05, then another top-half finish should be possible, although it's difficult to see the squad threatening the Play-Offs.

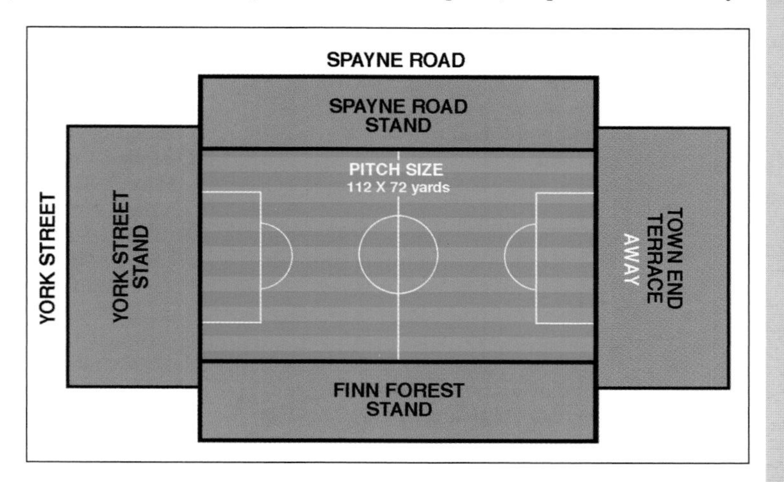

A.F.C. BOURNEMOUTH

The Fitness First Stadium at Dean Court, Bournemouth, Dorset, BH7 7AF

Tel No: 01202 726300
Advance Tickets Tel No: 0845 011 2322; 01202 726303
Fax: 01202 726301
E-Mail: enquiries@afcb.co.uk
Web Site: www.afcb.premiumtv.co.uk
League: League One
Brief History: Founded 1890 as Boscombe St. John's, changed to Boscombe (1899), Bournemouth & Boscombe Athletic (1923) and A.F.C. Bournemouth (1971). Former grounds Kings Park (twice) and Castlemain Road, Pokesdown. Moved to Dean Court in 1910. Record attendance 28,799; since rebuilding: 8,819
(Total) Current Capacity: 9,600 (all seated)
Visiting Supporters' Allocation: 1,160 in East Stand (can be increased to 2,000 if required)
Club Colours: Red and black shirts, black shorts
Nearest Railway Station: Bournemouth
Parking (Car): Large car park adjacent ground
Parking (Coach/Bus): Large car park adjacent ground
Police Force and Tel No: Dorset (01202 552099)
Disabled Visitors' Facilities:
Wheelchairs: 100 spaces
Blind: No special facility
Anticipated Development(s): Following the completion of the first three stands at the new Dean Court, attention has turned to the possibility of constructing the fourth stand. Once completed, this will take Dean Court's capacity to 12,000 all-seated (although there is some debate as to whether this new facility will be terraced). There is, however, no current time-scale for the work.

KEY

C Club Offices

⬆ North direction (approx)

1. Car Park
2. A338 Wessex Way
3. To Bournemouth BR Station (1½ miles)
4. To A31 & M27
5. Thistlebarrow Road
6. King's Park Drive
7. Littledown Avenue
8. North Stand
9. Main Stand
10. East Stand

Above: 695760; *Right:* 695749

Having been promoted at the end of 2002/03, Sean O'Driscoll's team might have considered success to have achieved no more than Second Division survival. However, despite the occasional set-back — such as losing away to non-league Accrington Stanley in the second round of the FA Cup on penalties — the team had a successful campaign in 2003/04, threatening, but never quite achieving, a Play-Off position. In the event, finishing 10th on 66 points, represents a good foundation for further progress in 2004/05 and there is every possibility that the team can do even better in the new season.

MAIN STAND
PITCH SIZE
112 X 74 yards
P
NORTH STAND
THISTLEBARROW ROAD
AWAY
EAST STAND

BRADFORD CITY

Valley Parade, Bradford, BD8 7DY

Tel No: 01274 773355
Advance Tickets Tel No: 01274 770022
Fax: 01274 773356
Web Site: www.bradfordcityfc.premiumtv.co.uk
E-Mail: bradfordcityfc@compuserve.com
League: League One
Brief History: Founded 1903 (formerly Manningham Northern Union Rugby Club founded in 1876). Continued use of Valley Parade, joined 2nd Division on re-formation. Record attendance: 39,146
(Total) Current Capacity: 25,136 (all seated)
Visiting Supporters' Allocation: 1,842 (all seated) in TL Dallas stand plus seats in Midland Road Stand if required
Club Colours: Claret and amber shirts, white shorts
Nearest Railway Station: Bradford Forster Square
Parking (Car): Street parking and car parks
Parking (Coach/Bus): As directed by Police
Police Force and Tel No: West Yorkshire (01274 723422)
Disabled Visitors' Facilities:
Wheelchairs: 110 places in Sunwin, CIBA and Carlsberg stands
Blind: Commentary available
Anticipated Development(s): With work on the Main (Sunwin) Stand now completed, Valley Parade has a slightly imbalanced look. The club has proposals for the reconstruction of the Midland Road (CIBA) Stand to take the ground's capacity to 30,000, although, given the club's current financial position, there is no time-scale.

KEY

- **C** Club Offices
- **S** Club Shop
- **E** Entrance(s) for visiting supporters
- **R** Refreshment bars for visiting supporters
- **T** Toilets for visiting supporters

⬆ North direction (approx)

1. Midland Road
2. Valley Parade
3. A650 Manningham Lane
4. To City Centre, Forster Square and Interchange BR Stations M606 & M62
5. To Keighley
6. Car Parks
7. Sunwin Stand
8. Midland (CIBA) Stand
9. TL Dallas Stand
10. Carlsberg Stand

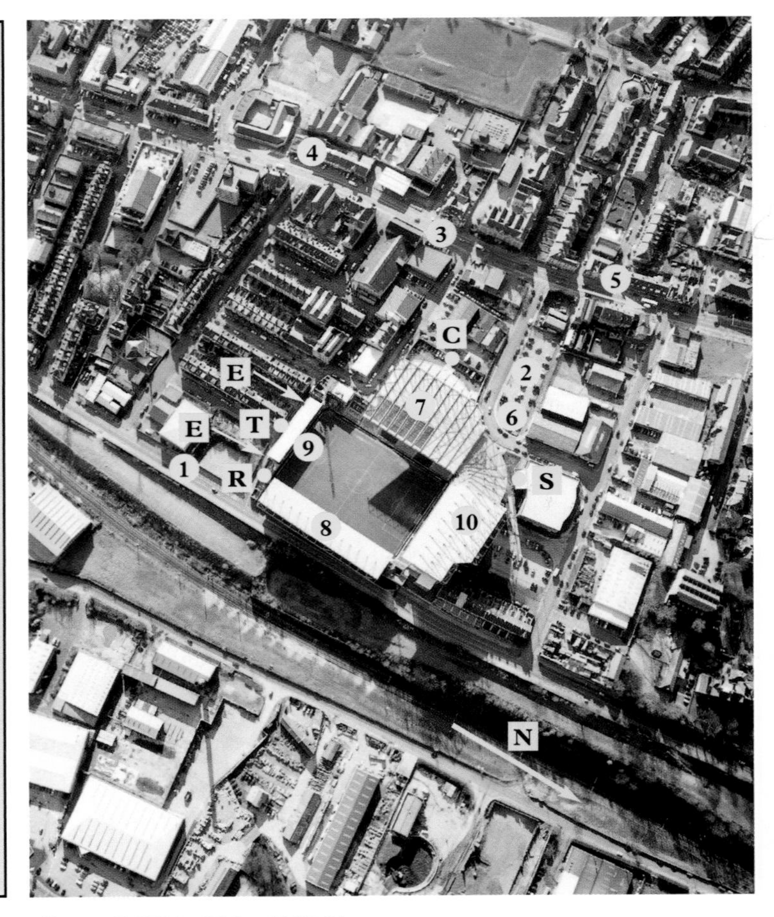

Above: 692550; *Right:* 692545

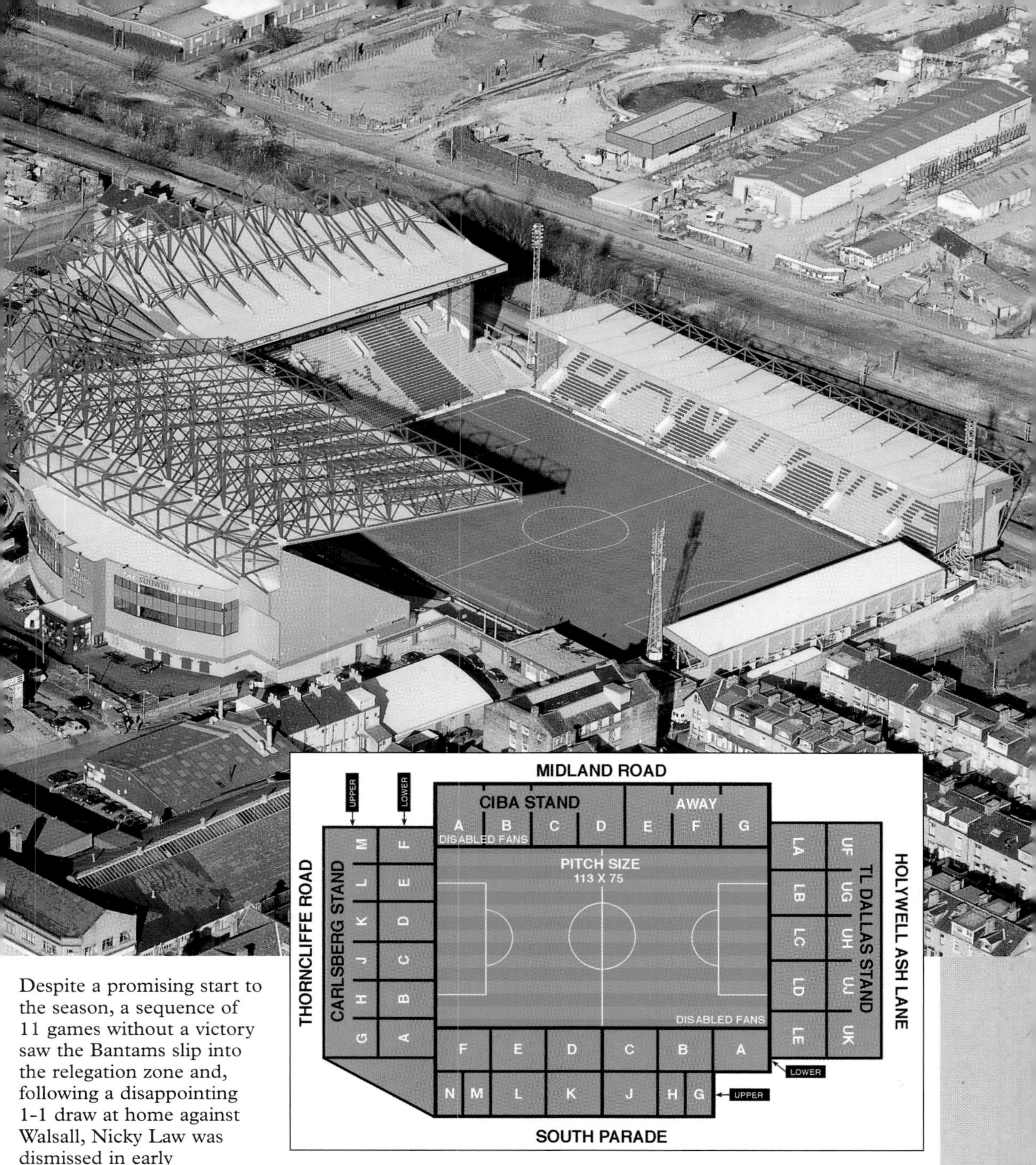

Despite a promising start to the season, a sequence of 11 games without a victory saw the Bantams slip into the relegation zone and, following a disappointing 1-1 draw at home against Walsall, Nicky Law was dismissed in early November. Towards the end of the month, following considerable speculation, ex-Boro boss Bryan Robson took over with Colin Todd arriving as his assistant. The immediate result was a first win, against Millwall, in 13 matches. However, the team's form continued to be poor and, despite the odd encouraging result — such as victory at leaders Norwich City — the club was relegated. With defeats in the two cup competitions against lower league teams and a return to Administration in February on top of relegation, the 2003/04 season is perhaps one that City's fans will probably want to forget. Other recent Premiership clubs — such as Sheffield Wednesday — have struggled in the Second Division, and it is hard to escape the conclusion that, under new manager Colin Todd the financial constraints that the club will be operating under makes an immediate return to the League Championship unlikely.

BRENTFORD

Griffin Park, Braemar Road, Brentford, Middlesex, TW8 0NT

Tel No: 020 8847 2511; 0870 900 9229
Advance Tickets Tel No: 0870 900 9229
Fax: 020 8380 9937
Web Site: www.brentfordfc.premiumtv.co.uk
E-Mail: enquiries@brentfordfc.co.uk
League: League One
Brief History: Founded 1889. Former Grounds: Clifden House Ground, Benn's Field (Little Ealing), Shotters Field, Cross Roads, Boston Park Cricket Ground, moved to Griffin Park in 1904. Founder-members Third Division (1920). Record attendance 38,678
(Total) Current Capacity: 13,870 (8,905 seated)
Visiting Supporters' Allocation: 2,200 on Ealing Road Terrace (open) and 600 seats in Block A of Braemar Road Stand
Club Colours: Red and white striped shirts, black shorts
Nearest Railway Station: Brentford, South Ealing (tube)
Parking (Car): Street parking (restricted)
Parking (Coach/Bus): Layton Road car park
Other Club Sharing Ground: London Broncos RLFC
Police Force and Tel No: Metropolitan (020 8577 1212)
Disabled Visitors' Facilities:
Wheelchairs: Braemar Road
Blind: Commentary available
Anticipated Development(s): After some years of debate, where relocation to Feltham seemed likely, the club announced in November 2002 that it was planning to relocate to a site near Kew, about a mile from Griffin Park. It is expected that Griffin Park will be sold and that the club will seek planning permission to construct a new 25,000-seat ground at the new site. There is, however, no confirmed timescale for the work. It is also likely that the new ground will be shared with the London Broncos RLFC, who are currently playing their home games at Griffin Park.

KEY

- **C** Club Offices
- **S** Club Shop
- ⬆ North direction (approx)

1. Ealing Road
2. Braemar Road
3. Brook Road South
4. To M4 (1/4 mile) & South Ealing Tube Station(1 mile)
5. Brentford BR Station
6. To A315 High Street & Kew Bridge
7. New Road
8. Ealing Road Terrace (away)
9. Brook Road Stand

Above: 695938; *Right:* 695940

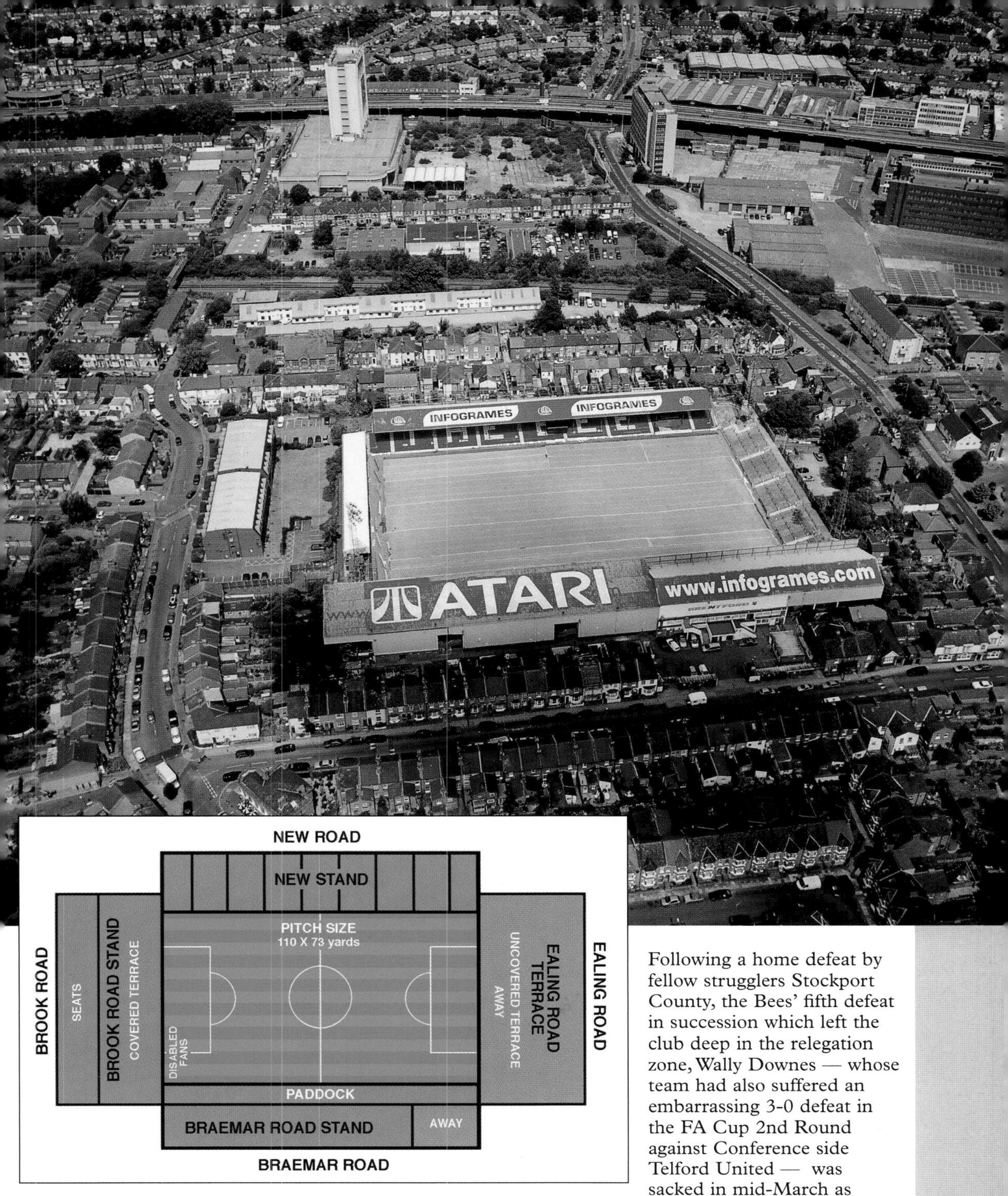

Following a home defeat by fellow strugglers Stockport County, the Bees' fifth defeat in succession which left the club deep in the relegation zone, Wally Downes — whose team had also suffered an embarrassing 3-0 defeat in the FA Cup 2nd Round against Conference side Telford United — was sacked in mid-March as manager. The club moved quickly to appoint Garry Thompson as caretaker, drawing his only game in charge, before ex-Barnet boss Martin Allen took over the permanent position. With Allen in charge, the reversal of the club's fortunes was immediate and a series of victories in the last 10 games ensured that League One football will again be on offer at Griffin Park. It was, however, a close run thing, with the Bees requiring a victory in a tense game against Bournemouth to be 100% certain of staying up.

BRIGHTON & HOVE ALBION

Withdean Stadium, Tongdean Lane, Brighton BN1 5JD

Tel No: 01273 778855
Fax: 01273 321095
Advance Ticket Tel No: 01273 776992
Web Site: www.seagulls.premiumtv.co.uk
E-Mail: seagulls@bhafc.co.uk
League: League Championship
Brief History: Founded 1900 as Brighton & Hove Rangers, changed to Brighton & Hove Albion 1902. Former grounds: Home Farm (Withdean), County Ground, Goldstone Ground (1902-1997), Priestfield Stadium (ground share with Gillingham) 1997-1999; moved to Withdean Stadium 1999. Founder members of the 3rd Division 1920. Record attendance (at Goldstone Ground): 36,747; at Withdean Stadium: 6,995.
(Total) Current Capacity: 7,053 (all seated)
Visiting Supporters' Allocation: 800 max on open North East Stand
Club Colours: Blue and white striped shirts, white shorts
Nearest Railway Station: Preston Park
Parking (Cars): Street parking in the immediate vicinity of the ground is residents' only. This will be strictly enforced and it is suggested that intending visitors should use parking facilities away from the ground and use the proposed park and ride bus services that will be provided.
Parking (Coach/Bus): As directed
Police Force and Tel No: Sussex (01273 778922)
Disabled Visitors' Facilities
Wheelchairs: Facilities in both North and South stands
Blind: No special facility
Anticipated Development(s): The ongoing saga of the construction of the new stadium at Falmer continues with the plans now in the hands of the Deputy Prime Minister, John Prescott. The club is hoping that its recent promotion to the League Championship will encourage the government to give the project the go-ahead, but in the meantime it is also hoping to undertake further work at the Withdean Stadium to increase capacity there by 2,000 in the short term. The new stadium is anticipated to cost £44 million and provide a 22,000 all-seated capacity eventually. The club is hoping to have the first phase of the new ground available for the start of the 2005/06 season but this depends on obtaining the necessary permissions.

KEY

Club Address:
8th Floor, Tower Point,
44 North Road, Brighton
BN1 1YR
Tel: 01273 695460
Fax: 01273 648179

Shop Address:
6 Queen's Road, Brighton

⬆ North direction (approx)

Note: All games at Withdean will be all-ticket with no cash admissions on the day.

1. Withdean Stadium
2. London-Brighton railway line
3. London Road (A23)
4. Tongdean Lane
5. Valley Drive
6. To Brighton town centre and main railway station (1.75 miles)
7. Tongdean Lane (with bridge under railway)
8. South Stand
9. A23 northwards to Crawley
10. To Preston Park railway station
11. North Stand

Above: 695745; *Right:* 695788

Despite the Seagulls flying high at the top of the Second Division, Steve Coppell departed as manager in early October to take over at Reading. Following a brief interregnum when Bob Booker acted as caretaker, ex-Millwall boss Mark McGhee took over at the end of the month. Under the experienced McGhee, Albion consolidated its push towards the Play-Offs, ultimately finishing in fourth spot, some six points below promoted QPR and facing a Play-Off semi-final against Swindon Town. Victory over the two legs in a tight contest with the Wiltshire side saw Albion head to Cardiff for a Millennium Stadium showdown with Bristol City. In another tight match, a 1-0 victory means that McGhee will again be managing a First Division (League Championship) team for the new season. The last time that Albion were promoted, after an appalling start, the club battled hard, but ultimately failed, to retain its hard-won status. It's hard to escape the conclusion that Albion will again struggle to remain a League Championship outfit but, in McGhee, the club has a manager with the knowledge to make a decent effort to stay up.

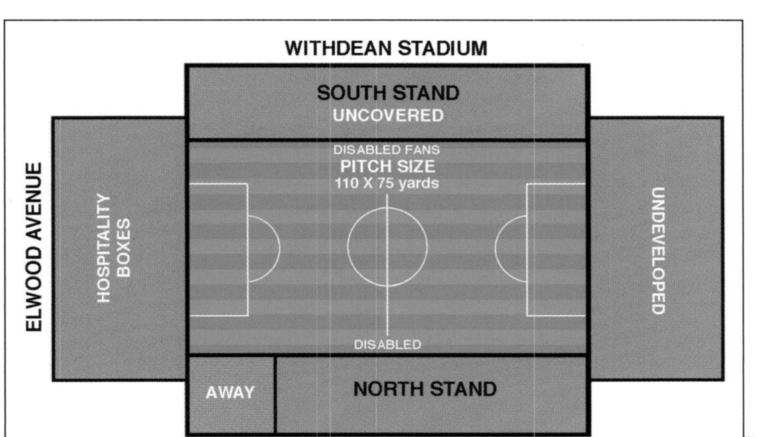

BRISTOL CITY

Ashton Gate Stadium, Ashton Road, Bristol BS3 2EJ

Tel No: 0117 963 0630
Advance Tickets Tel No: 0870 112 1897
Fax: 0117 963 0700
Web Site: www.bcfc.premiumtv.co.uk
E-Mail: commercial@bcfc.co.uk
League: League One
Brief History: Founded 1894 as Bristol South End changed to Bristol City in 1897. Former Ground: St John's Lane, Bedminster, moved to Ashton Gate in 1904. Record attendance 43,335
(Total) Current Capacity: 21,497 (all seated)
Visiting Supporters' Allocation: 3,000 in Wedlock End (all seated; can be increased to 5,500 if necessary)
Club Colours: Red shirts, white shorts
Nearest Railway Station: Bristol Temple Meads
Parking (Car): Street parking
Parking (Coach/Bus): Marsh Road
Police Force and Tel No: Avon/Somerset (0117 927 7777)
Disabled Visitors' Facilities:
Wheelchairs: Limited
Blind: Commentary available
Anticipated Development(s): The club is progressing with plans to redevelop the Williams, Wedlock and Dolman stands with work possibly starting in 2004.

KEY

- **C** Club Offices
- **S** Club Shop
- **E** Entrance(s) for visiting supporters

⬆ North direction (approx)

1. A370 Ashton Road
2. A3209 Winterstoke Road
3. To Temple Meads Station (1½ miles
4. To City Centre, A4, M32 & M4
5. Database Wedlock Stand
6. Atyeo Stand

Above: 692242; *Right:* 692240

Under Danny Wilson, City again challenged for automatic promotion from the Second Division with the final promotion place being determined by the final games of the season. City needed to defeat Blackpool at Ashton Gate whilst relying on Sheffield Wednesday to take at least a point off QPR at Hillsborough. In the event, both teams won with the result that QPR were promoted and City were consigned again to the Play-Offs, with a semi-final against the surprise package of the Second Division, Hartlepool United. Victory over the two legs saw City face Brighton in the Play-Off Final; however, a late penalty saw Albion secure promotion to the League Championshp and consign City to a further campaign in the League One. Having failed once again to get City promoted, Wilson was to pay with the loss of his job; the club moved quickly, appointing veteran Brian Tinnion to the position of player-manager. With the teams relegated from the First Division in 2003/04 looking pretty weak, City have the potential to again challenge for automatic promotion and, this season, should perhaps achieve it.

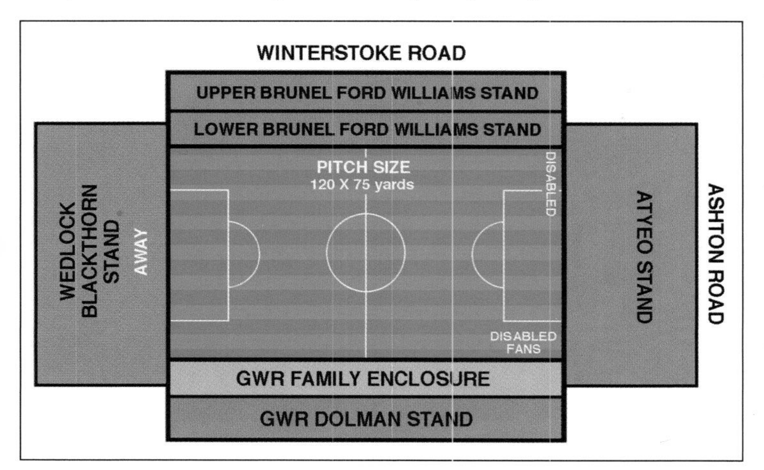

BRISTOL ROVERS

The Memorial Stadium, Filton Avenue, Horfield, Bristol BS7 0BF

Tel No: 0117 909 6648
Advance Tickets Tel No: 0117 909 6648
Fax: 0117 908 5530
Web Site: www.bristolrovers.premiumtv.co.uk
E-Mail: club@bristolrovers.co.uk
League: League Two
Brief History: Founded 1883 as Black Arabs, changed to Eastville Rovers (1884), Bristol Eastville Rovers (1896) and Bristol Rovers (1897). Former grounds: Purdown, Three Acres, The Downs (Horfield), Ridgeway, Bristol Stadium (Eastville), Twerton Park (1986-96), moved to The Memorial Ground 1996. Record attendance: (Eastville) 38,472, (Twerton Park) 9,813, (Memorial Ground) 9,274
(Total) Current Capacity: 11,917 (4,000 seated); standing capacity of 8,000 includes 500 on the Family Terrace
Visiting Supporters' Allocation: 1,132 (Centenary Stand Terrace; open)
Club Colours: Blue and white quartered shirts, white shorts
Nearest Railway Station: Filton or Stapleton Road
Parking (Car): Limited parking at ground for home fans only; street parking also available
Parking (Coach/Bus): As directed
Police Force and Tel No: Avon/Somerset (0117 927 7777)
Other Clubs Sharing Ground: Bristol RUFC
Disabled Visitors' Facilities:
Wheelchairs: 35 wheelchair positions
Blind: Limited provision
Anticipated Development(s): The club has ambitious plans for the development of the Memorial Ground. This work will probably include the replacement of the Centenary Stand and Terrace as well as the South Stand. The club is aiming for a stadium with a 20,000-seat capacity subject to finance. There is, as yet, no confirmed timescale for the work.

KEY

C Rugby Club offices
E Entrance(s) for visiting supporters
R Refrshments for visiting supporters
T Toilets for visiting supporters

⬆ North direction (approx)

1. Filton Avenue
2. Gloucester Road
3. Muller Road
4. To Bristol city centre (2.5 miles) and BR Temple Meads station (3 miles)
5. Downer Road
6. Car Park
7. To M32 J2 (1.5 miles)
8. Strathmore Road
9. To Filton (1.5 miles)
10. Centenary Stand
11. West Stand

Above: 692206; *Right:* 692197

Ray Graydon departed from the hot seat late 2003 to be replaced as caretaker by Phil Bater. Despite being more interested in the relegation fight than the promotion battle, Rovers had a direct influence on the latter when, in mid-March, it was announced that Oxford United boss Ian Atkins would take over at the Memorial Stadium at the end of the season. A furious United chairman suspended Atkins immediately. In the meantime, Rovers announced that Kevin Broadhurst and Russell Osman would take over as joint caretaker managers until the end of the season with Bater reverting to first team coach. Under the new management team, the Gasheads pulled away from the drop zone finally finishing in 15th position some 10 points off relegated Carlisle United. As to the future, Atkins will take over a club that has the potential to do better than be League Two relegation fodder, but two seasons at the wrong end of the division do not bode well for the future. Unless Atkins is able to turn things round rapidly another season of mid-table mediocrity, at best, beckons.

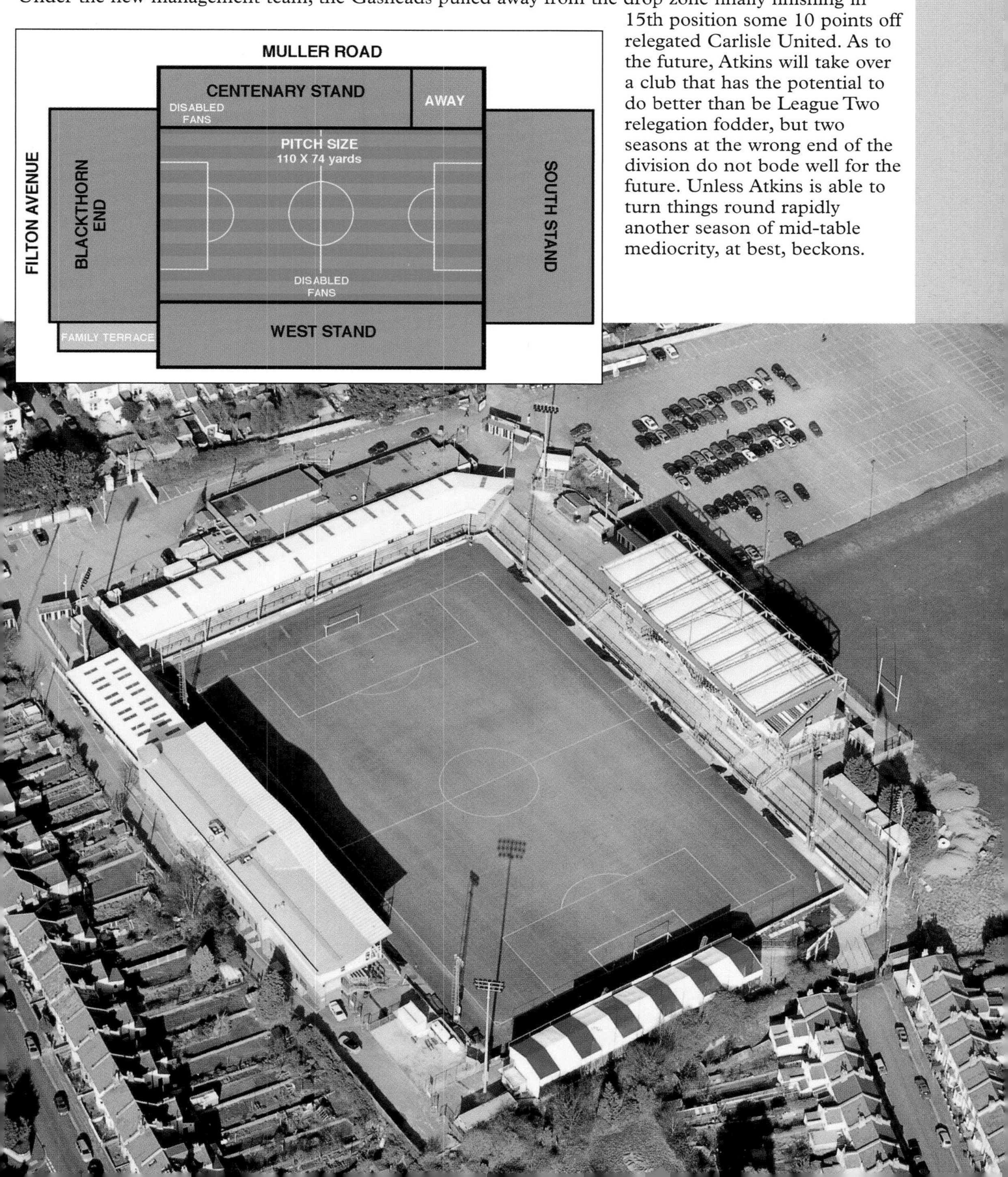

BURNLEY

Turf Moor, Harry Potts Way, Burnley, Lancs, BB10 4BX

Tel No: 0870 443 1882
Advance Tickets Tel No: 0870 443 1914
Fax: 01282 700014
Web Site: www.burnleyfootballclub.premium.co.uk
E-Mail: info@burnleyfootballclub.net
League: League Championship
Brief History: Founded 1882, Burnley Rovers (Rugby Club) combined with another Rugby Club, changed to soccer and name to Burnley. Moved from Calder Vale to Turf Moor in 1882. Founder-members Football League (1888). Record attendance 54,775
(Total) Current Capacity: 22,546 (all seated)
Visiting Supporters' Allocation: 4,125 (all seated in Lookers [Cricket Field] Stand)
Club Colours: Claret with blue sleeved shirts, white with claret and blue trim shorts
Nearest Railway Station: Burnley Central
Parking (Car): Church Street and Fulledge Rec. (car parks)
Parking (Coach/Bus): As directed by Police
Police Force and Tel No: Lancashire (01282 425001)
Disabled Visitors' Facilities:
Wheelchairs: Places available in North, East and Cricket Field stands
Blind: Headsets provided with commentary
Anticipated Development(s): The club has proposals for the redevelopment of the Cricket Field (Lookers) Stand but this depends on the relocation of the cricket club. The new structure would provide seating for some 7,000. In the event of this option not proving practical attention will turn to the expansion of the Bob Lord Stand.

KEY

- **C** Club Offices
- **S** Club Shop
- **E** Entrance(s) for visiting supporters

- ⬆ North direction (approx)

1. Brunshaw Road
2. Belvedere Road
3. Burnley Central BR Station (1/2 mile)
4. Cricket Ground
5. Cricket Field Stand
6. East (Jimmy McIlroy) Stand
7. Bob Lord Stand
8. North (James Hargreaves) Stand

Above: 696988; *Right:* 696994

A further disappointing season at Turf Moor saw the Clarets hovering just above the relegation zone for much of the campaign and, although First Division safety was assured, the club announced in early May that Stan Ternent's contract as manager would not be renewed for 2004/05. Ternent had held the Turf Moor job for six years, guiding the team back into the First Division and ensuring its survival. The new manager, the experienced Steve Cotterill, will inherit a team that will probably again struggle to make an impact in the League Championship in 2004/05.

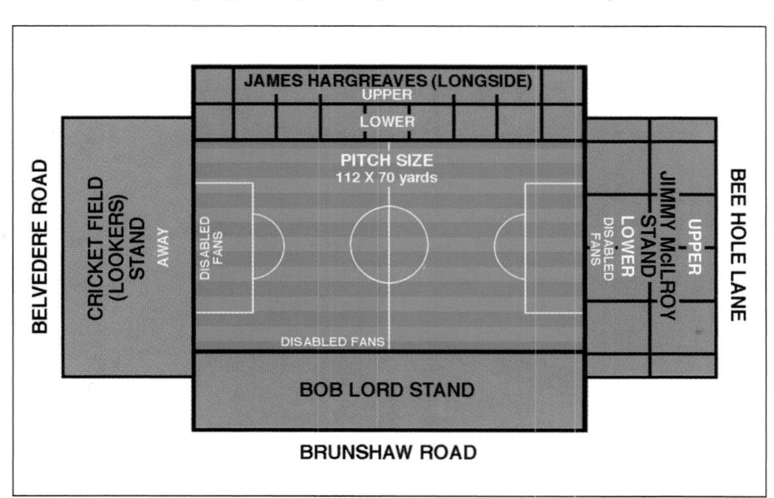

BURY

Gigg Lane, Bury, Lancashire, BL9 9HR

Tel No: 0161 764 4881
Advance Tickets Tel No: 0161 705 2144
Fax: 0161 764 5521
Web Site: www.buryfc.co.uk
E-Mail: info@buryfc.premiumtv.co.uk
League: League Two
Brief History: Founded 1885, no former names or former grounds. Record attendance 35,000
(Total) Current Capacity: 11,669 (all seated)
Visiting Supporters' Allocation: 2,676 (all seated) in West Stand
Club Colours: White shirts, royal blue shorts
Nearest Railway Station: Bury Interchange
Parking (Car): Street parking
Parking (Coach/Bus): As directed by Police
Police Force and Tel No: Greater Manchester (0161 872 5050)
Disabled Visitors' Facilities:
Wheelchairs: South Stand (home) and West Stand (away)
Blind: Commentary available
Anticipated Development(s): The completion of the rebuilt Cemetery End means that current plans for the redevelopment of Gigg Lane have been completed.

KEY

- **C** Club Offices
- **S** Club Shop
- **E** Entrance(s) for visiting supporters
- ⬆ North direction (approx)
- ❶ Car Park
- ❷ Gigg Lane
- ❸ A56 Manchester Road
- ❹ Town Centre & Bury Interchange (Metrolink) (3/4 mile)
- ❺ West (Manchester Road) Stand
- ❻ Cemetery End

Above: 696978; *Right:* 696984

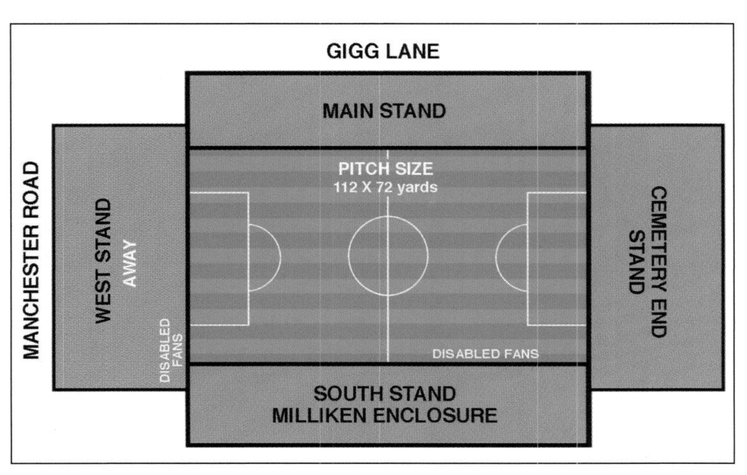

With the club in mid-table, Andy Preece was sacked as manager in mid-December, having held the job since May 2000. He was replaced, as caretaker manager, by Graham Barrow. Whilst Preece went off to Carlisle and was influential in their ultimately fruitless campaign to retain their League status, Barrow was able to secure a top-half finish — just (Bury finished in 12th position, 11 points above Carlisle but 18 below the Play-Offs). For 2004/05 the probability is that a top-half finish is perhaps the best that the Gigg Lane faithful can look forward to.

CAMBRIDGE UNITED

Abbey Stadium, Newmarket Road, Cambridge, CB5 8LN

Tel No: 01223 566500
Advance Tickets Tel No: 01223 566500
Fax: 01223 566502
Web Site: www.cambridge-united.premiumtv.co.uk
E-mail: commercial@cambridge-united.co.uk
League: League Two
Brief History: Founded 1913 as Abbey United, changed to Cambridge United in 1951. Former Grounds: Midsummer Common, Stourbridge Common, Station Farm Barnwell (The Celery Trenches) & Parker's Piece, moved to Abbey Stadium in 1933. Record attendance 14,000
(Total) Current Capacity: 9,617 (4,784 seated)
Visiting Supporters' Allocation: c1,000 (covered terrace on south end of the Habbin Stand) or 1,600 seats on the new South Stand.
Club Colours: Amber and black shirts, amber shorts
Nearest Railway Station: Cambridge (2 miles)
Parking (Car): Coldhams Common
Parking (Coach/Bus): Coldhams Common
Police Force and Tel No: Cambridge (01223 358966)
Disabled Visitors' Facilities:
Wheelchairs: Limited number that should be pre-booked
Blind: No special facility
Anticipated Development(s): The new South Stand has now been completed. This is the first stage of a plan to turn the ground into a 10,000-capacity all-seater stadium. The new stand has been moved some 15m to the south, thereby allowing for a slight adjustment to the pitch. The next phase in the redevelopment will cover the North Stand, which will be replaced by a 3,500-seat structure that will also include executive boxes. Planning permission for the next phase of work at the ground was given in early June 2004 although there was no confirmed timescale for the work at the time of going to press.

KEY

- **E** Entrance(s) for visiting supporters
- **R** Refreshment bars for visiting supporters
- **T** Toilets for visiting supporters
- ⬆ North direction (approx)

1. A1134 Newmarket Road
2. To A11 for Newmarket
3. To City Centre, Cambridge BR Station (2 miles) and M11
4. Whitehill Road
5. South Stand
6. Habbin Stand
7. Main Stand
8. North Terrace

Above: 695786; *Right:* 695782

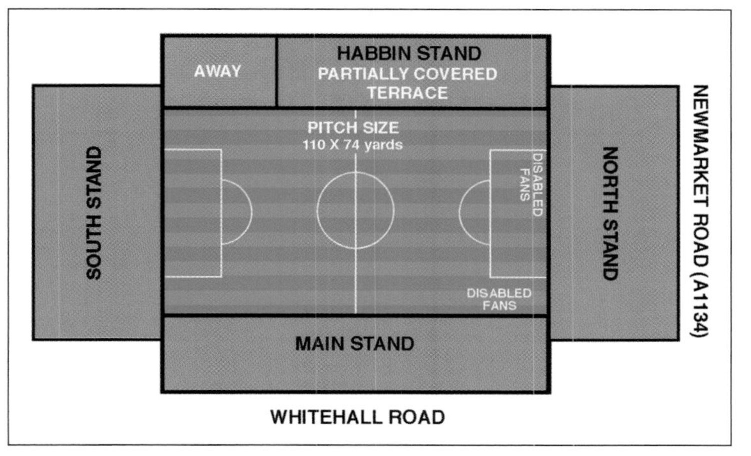

After just over two years in the managerial hot seat, during which time the club had been relegated to the Third Division, John Taylor departed in mid-March with the club hovering just above the Third Division drop zone, only six points above relegation-threatened Macclesfield Town. Although initially denying the fact that he was bound to join United, Frenchman Claude le Roy took over later in the month. Under le Roy, United moved away from the drop zone, ultimately finishing in 13th position, 11 points above relegated Carlisle United. At the end of the season le Roy became Director of Football with Herve Renhard taking over as manager.

CARDIFF CITY

Ninian Park, Sloper Road, Cardiff, CF11 8SX

Tel No: 029 2022 1001
Advance Tickets Tel No: 0845 345 1400
Fax: 029 2034 1148
Web Site: www.cardiffcityfc.premiumtv.co.uk
E-mail: reception@cardiffcityfc.co.uk
League: League Championship
Brief History: Founded 1899. Former Grounds: Riverside Cricket Club, Roath, Sophia Gardens, Cardiff Arms Park and The Harlequins Rugby Ground, moved to Ninian Park in 1910. Ground record attendance 61,566 (Wales v. England, 1961)
(Total) Current Capacity: 20,000 (12,647 seated)
Visiting Supporters' Allocation: 2,000 maximum in John Smiths Grange End Terrace (limited seating)
Club Colours: Blue shirts, blue shorts
Nearest Railway Station: Ninian Park (adjacent) (Cardiff Central 1 mile)
Parking (Car): Opposite Ground, no street parking around ground
Parking (Coach/Bus): Leckwith Stadium car park
Police Force and Tel No: South Wales (029 2022 2111)
Disabled Visitors' Facilities:
Wheelchairs: Corner Canton Stand/Popular Bank (covered)
Blind: No special facility
Anticipated Development(s): The club is progressing with the proposals to relocate to a new stadium at Leckwith, a project that received planning permission in December 2003. The £40 million project will provide a capacity of 30,000 initially (but upto to 60,000 ultimately) and is scheduled for completion for the start of the 2006/07 season. Work on the new stadium, which should have started in the first half of 2004, has, however, been slightly delayed and should begin in August 2004. Once the club relocates, Ninian Park will be sold for housing.

KEY

- **C** Club Offices
- **S** Club Shop
- **E** Entrance(s) for visiting supporters
- **R** Refreshment bars for visiting supporters
- **T** Toilets for visiting supporters (Terrace only, when used)

- ↑ North direction (approx)

1. Sloper Road
2. B4267 Leckwith Road
3. Car Park
4. To A4232 & M4 Junction 33 (8 miles)
5. Ninian Park Road
6. To City Centre & Cardiff Central BR Station (1 mile)
7. To A48 Western Avenue, A49M, and M4 Junction 32 and 29
8. Ninian Park BR station

Above: 693234; *Right:* 693243

A season of consolidation in the First Division saw Lennie Lawrence's team ultimately finish in mid table, never being threatened with relegation nor threatening to reach the Play-offs. At the start of the campaign fans would have been happy to have achieved a place above the drop zone but, having had a good start to the season, the failure to make more of an impact may have rankled with the Ninian Park faithful. Whilst not universally appreciated, Lawrence is an experienced manager and perhaps one who is suited to making sure that City's position in the League Championship is cemented. For 2004/05 there is every chance that Cardiff will make progress and whilst automatic promotion looks beyond the team, a Play-Off berth should certainly be a possibility.

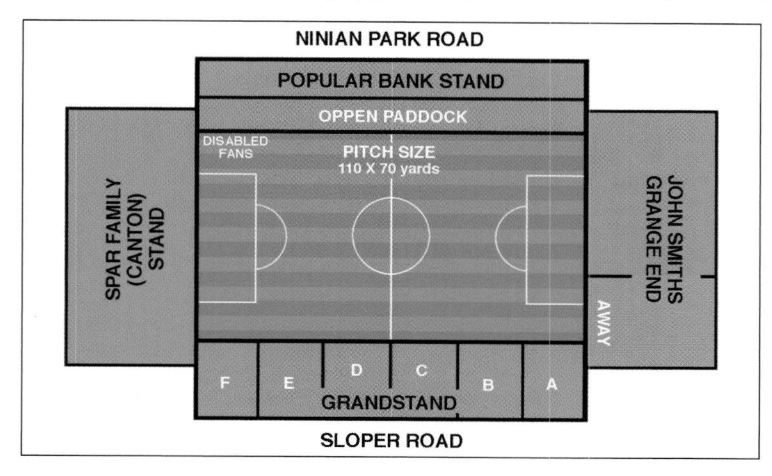

CHARLTON ATHLETIC

The Valley, Floyd Road, Charlton, London, SE7 8BL

Tel No: 020 8333 4000
Advance Tickets Tel No: 020 8333 4010
Fax: 020 8333 4001
Web Site: www.cafc.co.uk
E-Mail: info@cafc.co.uk
League: F.A. Premier
Brief History: Founded 1905. Former grounds: Siemens Meadows, Woolwich Common, Pound Park, Angerstein Athletic Ground, The Mount Catford, Selhurst Park (Crystal Palace FC), Boleyn Ground (West Ham United FC), The Valley (1912-23, 1924-85, 1992-date). Founder Members 3rd Division South. Record attendance 75,031
(Total) Current Capacity: 26,875 (all seated)
Visiting Supporters' Allocation: 3,000 (maximum; all seated in South Stand)
Club Colours: Red shirts, white shorts
Nearest Railway Station: Charlton
Parking (Car): Street parking
Parking (Coach/Bus): As directed by Police
Police Force and Tel No: Metropolitan (020 8853 8212)
Disabled Visitors' Facilities:
Wheelchairs: East/West/South stands
Blind: Commentary, 12 spaces
Anticipated Development(s): The club announced plans in late 2003 for the expansion of The Valley from its current capacity of 26,875 to 40,600. However, this works requires Planning Permission from Greenwich Council and the club is talking to the council about the further development of the ground.

KEY

E Entrance(s) for visiting supporters
R Refreshment bars for visiting supporters
T Toilets for visiting supporters

⬆ North Direction (approx)

1. Harvey Gardens
2. A206 Woolwich Road
3. Valley Grove
4. Floyd Road
5. Charlton BR Station
6. East Stand
7. North Stand
8. West stand
9. South stand (away)
10. Charlton Church Lane
11. Charlton Lane

Above: 692147; *Right:* 692140

Charlton seem to have a slightly strange view of the football season: for the first half of the campaign the club seems to promise that it will push towards achieving a European place but for the second half the team seems to evince form that would, if replicated for the full season, lead to automatic relegation. The 2003/04 season was to exemplify this to the extent that, for much of the season, the pundits were suggesting that the team could have pipped either Liverpool or Newcastle for the final Champions League position but in the event the club finished in seventh position. Another negative was the fact that the club was defeated 3-2 away at First Division Gillingham in the Third Round of the FA Cup. If Alan Curbishley could ensure that his squad played for the full 38 games then again the team should challenge for Europe in 2004/05 but it's hard to escape the conclusion that, once again, Charlton will be one of the also rans.

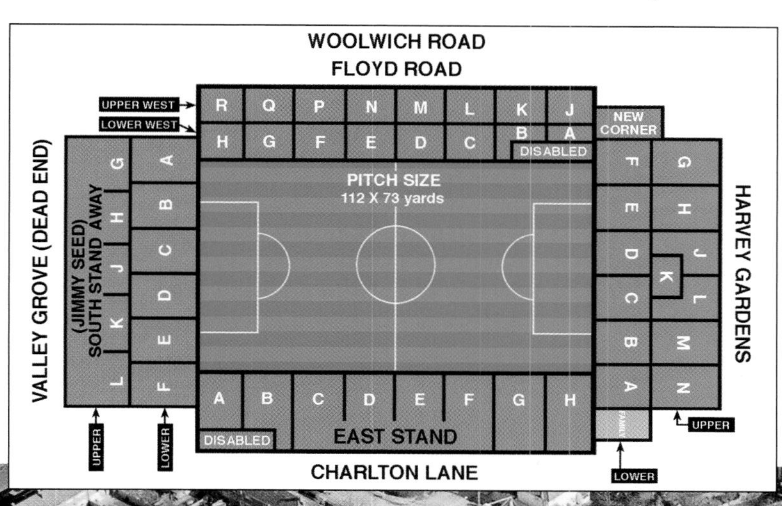

CHELSEA

Stamford Bridge, Fulham Road, London, SW6 1HS

Tel No: 020 7385 5545
Advance Tickets Tel No: 020 7386 7799
Fax: 020 7381 4831
E-Mail: Accessed from web-site
Web Site: www.chelseafc.com
League: F.A. Premier
Brief History: Founded 1905. Admitted to Football League (2nd Division) on formation. Stamford Bridge venue for F.A. Cup Finals 1919-22. Record attendance 82,905
(Total) Current Capacity: 42,449 (all seated)
Visiting Supporters' Allocation: Approx. 1,600 (East Stand Lower; can be increased to 3,200 if required or 5,200 if part of the Matthew Harding Stand [lower tier] is allocated)
Club Colours: Blue shirts, blue shorts
Nearest Railway Station: Fulham Broadway or West Brompton
Parking (Car): Street parking and underground car park at ground
Parking (Coach/Bus): As directed by Police
Police Force and Tel No: Metropolitan (020 7385 1212)
Disabled Visitors' Facilities:
Wheelchairs: East Stand
Blind: No special facility
Anticipated Development(s): With the long awaited completion of the second tier of the West Stand now achieved, redevelopment of Stamford Bridge as a stadium is now complete.

KEY

⬆ North direction (approx)

❶ A308 Fulham Road
❷ Central London
❸ To Fulham Broadway Tube Station
❹ Mathew Harding Stand
❺ East Stand
❻ West Stand
❼ South (Shed) Stand
❽ West Brompton Station

Above: 697396; *Right:* 697393

The first year of the Roman occupation of Stamford Bridge saw considerable investment in the squad and some success on the field: finishing second in the Premiership, the club's highest league position since winning the Championship in the 1950s, and the semi-finals of the Champions League. Normally, success of this nature would result in the manager being lauded and offered job security; however, most of the news from Chelski during the past season was not on when Claudio 'Tinkerman' Ranieri was to be dismissed but which high-profile coach would replace him. The dignity with which Ranieri conducted himself in these circumstances was impressive but the distraction of constantly having to defend his position must have made the job even more difficult than in normal circumstances. It was interesting to note that, as the pressure on the team built, Ranieri relied increasingly on the squad that he'd acquired before Abramovitch's millions arrived and that many of the expensive acquisitions after the change off ownership flattered to deceive. At the end of May, the worst kept secret in football was confirmed with Ranieri's dismissal and the appointment of ex-Porto boss Jose Mourinho to replace him. Perhaps, however, the one lesson from 2003/04 is that whilst you can spend a fortune, you can't necessarily convert disparate talents into a coherent unit. Undoubtedly, simply because of the size and strength of the squad, Chelsea will again challenge on all fronts, but will the new manager and players gel quickly enough to be able to challenge Arsenal for English supremacy?

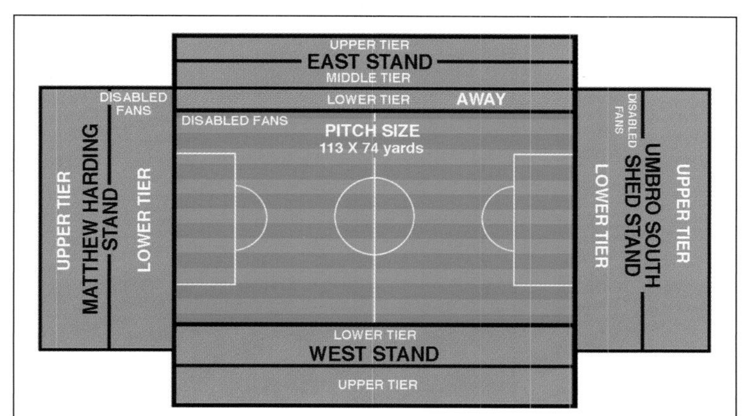

CHELTENHAM TOWN

Whaddon Road, Cheltenham, Gloucestershire GL52 5NA

Tel No: 01242 573558
Advance Tickets Tel No: 01242 573558
Fax: 01242 224675
Web Site: www.cheltenhamtownfc.com
E-Mail: info@cheltenhamtownfc.premiumtv.co.uk
League: League Two
Brief History: Cheltenham Town was founded in 1892. It moved to Whaddon Road in 1932 having previously played at Carter's Field. After two seasons in the Conference it achieved Nationwide League status at the end of the 1998/99 season. Record attendance 8,326
(Total) Current Capacity: 7,407 (3,139 seated)
Visiting Supporters' Allocation: 2,100 (maximum) in Whaddon Road Terrace – uncovered – and in Wymans Road (In2Print) Stand
Club Colours: Red and white striped shirts, white shorts
Nearest Railway Station: Cheltenham (1.5 miles)
Parking (Car): Limited parking at ground; otherwise on-street
Parking (Coach/Bus): As directed by Police
Police Force and Tel No: Gloucestershire (01242 521321)
Disabled Visitors' Facilities:
Wheelchairs: Six spaces in front of Main Stand
Blind: No special facility
Anticipated Development(s): The long-awaited cover over the open Whaddon Road Terrace has, despite earlier forecasts, yet to be completed. Once this work has been undertaken the next phase in the development of the ground will be the rebuilding of the Main Stand, although there is no time-scale for this work.

KEY

C Club Offices
E Entrance(s) for visiting supporters

⬆ North direction (approx)

1. B4632 Prestbury Road
2. Cromwell Road
3. Whaddon Road
4. Wymans Road
5. To B4075 Priors Road
6. To B4075 Prior Road
7. To Cheltenham town centre and railway station (1.5 and 2 miles respectively)
8. Main Stand
9. Wymans Road Stand
10. Prestbury Road End
11. Whaddon Road End

Above: 695569; *Right:* 695566

As a result of a disappointing run, which had seen the team lose six out of its last seven games, culminating in a 2-0 home defeat by Rochdale, Bobby Gould resigned as manager in late October. The club moved quickly to appoint his successor, John Ward taking over in early November, with caretaker boss Bob Bloomer remaining as assistant. Under Ward, the club achieved a position of mid-table mediocrity, finishing in 14th position — 18 points below the Play-Offs but 17 points above the drop zone. Providing that the club can maintain the progress shown in the second half of 2003/04 there is every possibility that the team will be able to make a serious challenge for the Play-Offs at worst.

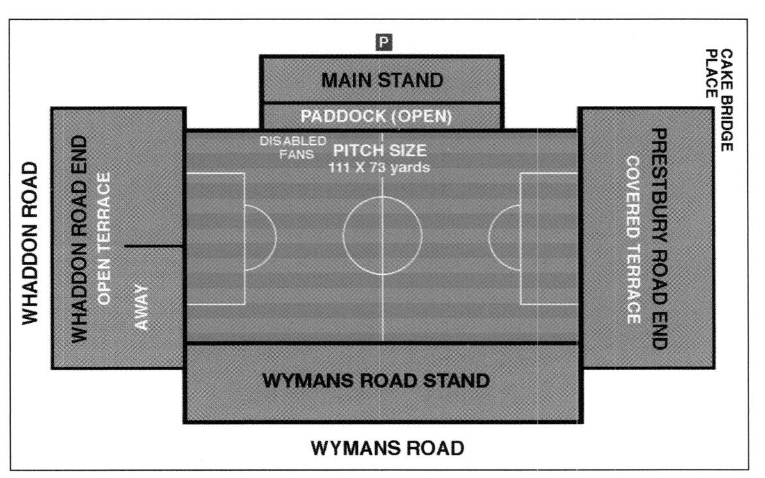

CHESTER CITY

The Deva Stadium, Bumpers Lane, Chester, CH1 4LT

Tel No: 01244 371376
Advance Tickets Tel No: 01244 371376
Fax: 01244 390265
Web-site: www.chesterfieldfc.net
E-mail: via web site
League: League Two
Brief History: Founded 1884 from amalgamation of Chester Wanderers and Chester Rovers. Former Grounds: Faulkner Street, Lightfoot Street, Whipcord Lane, Sealand Road Moss Lane (Macclesfield Town FC), moved to Deva Stadium 1992. Record attendance (Sealand Road) 20,500; (Deva Stadium) 5,987
(Total) Current Capacity: 6,012 (3,284) seated
Visiting Supporters' Allocation: 1,896 maximum (seated 600 maximum)
Club Colours: Blue/White striped shirts, Blue shorts
Nearest Railway Station: Chester (three miles)
Parking (Car): Car park at ground
Parking(Coach/Bus): Car park at ground
Police Force and Tel No: Cheshire (01244 350222)
Disabled Visitors' Facilities:
Wheelchairs: West and East Stand
Blind: Facility Available
Anticipated Development(s):

KEY

C Club Offices
S Club Shop
E Entrance(s) for visiting supporters
R Refreshment bars for visiting supporters
T Toilets for visiting supporters

⬆ North direction (approx)

❶ Bumpers Lane
❷ To City centre and Chester railway station (1.5 miles)
❸ Car park

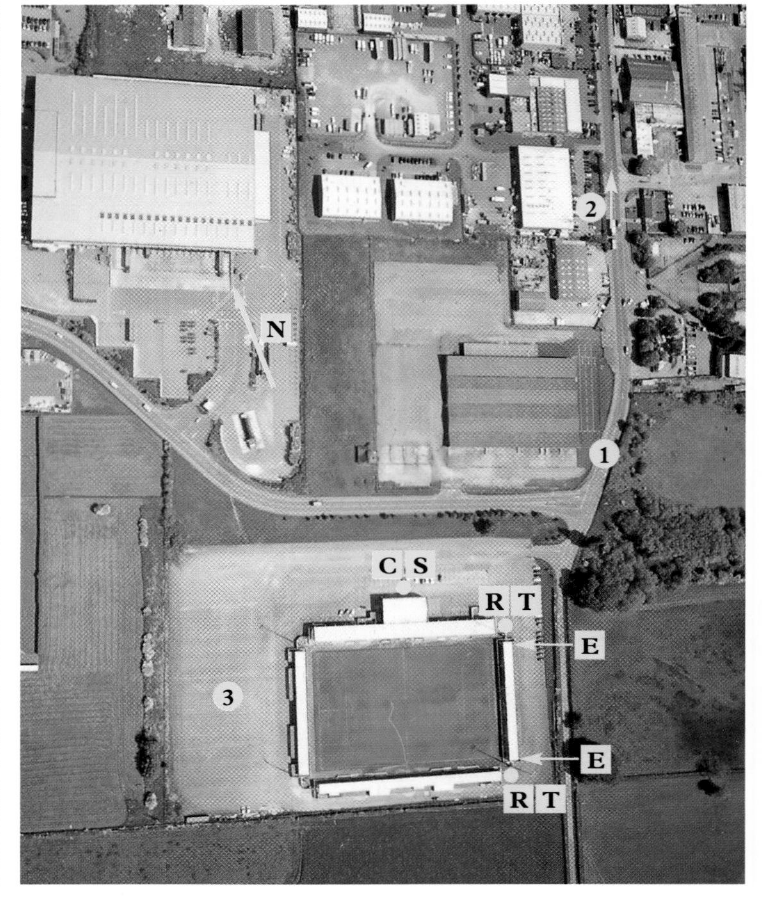

Above: 697211; *Right:* 697204

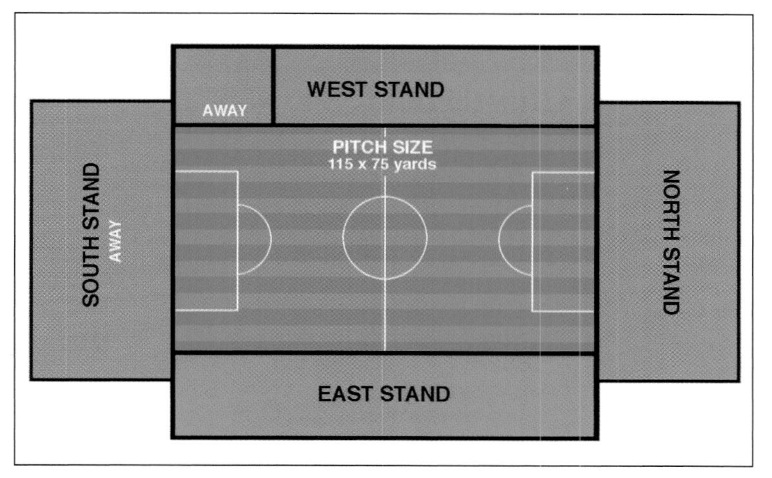

Four years after Chester lost their League status — four years in which the club's very survival was open to doubt at one stage — League football returns to the Deva Stadium as a result of City's success in winning the Nationwide Conference. Mark Wright's team was top of the table for virtually the entire season, with the only realistic challenge to its dominance coming from another ex-League team, Hereford United. In recent years, teams promoted from the Conference have gone on to do well at the higher level — witness Doncaster Rovers immediate promotion to League One in 2003/04 — and hopes will be high that City can emulate the feat. It may well be, however, that the best the club can aspire to is to challenge for a Play-Off place, but even this will represent a startling turn round for a club that might not have survived into the 21st century.

CHESTERFIELD

Recreation Ground, Saltergate, Chesterfield, S40 4SX

Tel No: 01246 209765
Advance Tickets Tel No: 01246 209765
Fax: 01246 556799
Web Site: www.chesterfield-fc.premiumtv.co.uk
E-Mail: reception@chesterfield-fc.co.uk
League: League One
Brief History: Found 1886. Former Ground: Spital Vale. Formerly named Chesterfield Town. Record attendance 30,968
(Total) Current Capacity: 8,300 (2,674 seated)
Visiting Supporters' Allocation: 2,200 maximum (maximum 800 seated)
Club Colours: Blue and white shirts, white shorts
Nearest Railway Station: Chesterfield
Parking (Car): Saltergate car park, street parking
Parking (Coach/Bus): As directed by Police
Police Force and Tel No: Derbyshire (01246 220100)
Disabled Visitors' Facilities:
Wheelchairs: Saltergate Stand
Blind: No special facility
Anticipated Development(s): The club's supporters voted in favour of relocation in the summer of 2003 and the club is now actively pursuing relocation to the site of a former greyhound stadium at Brinington for which planning permission has now been granted.

KEY

- **C** Club Offices
- **S** Club Shop
- **E** Entrance(s) for visiting supporters
- **R** Refreshment bars for visiting supporters
- **T** Toilets for visiting supporters
- ⬆ North direction (approx)

1. Saltergate
2. Cross Street
3. St Margaret's Drive
4. West Bars
5. To A617 & M1 Junction 29
6. To station and town centre
7. Compton Street Terrace
8. Cross Street End (away)

Above: 695552; *Right:* 695550

As forecast, Chesterfield did experience another battle against relegation in 2003/04, with its ultimate fate depending upon results on the last day of the season. On the last day, one of three teams — Grimsby, Rushden or Chesterfield — could survive with the other two being consigned to League Two. In the event, both Grimsby and Rushden lost and the Spireites defeated Luton 1-0 at the Recreation Ground thus ensuring another season of League One football for Roy McFarland's team. In the great escape, the team was undoubtedly assisted by Rushden's freefall during the latter part of the season; without this, it's probable that Chesterfield would have been relegated and it's hard to escape the conclusion that once again the new season will see the team battling to avoid the drop.

COLCHESTER UNITED

Layer Road Ground, Colchester, CO2 7JJ

Tel No: 0845 330 2975
Advance Tickets Tel No: 0845 330 2975
Fax: 01206 715327
Web Site: www.cu-fc.premiumtv.co.uk
E-Mail: commercial@colchesterunited.net
League: League One
Brief History: Founded 1937, joined Football League 1950, relegated 1990, promoted 1992. Record attendance 19,072
(Total) Current Capacity: 7,556 (1,877 seated)
Visiting Supporters' Allocation: 650 in Layer Road End (standing) plus 200 seats (East Coast Cable Stand)
Club Colours: Royal blue and white shirts, blue shorts
Nearest Railway Station: Colchester Town
Parking (Car): Street parking
Parking (Coach/Bus): Boadicea Way
Police Force and Tel No: Essex (01206 762212)
Disabled Visitors' Facilities:
Wheelchairs: Space for 12 in front of terrace (next to Main Stand)
Blind: Space for 3 blind persons and 3 guides (two regularly occupied by home supporters)
Anticipated Development(s): The club is progressing with its plans for the construction of a new 10,000-seat stadium at Cuckoo Farm close to the A12 although the planned opening date has yet to be confirmed.

KEY

- **C** Club Offices
- **S** Club Shop
- **E** Entrance(s) for visiting supporters
- **R** Refreshment bars for visiting supporters
- **T** Toilets for visiting supporters
- ⬆ North direction (approx)

- ❶ B1026 Layer Road
- ❷ Town Centre & Colchester Town BR Station (2 miles)
- ❸ Evening Gazette Main Stand
- ❹ Barside Popular Side
- ❺ East Coast Cable Stand

Above: 697285; *Right:* 697277

Under Phil Parkinson, United did manage to make some limited progress in 2003/04, finishing in 11th position rather than the 12th of the previous season. One of the high points of the campaign was victory over First Division Coventry City 3-1 in an FA Cup Fourth Round replay at Layer Road. Never quite good enough to make a serious challenge for the Play-Offs in 2003/04, the relative lack of strength in the three teams relegated from the First Division in 2003/04 means that the chasing pack in League One may well find that 2004/05 represents their best chance of promotion. As one of the chasing pack, United could be closer to the Play-offs than in previous years.

COVENTRY CITY

Highfield Road Stadium, King Richard Street, Coventry CV2 4FW

Tel No: 02476 234000
Advance Tickets Tel No: 02476 234020
Fax: 02476 234099
Web Site: www.ccfc.co.uk
E-Mail: info@ccfc.co.uk
League: League Championship
Brief History: Founded 1883 as Singers F.C., changed name to Coventry City in 1898. Former grounds: Dowell's Field, Stoke Road Ground, moved to Highfield Road in 1899. Record attendance 51,455
(Total) Current Capacity: 23,627 all seated
Visiting Supporters' Allocation: 4,148 all seated in Mitchells & Butler Stand
Club Colours: Sky blue shirts, dark blue shorts
Nearest Railway Station: Coventry
Parking (Car): Street parking
Parking (Coach/Bus): Gosford Green Coach Park
Police Force and Tel No: West Midlands (02476 539010)
Disabled Visitors' Facilities:
Wheelchairs: Clock Stand and East Stand
Blind: Clock Stand (booking necessary)
Anticipated Development(s): If all goes according to plan 2004/05 will be City's last season at Highfield Road as work has started on the development of the club's new home at Foleshill. The multi-million pound development, part funded by the local council, also includes a new railway station and supermarket. The club will lease the new stadium and Highfield Road has been sold for redevelopment once the new ground is functioning.

KEY

- **C** Club Offices
- **S** Club Shop
- **E** Entrance(s) for visiting supporters
- **R** Refreshment bars for visiting supporters
- **T** Toilets for visiting supporters

- ⬆ North direction (approx)

1. Swan Lane
2. Thackhall Street
3. Nicholls Street
4. Catherine Street
5. A444 Phoenix Way
6. Heath Road
7. To M6 Junction 3
8. To A428 Binley Road
9. To Gosford Green coach park
10. To Coventry station (one mile)
11. M&B Stand

Above: 688720; *Right:* 688710

In early December, Gary McAllister stood down temporarily as manager for family reasons with his assistant, Eric Black, taking over as caretaker. In early January, however, McAllister announced his resignation to enable the club to focus on the future and the club moved quickly to appoint a successor, confirming Eric Black in post until the end of the 2004/05 season. However, despite a 5-2 away win at Gillingham in the penultimate game of the season, inconsistent form meant that Eric Black was dismissed in early May, with Peter Reid being quickly appointed to take over. Reid's experience should help City in the new campaign, but the competition for automatic promotion and the Play-Offs is certain to be as intense as ever in 2004/05 and it's difficult to see City as anything other than potential Play-Off candidates at best.

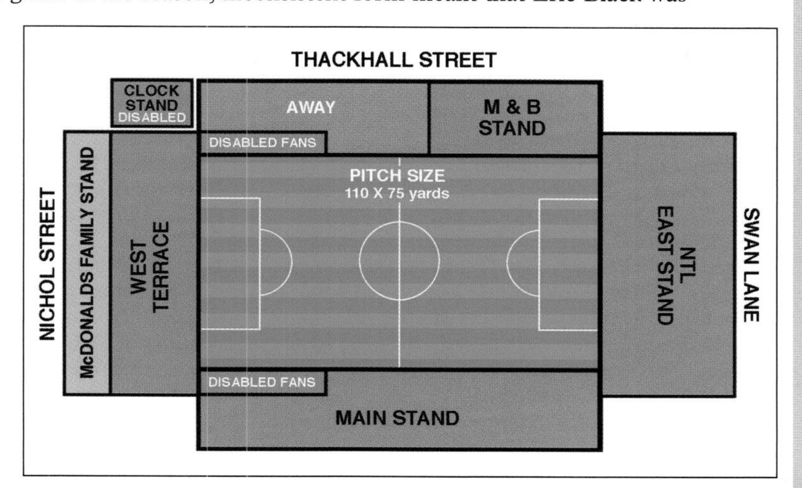

CRECREWE ALEXANDRA

The Alexandra Stadium, Gresty Road, Crewe, Cheshire, CW2 6EB

Tel No: 01270 213014
Advance Tickets Tel No: 01270 252610
Fax: 01270 216320
Website: www.crewealex.net
E-Mail: info@crewealex.premiertv.co.uk
League: League Championship
Brief History: Founded 1877. Former Grounds: Alexandra Recreation Ground (Nantwich Road), Earle Street Cricket Ground, Edleston Road, Old Sheds Fields, Gresty Road (Adjacent to current Ground), moved to current Ground in 1906. Founder members of 2nd Division (1892) until 1896. Founder members of 3rd Division North (1921). Record attendance 20,000
(Total) Current Capacity: 10,100 all seated
Visiting Supporters' Allocation: 1,694 (Blue Bell BMW Stand)
Club Colours: Red shirts, white shorts
Nearest Railway Station: Crewe
Parking (car): There is a car park adjacent to the ground. It should be noted that there is a residents' only scheme in operation in the streets surrounding the ground.
Parking (Coach/Bus): As directed by Police
Police Force and Tel No: Cheshire (01270 500222)
Disabled Visitors' Facilities:
Wheelchairs: Available on all four sides
Blind: Commentary available
Anticipated Development(s): The club has long term plans for the construction of a new two-tier stand to replace the Blue Bell (BMW) Stand, although there is no confirmed timescale for the work.

KEY

- **C** Club Offices
- **S** Club Shop
- **E** Entrance(s) for visiting supporters
- ⬆ North direction (approx)
- ❶ Crewe BR Station
- ❷ Gresty Road
- ❸ Gresty Road
- ❹ A534 Nantwich Road
- ❺ To A5020 to M6 Junction 16
- ❻ To M6 Junction 17 [follow directions at roundabout to M6 J16/J17]
- ❼ Main Stand
- ❽ Gresty Road (Adtranz) Stand
- ❾ Railway End
- ❿ Ringways Stand (Blue Bell BMW)(away)
- ⓫ Car Park

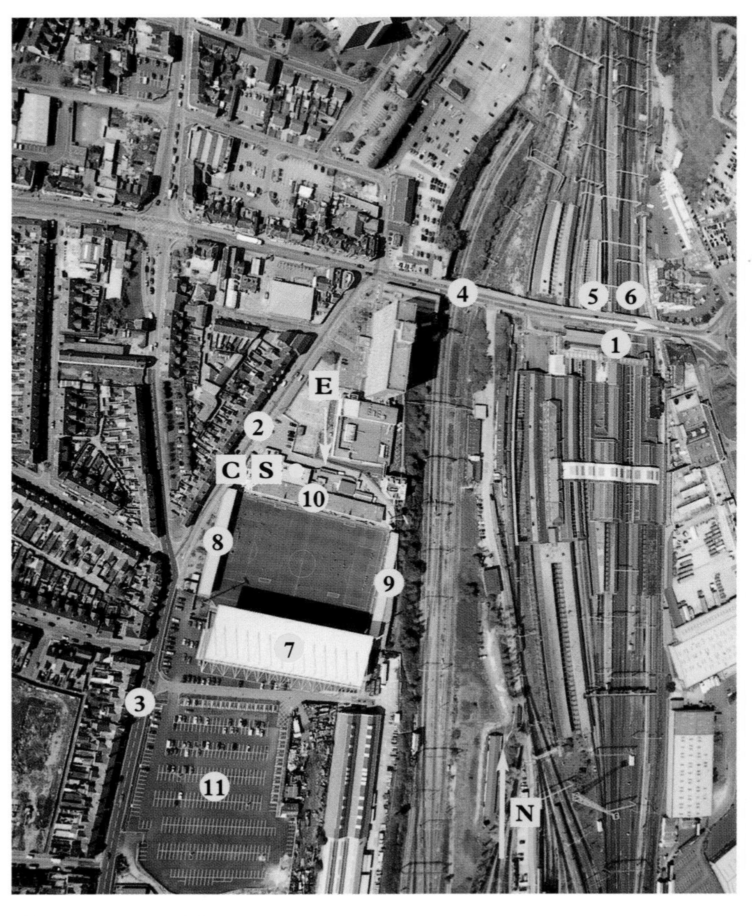

Above: 684966; *Right:* 684958

Having secured promotion at the end of 2002/03, the Railwaymen defied the odds and, for the first part of the season, looked like serious contenders for a Play-Off position. However, as the season wore on, performances took a dip and the team gradually slipped down the table and, ultimately finished in 18th position only two points off the drop zone. Another negative during the season was the defeat 1-0 at home against non-league Telford United in the Third Round of the FA Cup. Dario Gradi has now been at Crewe for more than two decades and, in that time, has fostered some of the most talented young players and has, despite the odds, ensured that Crewe play attractive football. No doubt the new season will again see the club face a struggle to survive, a struggle that may be more difficult in 2004/05 as the League Championship arguably looks stronger than that of 2003/04. Survival at best is perhaps the most that the Gresty Road faithful can look forward to in the new season.

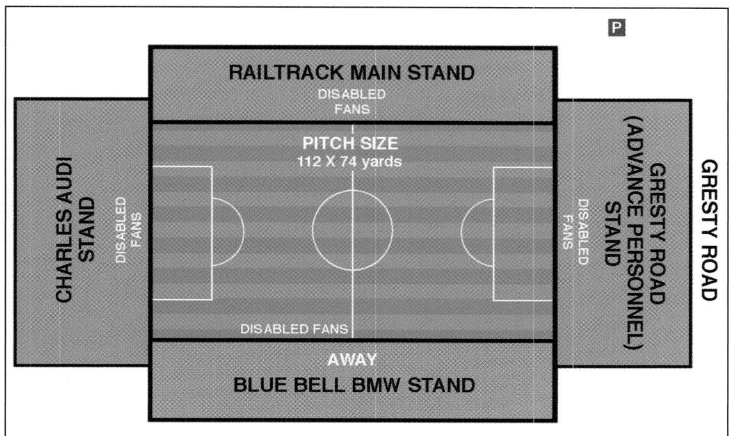

CRYSTAL PALACE

Selhurst Park, London, SE25 6PU

Tel No: 020 8768 6000
Advance Tickets Tel No: 08712 000071
Fax: 020 8771 5311
Web Site: www.cpfc.premiumtv.co.uk
E-Mail: info@cpfc.co.uk
Ticket Office/Fax: 020 8653 4708
League: FA Premiership
Brief History: Founded 1905. Former Grounds: The Crystal Palace (F.A. Cup Finals venue), London County Athletic Ground (Herne Hill), The Nest (Croydon Common Athletic Ground), moved to Selhurst Park in 1924. Founder members 3rd Division (1920). Record attendance 51,482
(Total) Current Capacity: 26,400 all seated
Visiting Supporters' Allocation: Approx 2,000 in Arthur Wait Stand
Club Colours: Blue and red striped shirts, red shorts
Nearest Railway Station: Selhurst, Norwood Junction and Thornton Heath
Parking (Car): Street parking and Sainsbury's car park
Parking (Coach/Bus): Thornton Heath
Police Force and Tel No: Metropolitan (020 8653 8568)
Disabled Visitors' Facilities:
Wheelchairs: 56 spaces in Arthur Wait and Holmesdale Stands
Blind: Commentary available
Anticipated Development(s): Although the club had plans to reconstruct the Main Stand — indeed had Planning Permission for the work — local opposition has meant that no work has been undertaken. Serious thought is now being given to relocation.

KEY

- **C** Club Offices
- **S** Club Shop
- **E** Entrance(s) for visiting supporters
- **T** Toilets for visiting supporters
- ⬆ North direction (approx)

1. Whitehorse Lane
2. Park Road
3. A213 Selhurst Road
4. Selhurst BR Station (1/2 mile)
5. Norwood Junction BR Station (1/4 mile)
6. Thornton Heath BR Station (1/2 mile)
7. Car Park (Sainsbury's)

Above: 695773; *Right:* 695766

After a sequence of only one win in 13 games, Steve Kember lost the managership in early November with the team just above the drop zone. He was replaced on a caretaker basis by Kit Symons but ex-Oldham boss Iain Dowie, who was once a player with Palace, took over the reins full-time just before Christmas. The turn round in form was impressive, with the team moving rapidly up the table. Sneaking into the Play-Offs towards the end — for much of the final day it appeared that Wigan held the all-important position — Palace ultimately finished in sixth position and faced Sunderland in the Play-Offs. Victory over the two legs took the Londoners to a final in Cardiff against West Ham. Victory, 1-0, saw the Eagles soar into the Premiership at the Hammers' expense. Palace will undoubtedly be one of the pre-season favourites for an immediate return to the League Championship and it is difficult to gainsay the argument. However, Iain Dowie may well engender enough spirit to ensure that the club makes a decent effort and, if the confidence is there, the club might still sneak another success and survive.

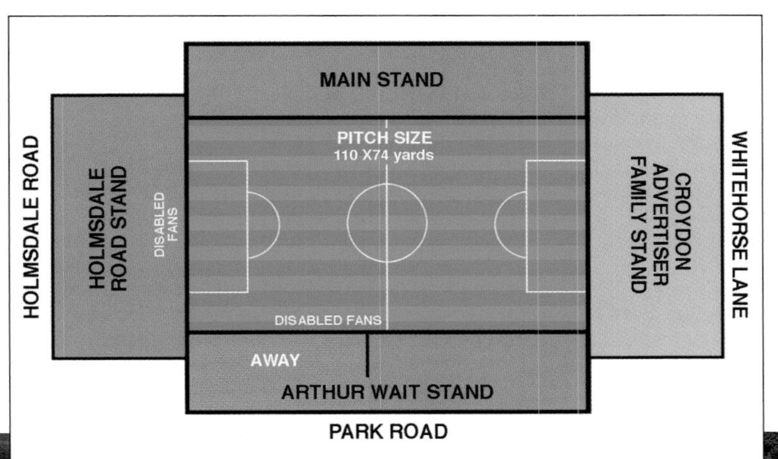

DARLINGTON

The New Stadium, Neasham Road, Darlington DL2 1GR

Tel No: 01325 387000
Advance Tickets Tel No: 01325 387030
Fax: 01325 387050
Web Site: www.darlington-fc.premiumtv.co.uk
E-mail: carol@newstadium.fs.net
League: League Two
Brief History: Founded 1883. Founder members of 3rd Division (North) 1921. Relegated from 4th Division 1989. Promoted from GM Vauxhall Conference in 1990. Previous Ground: Fathoms; moving to Neasham Road in 2003. Record attendance (at Feethams) 21,023; (at Neasham Road) 11,600
(Total) Current Capacity: 25,000
Visiting Supporters' Allocation: 3,000 in East Stand
Club Colours: White and black shirts, black shorts
Nearest Railway Station: Darlington Bank Top
Parking (Car): Spaces available in adjacent car park (£5.00 fee)
Parking (Coach/Bus): As directed
Police Force and Tel No: Durham (01235 467681)
Disabled Visitors Facilities:
Wheelchairs: 165 places
Blind: tbc
Anticipated Developments: The club finally moved into the new stadium, at that date called 'The Reynolds Arena', in August 2003. However, the club's financial problems suggested that, at one stage, it would return to Feethams; however, this now seems unlikely. With the construction of the new ground, there are no further plans for development as the existing ground's capacity is more than adequate for League Two.

⬆ North direction (approx)

❶ A66
❷ To Stockton
❸ To A66(M) and A1(M)
❹ Neasham Road
❺ To Darlington town centre and railway station (one mile)
❻ To Neasham
❼ Snipe Lane

Above: 695517; *Right:* 695507

At the end of October, with the Quakers towards the wrong end of the Third Division, Mick Tait stood down as manager, although remaining at the club in another capacity, to be replaced by David Hodgson, who returned to the club for his third spell in charge. Just before Christmas the club entered Administration and for a period the very future of the club seemed in doubt as a result of disagreements between erstwhile chairman, George Reynolds, and the consortium seeking to acquire the club. Towards the end of the season, these differences seemed to have been resolved, with a CVA being agreed at the end of May, and thus fans of the Quakers can look forward to a further season of League Two football thankful that they still have a team to support. On the field, Darlington dallied too close to the drop zone for much of the season but ultimately were to finish in 18th position. With stability, hopefully, ensured off the field, perhaps the club can concentrate on football in 2004/05 and fans will be expecting a distinct improvement on the story of 2003/04.

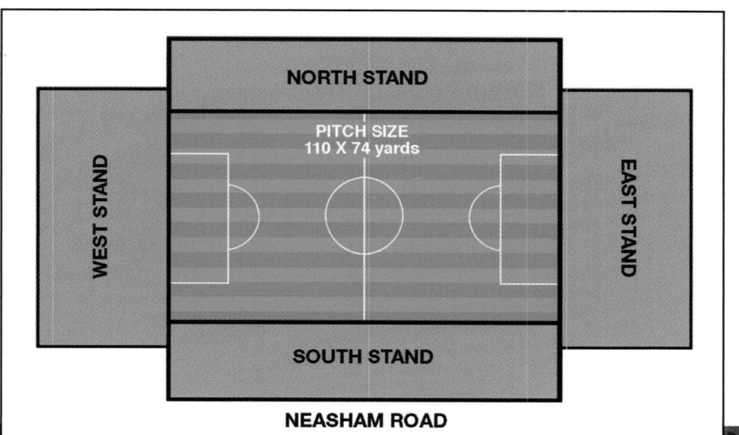

DERBY COUNTY

Pride Park, Derby, Derbyshire DE24 8XL

Tel No: 0870 444 1884
Advance Tickets Tel No: 0870 444 1884
Fax: 01332 667540
Web Site: www.dcfc.co.uk
E-Mail: derby.county@dcfc.premiumtv.co.uk
League: League Championship
Brief History: Founded 1884. Former grounds: The Racecourse Ground, the Baseball Ground (1894-1997), moved to Pride Park 1997. Founder members of the Football League (1888). Record capacity at the Baseball Ground: 41,826; at Pride Park: 33,597
(Total) Current Capacity: 33,597
Visiting Supporters' Allocation: 4,800 in the South Stand
Club Colours: White shirts and black shorts
Nearest Railway Station: Derby
Parking (Car): 2,300 places at the ground designated for season ticket holders. Also two 1,000 car parks on the A6/A52 link road. No on-street parking
Parking (Coach/Bus): As directed
Police Force and Tel No: Derbyshire (01332 290100)
Disabled Visitors' Facilities:
Wheelchairs: 70 home/30 away spaces
Blind: Commentary available
Anticipated Development(s): There are no definite plans for the further development of Pride Park following the completion of the southwest corner.

KEY

- **C** Club Offices
- **S** Club Shop
- **E** Entrance(s) for visiting supporters
- ⬆ North direction (approx)
- ❶ To Derby Midland BR station
- ❷ North Stand
- ❸ Toyota West Stand
- ❹ South (McArthur Glen) Stand (away)
- ❺ Bombardier East Stand
- ❻ Derwent Parade
- ❼ To A52/M1
- ❽ To City Centre and A6
- ❾ A52

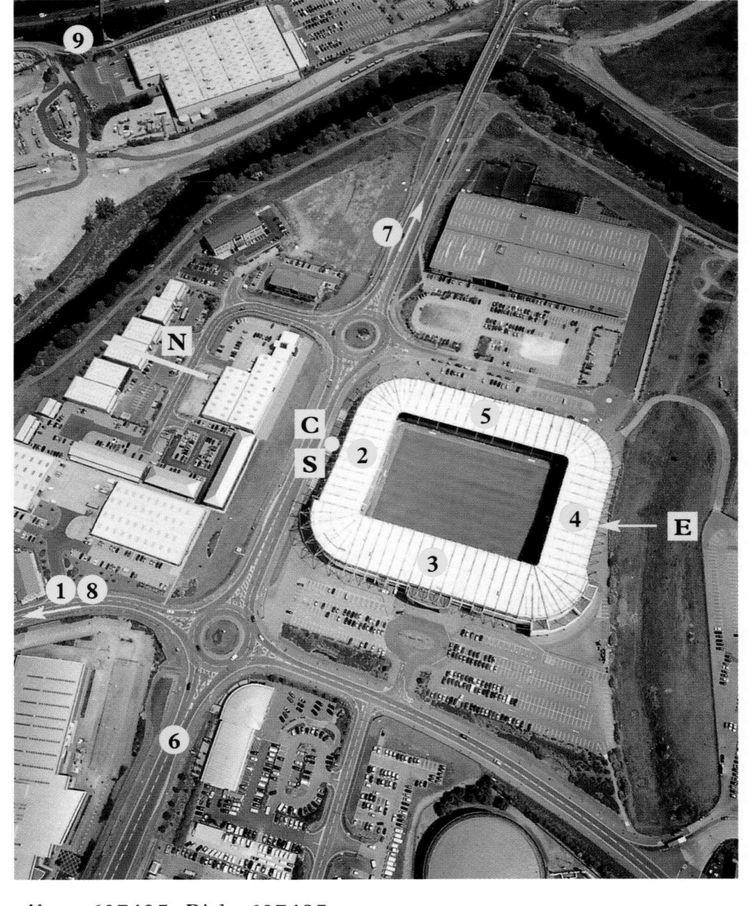

Above: 697495; *Right:* 697485

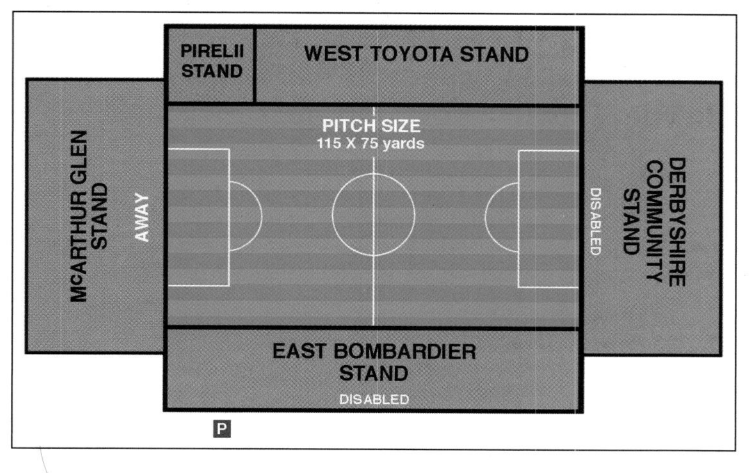

A worrying season at Pride Park saw George Burley's team in or close to the First Division drop zone for much of the year and it was only results towards the end of the campaign that ensured League Championship football for another year. With the club still financially-stretched as a result of its years in the Premiership, it's likely that the team will face a further season of adversity in 2004/05, particularly as, in Plymouth and QPR, the new arrivals in this division look better placed than usual to survive at this higher level.

DONCASTER ROVERS

The Earth Stadium, Belle Vue, Bawtry Road, Doncaster, DN4 5HT

Tel No: 01302 539441
Advance Tickets Tel No: 01302 379329
Fax: 01302 539679
Web Site: www.doncasterroversfc.premiumtv.co.uk
E-mail: info@doncasterroversfc.co.uk
League: League One
Brief History: Founded 1879, Former grounds: Town Moor, Belle Vue (not current ground), Deaf School Playing Field (later name Intake Ground), Bennetthorpe, moved to Belle Vue (former name Low Pasture) in 1922. Returned to Football League after a five-year absence in 2003. Record attendance 37,149
(Total) Current Capacity: 9,706 (1,259 seated)
Visiting Supporters' Allocation: 1,900 on Rossington End terrace (open, standing), plus 800 (300 seated) in Main Stand if required
Club Colours: Red and white shirts, red shorts
Nearest Railway Station: Doncaster
Parking (Car): Car park at ground
Parking (Coach/Bus): Car park at ground
Other Clubs Sharing Ground: Doncaster Dragons RLFC and Doncaster Belles Ladies FC
Police Force and Tel No: South Yorkshire (01302 366744)
Disabled Visitors' facilities:
Wheelchairs: Bawtry Road
Blind: No special facility
Anticipated Development(s): The council is backing a proposal for the construction of a new £20 million stadium, providing seats for 10,000, to be shared between Rovers, Doncaster Dragons RLFC and Doncaster Belles Ladies FC. The current plan envisages this being available from the start of the 2005/06 season.

KEY

⬆ North direction (approx)

1. Doncaster Racecourse
2. A638 Bawtry Road
3. To Bawtry
4. To Doncaster town centre and railway station (1.5 miles)
5. Carr House Road
6. Car Park
7. Main Stand
8. Rossington End (away)

Above: 695664; *Right:* 695660

The club's first season back in the Football League proved to be a considerable triumph, with Dave Penney's team looking like promotion candidates throughout the campaign and ultimately winning the Third Division title ahead of more fancied teams. It wasn't all positive however, as the team managed to lose 1-0 away to Scarborough in first round of FA Cup. Two promotions in two seasons have often proved to be one promotion too far for other clubs and it is hard to escape the conclusion that Rovers may well struggle in League One. Perhaps the best that can be hoped for is a season of consolidation but more likely is a battle against relegation.

TERRACE) (OPEN
MAIN STAND
(AWAY) TERRACE) (OPEN
PITCH SIZE
TOWN END (OPEN TERRACE)
ROSSINGTON END TERRACE (OPEN) (AWAY)
POPULAR TERRACE (COVERED TERRACE)

EVERTON

Goodison Park, Goodison Road, Liverpool, L4 4EL

Tel No: 0151 330 2200
Advance Tickets Tel No: 0151 330 2300
Fax: 0151 286 9112
Web Site: www.everton.fc.com
E-Mail: everton@evertonfc.com
League: F.A. Premier
Brief History: Founded 1879 as St. Domingo, changed to Everton in 1880. Former grounds: Stanley Park, Priory Road and Anfield (Liverpool F.C. Ground), moved to Goodison Park in 1892. Founder-members Football League (1888). Record attendance 78,299
(Total) Current Capacity: 40,170 all seated
Visiting Supporters' Allocation: 3,000 (part of Bullens Road Stand) maximum
Club Colours: Blue and white shirts, white shorts
Nearest Railway Station: Liverpool Lime Street
Parking (Car): Corner of Utting Avenue and Priory Road
Parking (Coach/Bus): Priory Road
Police Force and Tel No: Merseyside (0151 709 6010)
Disabled Visitors' Facilities:
Wheelchairs: Bullens Road Stand
Blind: Commentary available
Anticipated Development(s): Having abandoned earlier proposals to relocate to a new stadium in the King's Dock area, the club is still keen to move from Goodison and is now investigating the possibility of constructing a 55,000-seat stadium in the Central docks area. This is, however, only a tentative proposal at this stage and much will depend on getting the funding in place. Another recent proposal is for the club to share Liverpool FC's planned new ground. Expect Everton to remain at Goodison for probably for at least two or three seasons at least.

KEY

- **C** Club Offices
- **S** Club Shop
- **E** Entrance(s) for visiting supporters
- **R** Refreshment bars for visiting supporters
- **T** Toilets for visiting supporters
- ⬆ North direction (approx)

1. A580 Walton Road
2. Bullen Road
3. Goodison Road
4. Car Park
5. Liverpool Lime Street BR Station (2 miles)
6. To M57 Junction 2, 4 and 5
7. Stanley Park

Above: 695687; *Right:* 695678

A disappointing season for fans of the Toffees after the near miss at the end of 2002/03 when the club just missed out of reaching the UEFA Cup. In 2003/04 David Moyes' team reverted to type and were more interested in events at Leeds, Wolves and Leicester than at Old Trafford, Highbury and Stamford Bridge. Although Premiership survival was again assured, the team's proximity to the drop zone will not be regarded as acceptable by manager, players and fans. Although the team does possess players of some talent, it seems to lack the consistency required to make a serious and sustained challenge for the top half of the table. Whilst the promoted teams in 2004/05 look unlikely to pose a serious challenge to the established Premiership order, Everton is one of those teams that could be looking nervously over its shoulders as the new campaign draws to a close if any of the new trio show the same sort of fighting spirit evinced by Portsmouth and, to a lesser extent, by Wolves and Leicester.

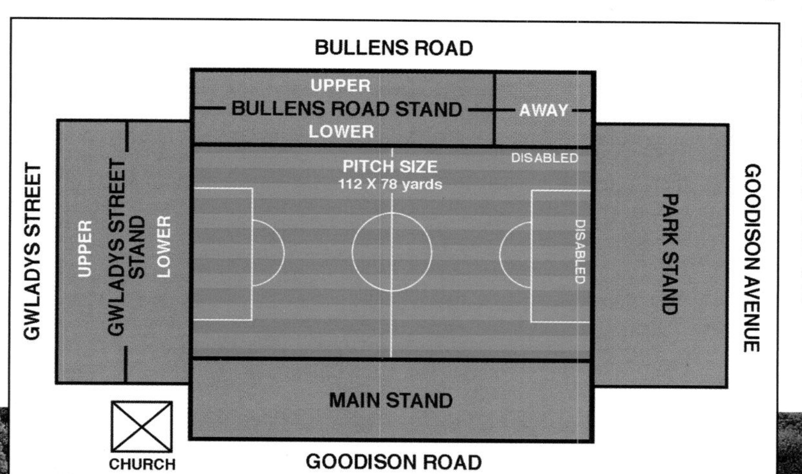

FULHAM

Craven Cottage, Stevenage Road, Fulham, London SW6 6HH

Tel No: 020 7893 8383
Advance Tickets Tel No: 020 7384 4710
Fax: 020 7384 4715
Web-site: www.fulhamfc.co.uk
E-mail:
League: F.A. Premiership
Brief History: Founded in 1879 at St. Andrews Fulham, changed name to Fulham in 1898. Former grounds: Star Road, Ranelagh Club, Lillie Road, Eel Brook Common, Purer's Cross, Barn Elms, Half Moon (Wasps Rugby Football Ground, Craven Cottage (from 1894), moved to Loftus Road 2002 and returned to Craven Cottage for start of the 2004/05 season. Record Attendance: Craven Cottage (49,335)
(Total) Current Capacity: 22,000
Visiting Supporters' Allocation: 3,000 in Putney End
Club Colours: White shirts, black shorts
Nearest Railway Station: Putney Bridge (Tube)
Parking (Car): Street parking
Parking(Coach/Bus): Stevenage Road
Police Force and Tel No: Metropolitan (020 7741 6212)
Disabled Visitors' Facilities:
Wheelchairs: Main Stand and Hammersmith End
Blind: No special facility
Anticipated Development(s): It was announced in mid-December that the club had obtained planning permission for a limited £5.4 million upgrade to Craven Cottage. The work, with a completion date of July 2004, includes the bolting on of seats to the existing terraces and the provision of new floodlighting. After the work is completed, the ground's capacity will be 22,000 all-seated. The club's long term aim, however, remains to relocate within the west London area provided that a suitable site can be identified.

KEY

- **C** QPR club offices
- **S** Club shop
- **E** Entrance(s) for visiting supporters
- **R** Refreshment bars for visiting supporters
- **T** Toilets for visiting supporters

⬆ North direction (approx)

1. River Thames
2. Stevenage Road
3. Finlay Street
4. Putney Bridge Tube Station (0.5 mile)
5. Putney End (away)
6. Riverside Stand
7. Main Stand
8. Hammersmith End
9. Craven Cottage

Above: 697373; *Right:* 697364

Many pundits expected Fulham to struggle in the Premiership under tyro manager Chris Coleman, but the team did far better than most expected during 2003/04. Indeed, for much of the season, a European spot was a very real possibility. However, form towards the end of the campaign was variable and the team ultimately finished in ninth position, but only four points below Newcastle who finished fifth and took the final UEFA Cup spot. With the team returning to Craven Cottage for 2004/05, optimism will be high that Coleman's first season in charge has laid the basis of a further successful campaign in the new season. Whilst it's difficult to see the team hitting a place in the top five and thus guaranteeing European football, the team should undoubtedly be one of the chasing pack that will snap at the heels of the top five teams.

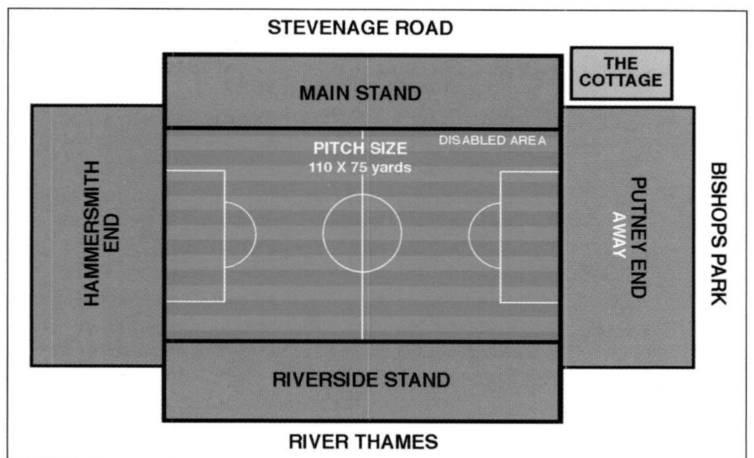

GILLINGHAM

Priestfield Stadium, Redfern Avenue, Gillingham, Kent, ME7 4DD

Tel No: 01634 300000
Advance Tickets Tel No: 01634 300000
Fax: 01634 850986
Web Site: www.gillinghamfootballclub.premiumtv.co.uk
E-mail: info@gillinghamfootballclub.com
League: League Championship
Brief History: Founded 1893, as New Brompton, changed name to Gillingham in 1913. Founder-members Third Division (1920). Lost Football League status (1938), re-elected to Third Division South (1950). Record attendance 23,002
(Total) Current Capacity: 10,952 (all seated)
Visiting Supporters' Allocation: 1,300 (in Gillingham End)
Club Colours: Blue and black hooped shirts, blue shorts
Nearest Railway Station: Gillingham
Parking (Car): Street parking
Parking (Coach/Bus): As directed by Police
Police Force and Tel No: Kent (01634 234488)
Disabled Visitors' Facilities:
Wheelchairs: Redfern Avenue (Main) Stand
Blind: No special facility
Anticipated Development(s): The old open Town End Terrace was demolished during 2003 and replaced by a new temporary open stand. Planning Permission was granted in 2003 for the construction of a new 3,500-seat stand, to be named after noted fan the late Brian Moore, and it hoped that this will be available by the start of the 2004/05 season. Despite the investment at Priestfield, however, the club is investigating, in conjunction with the local council, the possibility of constructing a new stadium at Temple Marsh.

KEY

E Entrance(s) for visiting supporters

⬆ North direction (approx)

1. Redfern Avenue
2. Toronto Road
3. Gordon Road
4. Gillingham BR station (1/4 mile)
5. Gordon Street Stand
6. New two-tier Main (Medway) Stand
7. New Rainham End Stand
8. Gillingham End; uncovered seating (away)

Above: 697309; *Right:* 697302

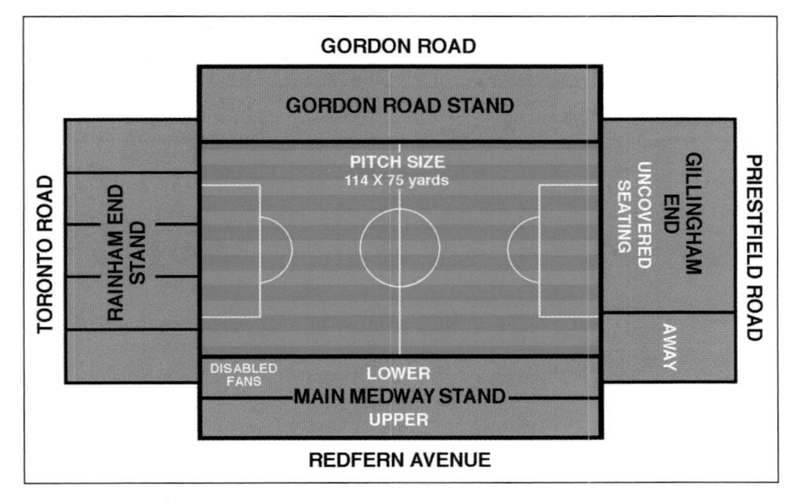

A somewhat difficult season for Andy Hessenthaler and his Gillingham team, saw the Gills hovering just above the relegation zone for much of the campaign. Indeed, it was a draw away at Stoke City in the final game of the season that ensured League Championship football again at the Priestfield Stadium in 2004/05 as the team survived on goal difference over relegated Walsall. With money being tight and with a stretched squad if (and when) injuries intervene, it is hard to escape the conclusion that the Gills will again face a struggle to avoid the drop and, perhaps, this forthcoming campaign may well be a battle too far to escape once again. In an otherwise pretty disappointing season, the one high spot was perhaps defeating Charlton Athletic in the Third Round of the FA Cup.

GRIMSBY TOWN

Blundell Park, Cleethorpes, DN35 7PY

Tel No: 01472 605050
Advance Tickets Tel No: 01472 605050
Fax: 01472 693665
Web Site: www.grimsby-townfc.premiumtv.co.uk
E-Mail: enquiries@gtfc.co.uk
League: League Two
Brief History: Founded in 1878, as Grimsby Pelham, changed name to Grimsby Town in 1879. Former Grounds: Clee Park (two adjacent fields) and Abbey Park, moved to Blundell Park in 1899. Founder-members 2nd Division (1892). Record attendance 31,651
(Total) Current Capacity: 10,033 (all seated)
Visiting Supporters' Allocation: 2,200 in Osmond Stand
Club Colours: Black and white striped shirts, black shorts
Nearest Railway Station: Cleethorpes
Parking (Car): Street parking
Parking (Coach/Bus): Harrington Street
Police Force and Tel No: Humberside (01472 359171)
Disabled Visitors' Facilities:
Wheelchairs: Harrington Street (Main) Stand
Blind: Commentary available
Anticipated Development(s): The club's proposed relocation to a new £14 million stadium at Great Coates is proving problematic, with the latest difficulty being its inability to acquire the site. If the Great Coates scheme collapses, then the club will probably seek an alternative site for relocation.

KEY

- **C** Club Offices
- **S** Club Shop
- **E** Entrance(s) for visiting supporters
- **R** Refreshment bars for visiting supporters
- **T** Toilets for visiting supporters

⬆ North direction (approx)

1. A180 Grimsby Road
2. Cleethorpes BR Station (1½ miles)
3. To Grimsby and M180 Junction 5
4. Harrington Street
5. Constitutional Avenue
6. Humber Estuary

Following a 6-0 drubbing by Oldham Athletic, which meant that Town had failed to win in 10 games and stood in 20th position in the table only two points off the drop zone, Paul Groves was dismissed from the Blundell Park hot seat in early February, although he remained with the club in a playing capacity. In the short term he was replaced by Graham Rodger and Neil Woods on a caretaker basis. In early March, ex-Bradford City manager Nicky Law was appointed to the end of the season, with Graham Rodger remaining as his number two. However, Law was unable to arrest the team's gradual drift towards the Third Division, although it was results on the final day — with Grimsby losing 2-1 at Tranmere and Chesterfield defeating Luton — that confirmed the fact that the Mariners will be playing at the lower level in 2004/05 — the second relegation in two seasons. With relegation, Nicky Law paid the price of failure and was replaced shortly after the end of the season by ex-Scarborough boss Russell Slade. He will face a struggle to ensure that Town bounce back immediately.

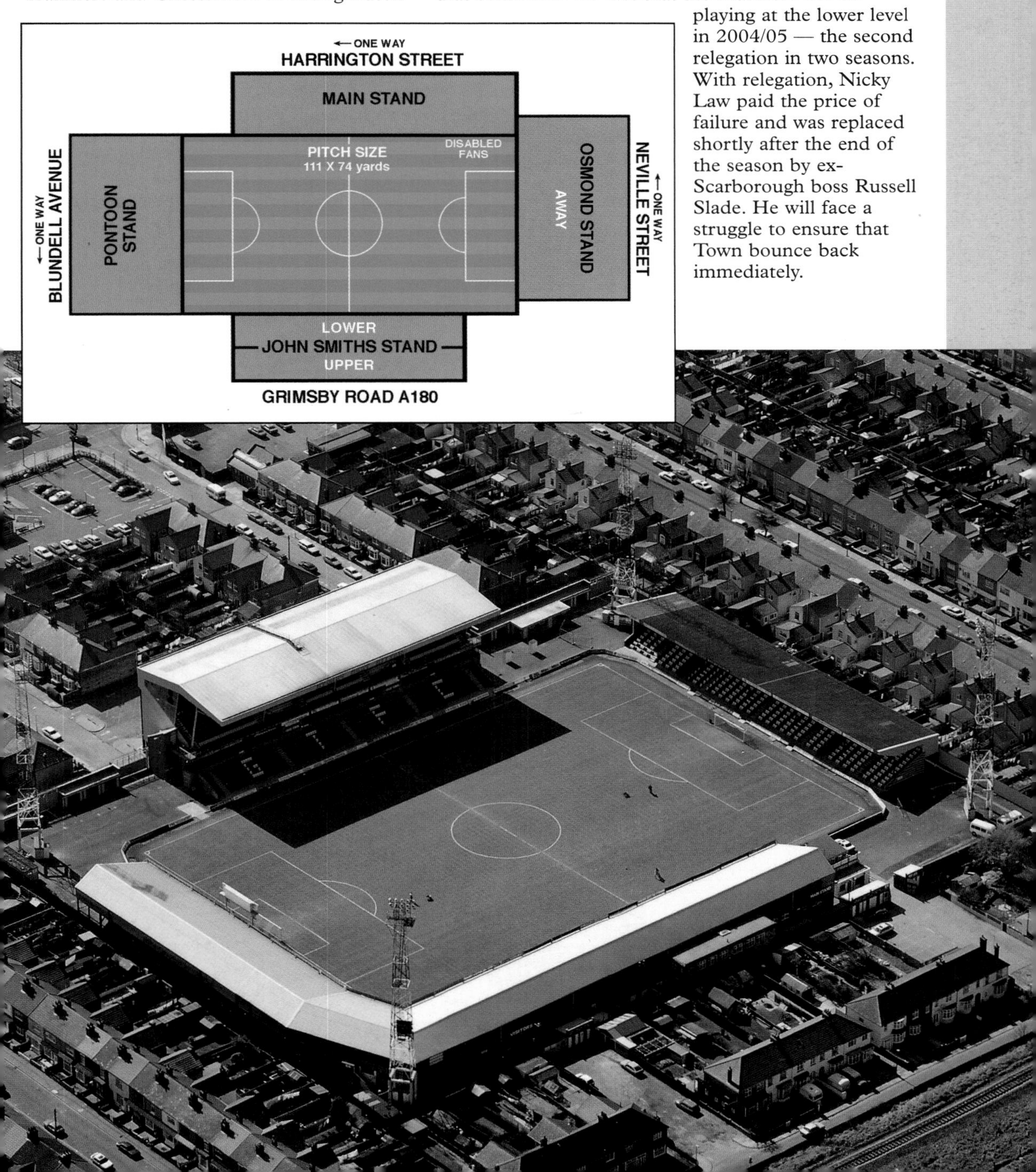

HARTLEPOOL UNITED

Victoria Park, Clarence Road, Hartlepool, TS24 8BZ

Tel No: 01429 272584
Advance Tickets Tel No: 01429 272584
Fax: 01429 863007
Web Site: www.hartlepoolunited.premiumtv.co.uk
E-Mail: info@hartlepoolunited.co.uk
Fax: 01429 863007
League: League One
Brief History: Founded 1808 as Hartlepools United, changed to Hartlepool (1968) and to Hartlepool United in 1977. Founder-members 3rd Division (1921). Record attendance 17,426
(Total) Current Capacity: 7,629 (3,966 seated)
Visiting Supporters' Allocation: 720 (located in Rink Stand)
Club Colours: Blue and white striped shirts, blue shorts
Nearest Railway Station: Hartlepool Church Street
Parking (Car): Street parking and rear of clock garage
Parking (Coach/Bus): As directed
Police Force and Tel No: Cleveland (01429 221151
Disabled Visitors' Facilities:
Wheelchairs: Cyril Knowles Stand and Rink End
Blind: Commentary available
Anticipated Development(s): The plans for the redevelopment of the Millhouse Stand are still progressing, although there is now no definite timescale. When this work does commence, the ground's capacity will be reduced to 5,000 temporarily.

KEY
- **C** Club Offices
- **S** Club Shop
- **E** Entrance(s) for visiting supporters

⬆ North direction (approx)

1. A179 Clarence Road
2. Hartlepool Church Street BR Station
3. Marina Way
4. Site of former Greyhound Stadium
5. To Middlesbrough A689 & A1(M)
6. To A19 North
7. Rink End Stand

Above: 695504; *Right:* 695500

Whilst finishing in the highest position ever achieved by Hartlepool — sixth in the Second Division — might be considered something of a triumph for Neale Cooper in his first season in charge (and in the club's first season back at this level), ultimately, the 2003/04 campaign will be regarded as something of a curate's egg by fans. The glow that will permeate as a result of the undoubted success of thriving at this higher level will be tinged by a sadness that the club was, ultimately not to progress further in the Play-Offs, being defeated by Bristol City over the two legs. Provided that Cooper can retain the bulk of his squad, and strengthen it where needed, Hartlepool could again provide a challenge for the Play-Offs in 2004/05. The danger, however, is that like a number of teams playing in their second season at a higher level, it will be difficult to emulate the success of the first.

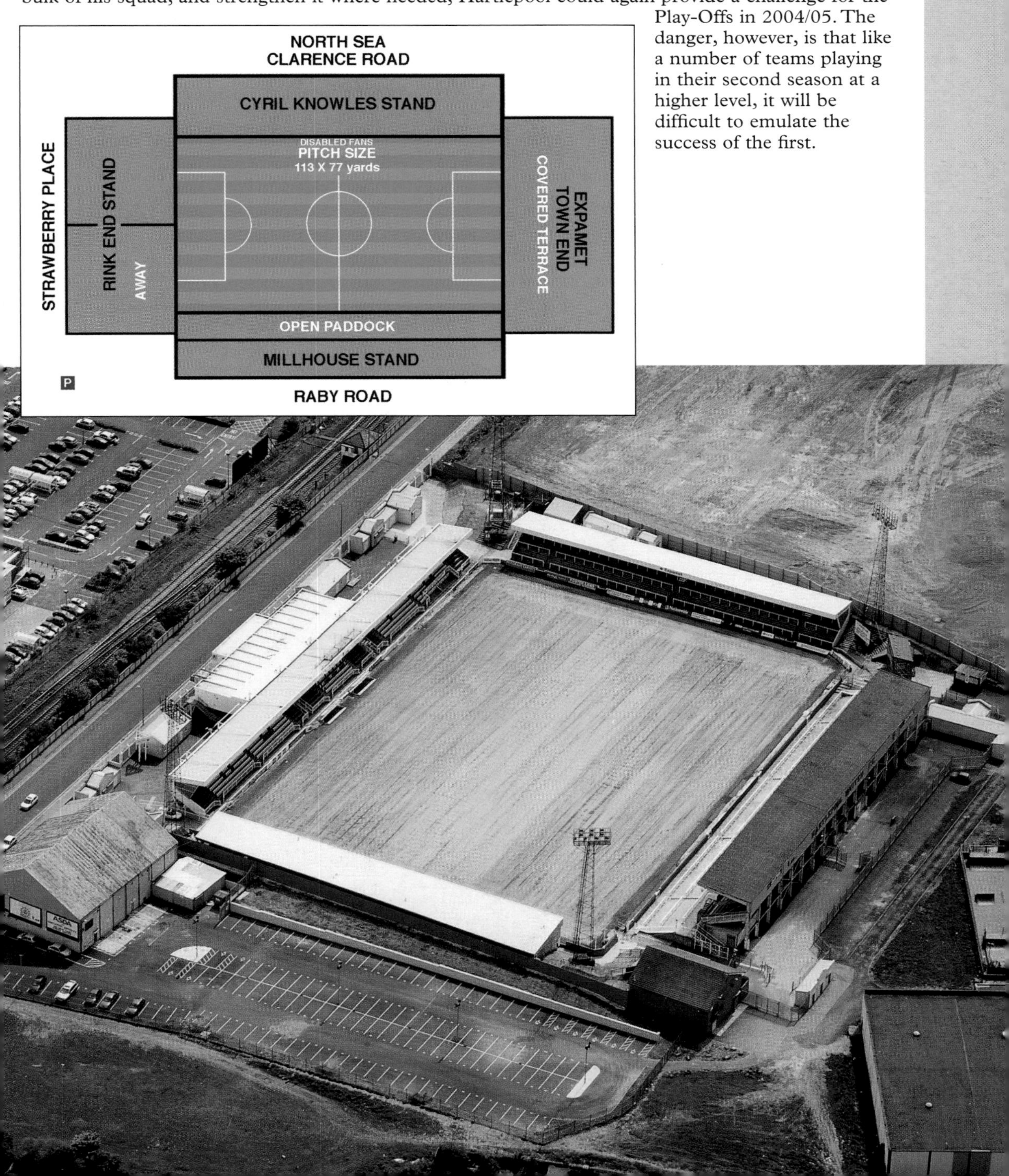

HUDDERSFIELD TOWN

The Alfred McAlpine Stadium, Leeds Road, Huddersfield, HD1 6PX

Tel No: 01484 484100
Advance Tickets Tel No: 01484 484123
Fax: 01484 484101
Web Site: www.htafc.premiumtv.co.uk
E-Mail: info@htafc.com
League: League One
Brief History: Founded 1908, elected to Football League in 1910. First Club to win the Football League Championship three years in succession. Moved from Leeds Road ground to Kirklees (Alfred McAlpine) Stadium 1994/95 season. Record attendance (Leeds Road) 67,037; McAlpine Stadium: 23,678
(Total) Current Capacity: 24,500 (all seated)
Visiting Supporters' Allocation: 4,037 (all seated)
Club Colours: Blue and white striped shirts , white shorts
Nearest Railway Station: Huddersfield
Parking (Car): Car parks (pre-sold) adjacent to ground
Parking (Coach/Bus): Car parks adjacent to ground
Other Clubs Sharing Ground: Huddersfield Giants RLFC
Police Force and Tel No: West Yorkshire (01484 422122)
Disabled Visitors' Facilities:
Wheelchairs: Three sides of Ground, at low levels and raised area, including toilet access
Blind: Area for Partially sighted with Hospital Radio commentary
Anticipated Development(s): With completion of the new North Stand, work on the McAlpine Stadium is over.

KEY

- **C** Club Offices
- **S** Club Shop
- **E** Entrance(s) for visiting supporters
- ⬆ North direction (approx)

1. To Leeds and M62 Junction 25
2. A62 Leeds Road
3. To Huddersfield BR station (1¼ miles)
4. Disabled parking
5. Town Avenue pay car park (on site of former ground)
6. North Stand
7. St Andrews pay car park
8. Coach park
9. South Stand (away)

Above: 695676; *Right:* 695671

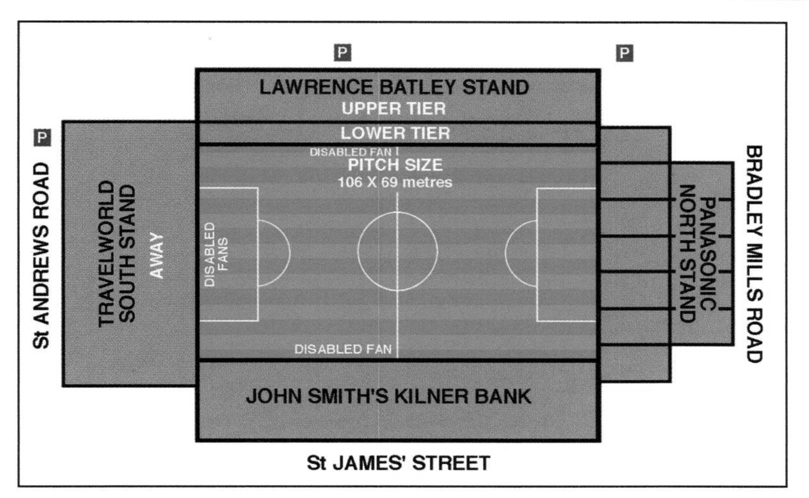

Having been relegated at the end of 2002/03, Town turned to erstwhile manager Peter Jackson for the team's first season in the Third Division. Despite the odd trauma away from the league — such as losing 1-0 away to non-league Accrington Stanley in the First Round of the FA Cup — in the more important arena Town were there or thereabouts all season. Unfortunately, results on the last day of the season, with Torquay defeating Southend and with Town drawing at Cheltenham, resulted in the Yorkshire team finishing fourth and thus in the Play-Offs. Victory over Lincoln saw Huddersfield face Mansfield in the Play-Off Final at the Millennium Stadium. With the score, after extra time, being 0-0, a penalty shoot out ensued with Town coming out victorious 4-1 to ensure that League One football was again on offer at the McAlpine Stadium in 2004/05. Under Jackson, Huddersfield should do more than consolidate their position at this higher level and a Play-Off position again should not be beyond the team.

HULL CITY

Kingston Communications Stadium, Walton Street, Hull, East Yorkshire HU3 6HU

Tel No: 0870 837 0003
Advance Tickets Tel No: 0870 837 0004
Fax: 01482 304882
Web Site: www.hullcityafc.premiumtv.co.uk
E-mail: info@hulltigers.com
League: League One
Brief History: Founded 1904. Former grounds: The Boulevard (Hull Rugby League Ground), Dairycoates, Anlaby Road Cricket Circle (Hull Cricket Ground), Anlaby Road, Boothferry Park (from 1946). Moved to Kingston Communications Stadium in late 2002. Record attendance (at Boothferry Park) 55,019; (at Kingston Communications Stadium) 22,319
(Total) Current Capacity: 25,404 (all-seated)
Visiting Supporters' Allocation: 4,000 all-seated in North Stand
Club Colours: Amber with black and white trim shirts, black shorts
Nearest Railway Station: Hull Paragon
Parking (Car): There are 1,800 spaces on the Walton Street Fairground for use on match days
Parking (Coach/Bus): As directed
Other Clubs Sharing Ground: Hull RLFC
Police Force and Tel No: Humberside (01482 220148)
Disabled Visitors' facilities:
Wheelchairs: tbc
Blind: tbc
Anticipated Development(s): The club moved into the new Kingston Communication Stadium towards the end of 2002. The ground is shared with Hull RLFC. The total cost of the 25,404-seat ground was £44million. The West Stand is provided with two tiers and there are plans for the construction of a second tier on the East Stand, taking the capacity to 30,000, if required.

KEY

⬆ North direction (approx)

1. A1105 Anlaby Road
2. Arnold Lane
3. West Stand
4. East Stand
5. Walton Street
6. To city centre and railway station
7. Car parks
8. Railway line towards Scarborough
9. Railway line towards Leeds
10. A1105 westwards towards A63 and M62

Above: 695565; *Right:* 695561

With the crowds turning out in force at the new stadium, to illustrate the great potential that Hull has as a footballing city, Peter Taylor's team did not disappoint on the field, winning promotion to the League One in finishing runners-up to Doncaster Rovers. With an astute manager and with the support of the crowd, the Tigers are probably better equipped to survive at this higher level than Doncaster Rovers. If Taylor remains at the club then the team must be fancied for an outside chance of the Play-Offs.

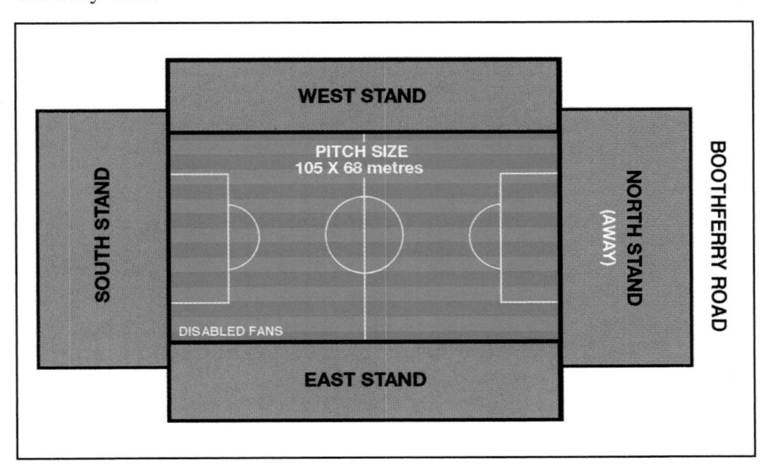

IPSWICH TOWN

Portman Road, Ipswich, IP1 2DA

Tel No: 01473 400500
Advance Tickets Tel No: 01473 400555
Fax: 01473 400040
Web Site: www.itfc.premiumtv.co.uk
E-Mail: enquiries@itfc.co.uk
League: League Championship
Brief History: Founded 1887 as Ipswich Association F.C., changed to Ipswich Town in 1888. Former Grounds: Broom Hill & Brookes Hall, moved to Portman Road in 1888. Record attendance 38,010
(Total) Current Capacity: 30,326 all seated
Visiting Supporters' Allocation: 1,771 all seated in Cobbold Stand
Club Colours: Blue shirts, white shorts
Nearest Railway Station: Ipswich
Parking (Car): Portman Road, Portman Walk & West End Road
Parking (Coach/Bus): West End Road
Police Force and Tel No: Suffolk (01473 611611)
Disabled Visitors' Facilities:
Wheelchairs: Lower Britannia Stand
Blind: Commentary available
Anticipated Development(s): The new Greene King (South) Stand has been followed by the construction of the new two-tier, 7,035-seat, North Stand, which was initially delayed as a result of legal action. The completion of the two stands takes Portman Road's capacity to more than 30,000.

KEY

- **C** Club Offices
- **E** Entrance(s) for visiting supporters
- **R** Refreshment bars for visiting supporters
- **T** Toilets for visiting supporters

⬆ North direction (approx)

1. A137 West End Road
2. Sir Alf Ramsay Way
3. Portman Road
4. Princes Street
5. To Ipswich BR Station
6. Car Parks
7. Cobbold Stand
8. Britannia Stand
9. North Stand
10. Greene King (South) Stand

Above: 694286; *Right:* 694275

Joe Royle's first full season at Portman Road started disastrously, with the team in the relegation zone early on, but a revival saw the club push towards automatic promotion. However, in the event, results against lower teams resulted in the club missing out and, in finishing fifth, faced West Ham in the Play-Offs. Unfortunately, however, a 1-0 victory at home was overturned by a 2-0 defeat away with the result that Town will again be in the League Championship in 2004/05. With the Premiership parachute now over, Royle will be under pressure to examine the squad and the club's position in the new campaign will be determined by how successful he is in retaining key players. Whilst fans will be bemoaning the success of neighbouring Norwich City, they will be expecting to pass the Canaries in changing divisions at the end of the season; objective assessment, however, would suggest that the Play-Offs are again perhaps the best that the club can aspire to.

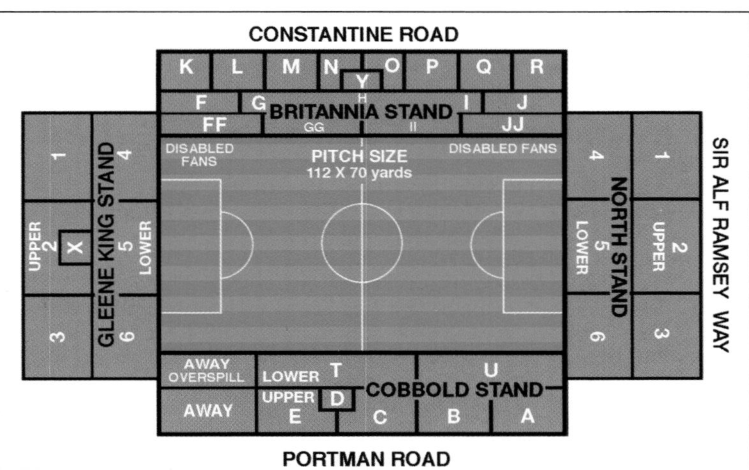

KIDDERMINSTER HARRIERS

Aggborough Stadium, Hoo Road, Kidderminster, Worcestershire DY10 1NB

Tel No: 01562 823931
Advance Tickets Tel No: 01562 823931
Fax: 01562 827329
Web Site: www.harriers.premiumtv.co.uk
E-Mail: info@harriers.co.uk
League: League Two
Brief History: The club was established in 1886. There have been no previous grounds. The team won the Nationwide Conference title at the end of the 1999/2000 season and entered the Nationwide League for 2000/01 season. Record attendance at Aggborough Stadium: 9,155
(Total) Current Capacity: 6,293 (3,150 seated)
Visiting Supporters' Allocation: 1,500 (all unseated in South [College End] Terrace), plus up to 760 seated in new East (William Greaves) Stand
Club Colours: Red shirts with white markings; red shorts
Nearest Railway Station: Kidderminster
Parking (Car): Limited at ground parking otherwise on-street
Parking (Coach/Bus): As directed
Police Force and Tel No: West Mercia (01562 820888
Disabled Visitors' Facilities:
Wheelchairs: Designated section in front of George Reynolds Stand
Blind: No special facility
Anticipated Development(s): The new William Greaves Stand was completed during the 2003/04 season and takes the ground's capacity to just under 7,000. There are no further plans present for the further development of the ground.

KEY

C Club Offices
S Club Shop
E Entrance(s) for visiting supporters

⬆ North direction (approx)

1. South (College) End – away
2. Kidderminster Town station (Severn Valley Railway)
3. Kidderminster station
4. Hoo Road
5. Constitution Hill Ringway
6. To Town Centre (half a mile)
7. Chester Road South
8. To A449 and M5 (14 miles)
9. Stadium Close
10. Car park
11. Harriers Trading Estate
12. Vicarage Close

Above: 696955; *Right:* 696963

With the team struggling in the Third Division, Ian Britton was dismissed as manager in October after a 0-0 draw at Swansea City, a result which left Harriers third from bottom. The club moved quickly to appoint ex-boss Jan Molby as Director of Football until the end of the season. The tactic worked in as much as Molby managed to keep the team from the drop. Finishing in 16th position on 55 points, 10 above relegated Carlisle United. Assuming Molby remains in charge for the new season, the club should improve on the form of 2003/04 and reach a top-half position.

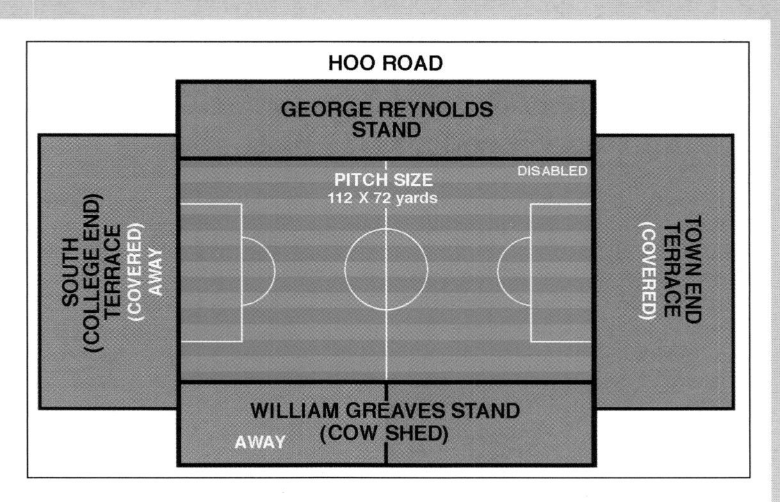

LEEDS UNITED

Elland Road, Leeds, LS11 0ES

Tel No: 0113 367 6000
Advance Tickets Tel No: 0845 121 1992
Fax: 0113 367 6050
Web Site: www.leedsunited.com
E-mail: admin@leedsunited.com
League: League Championship
Brief History: Founded 1919, formed from the former 'Leeds City' Club, who were disbanded following expulsion from the Football League in October 1919. Joined Football League in 1920. Record attendance 57,892
(Total) Current Capacity: 40,296 (all seated)
Visiting Supporters' Allocation: 1,725 in South East Corner (can be increased to 3,662 in South Stand if necessary)
Club Colours: White shirts, white shorts
Nearest Railway Station: Leeds City
Parking (Car): Car parks adjacent to ground
Parking (Coach/Bus): As directed by Police
Police Force and Tel No: West Yorkshire (0113 243 5353)
Disabled Visitors' Facilities:
Wheelchairs: West Stand and South Stand
Blind: Commentary available
Anticipated Development(s): Although the club had proposals for relocation to a new 50,000-seat stadium costing £60 million to be constructed close to the AI/M1 link road, given the club's high profile financial problems and recent relegation to the League Championship, it is unclear whether this work will proceed. In early July it was announced that the club intended to sell Elland Road and lease it back.

KEY
- **C** Club Offices
- **S** Club Shop
- **E** Entrance(s) for visiting supporters
- ⬆ North direction (approx)
- ❶ M621
- ❷ M621 Junction 2
- ❸ A643 Elland Road
- ❹ Lowfields Road
- ❺ To A58
- ❻ City Centre and BR station
- ❼ To M62 and M1

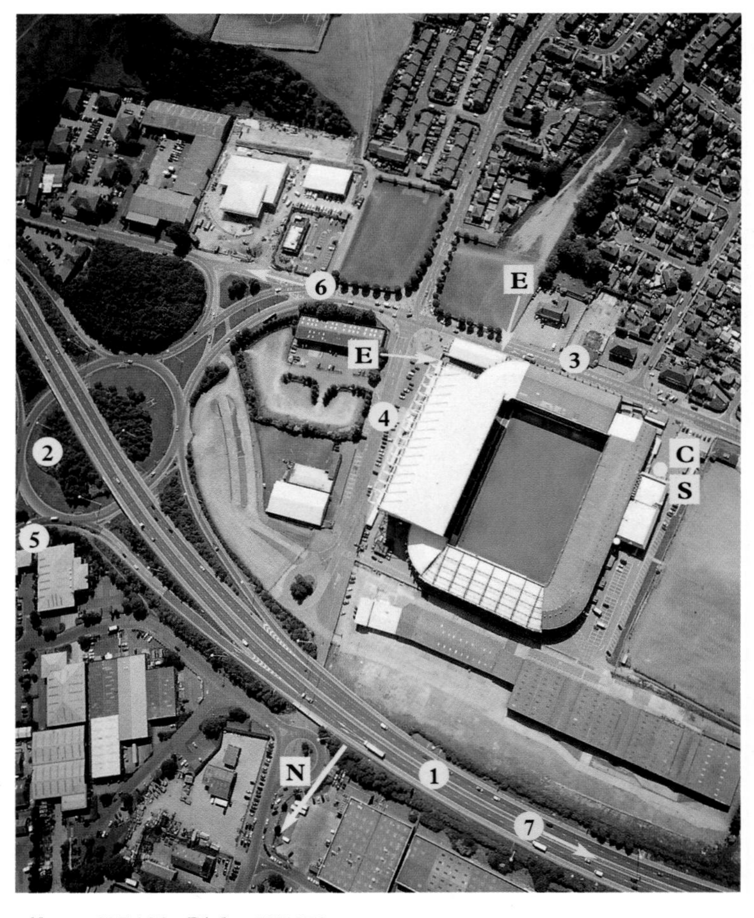

Above: 697482; *Right:* 697479

In early November, following a disastrous run culminating in a 6-1 defeat at Portsmouth, Peter Reid was sacked as manager with the club adrift in last place in the Premiership. Despite his lack of appropriate coaching qualifications, Eddie Gray took over as caretaker but, despite some decent performances, the club's appalling goal difference meant that relegation was guaranteed by a 4-1 defeat at Bolton Wanderers. Three years ago, United were challenging for the Champions League final; in 2004/05 visits to Rotherham and Crewe beckon for a team that were the last club outside the Manchester United/Arsenal axis to win the Premiership crown. The club's financial melt-down has been widely reported and relegation to the League Championship will undoubtedly add to the problems with many of the star players being sold to reduce both debt and salary levels. If, and it's a big if, Leeds can attract new investors prepared to put significant amounts of money into the team, then the manager, whoever it is (and Eddie Gray stood down before the final game of the season), will have a chance to push Leeds towards the Play-Offs or automatic promotion. But if not, the club has two local rivals — in Bradford City and Sheffield Wednesday — that illustrate what can happen to teams crippled with financial worries. With the season over, the club announced that Kevin Blackwell was to be appointed the new manager — he certainly has his work cut out!

LEICESTER CITY

Walkers Stadium, Filbert Way, Leicester, LE2 7FL

Tel No: 0870 040 6000
Advance Tickets Tel No: 0870 040 6000
Fax: 0116 291 1254
Web Site: www.lcfc.premiumtv.co.uk
E-mail: ticket.sales@lcfc.co.uk
League: League Championship
Brief History: Founded 1884 as Leicester Fosse, changed name to Leicester City in 1919. Former grounds: Fosse Road South, Victoria Road, Belgrave Cycle Track, Mill Lane, Aylstone Road Cricket Ground and Filbert Street (from 1891). The club moved to the new Walkers Stadium for the start of the 2002/03 season. Record attendance (at Filbert Street) 47,298; (at Walkers Stadium) 32,148
(Total) Current Capacity: 32,500
Visiting Supporters' Allocation: 3,000 (all seated) in North East of Ground
Club Colours: Blue shirts, white shorts
Nearest Railway Station: Leicester
Parking (Car): NCP car park
Parking (Coach/Bus): As directed
Police Force and Tel No: Leicester (0116 222 2222)
Disabled Visitors Facilities:
Wheelchairs: 186 spaces spread through all stands
Blind: Match commentary via hospital radio
Anticipated Developments: The club moved into the new 32,500-seat Walkers Stadium at the start of the 2002/03 season. Although there are no plans at present, the stadium design allows for the construction of a second tier to the East Stand, taking capacity to 40,000.

KEY

C Club Offices

⬆ North direction (approx)

1. Raw Dykes Road
2. Eastern Road
3. A426 Aylestone Road
4. Freeman's Common Road
5. To Lutterworth
6. To city centre and railway station (one mile)
7. Burnmoor Street
8. River Soar
9. Site of Filbert Street (old ground)

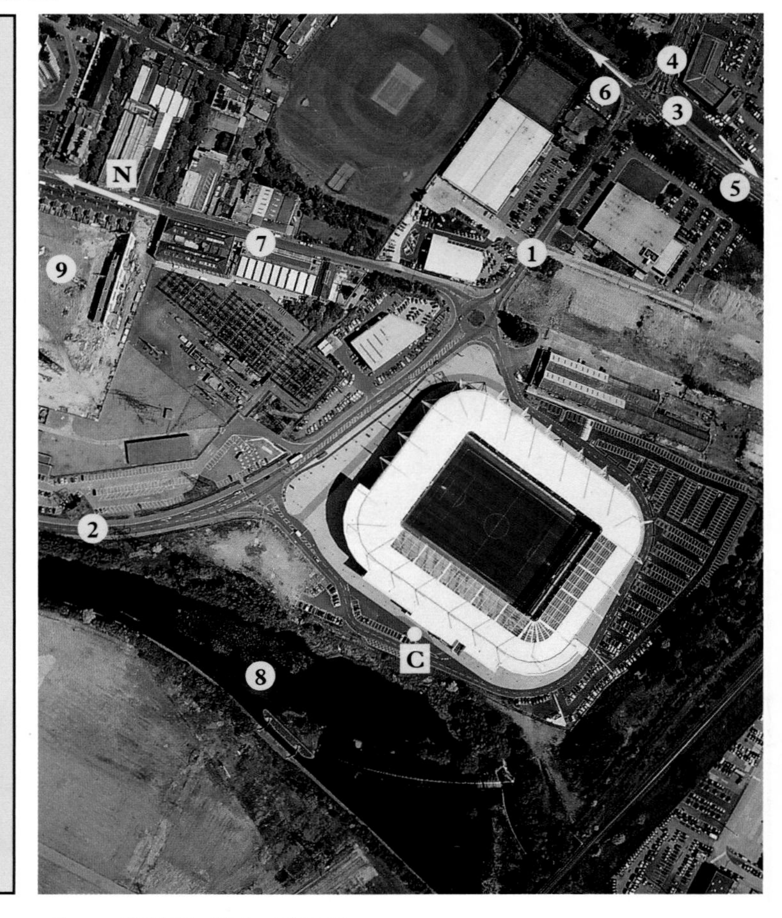

Above: 695615; *Right:* 695611

As widely predicted, the Foxes struggled to make an impact in the Premiership and it came as little surprise that Micky Adams side was relegated. There were occasional bright spots on the field, but the season as a whole was probably marred by events off it, particularly the well publicised accusations in Spain that resulted in a number of players spending time in jail. The loss of players at a crucial time, allied to the effect that the fiasco had on team morale, was undoubtedly a factor that saw the team's performances in the latter part of the season deteriorate and, ultimately, cost the team its Premiership status. The team, therefore, returns to the League Championship and will undoubtedly see a number of star players, such as Muzzy Izzet, depart during the close season. Last time City was relegated, despite Administration it bounced straight back; this time, with the League Championship having a number of much stronger and more ambitious teams, it could prove a struggle for Leicester to make an immediate return.

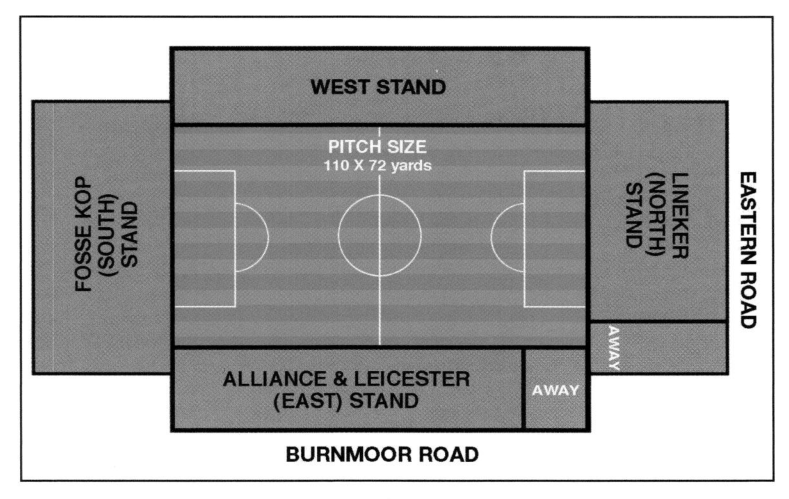

LEYTON ORIENT

Matchroom Stadium, Brisbane Road, Leyton, London, E10 5NF

Tel No: 020 8926 1111
Advance Tickets Tel No: 020 8926 1010
Fax: 020 8926 1110
Web Site: www.leytonorient.premiumtv.co.uk
E-Mail: info@leytonorient.net
League: League Two
Brief History: Founded 1887 as Clapton Orient, from Eagle Cricket Club (formerly Glyn Cricket Club formed in 1881). Changed name to Leyton Orient (1946), Orient (1966), Leyton Orient (1987). Former grounds: Glyn Road, Whittles Athletic Ground, Millfields Road, Lea Bridge Road, Wembley Stadium (2 games), moved to Brisbane Road in 1937. Record attendance 34,345
(Total) Current Capacity: 13,842 (7,027 seated) (prior to redevelopment); 5,200 once work starts
Visiting Supporters' Allocation: 1,500 (all seated) in East Stand/Terrace
Club Colours: Red shirts, red shorts
Nearest Railway Station: Leyton (tube), Leyton Midland Road
Parking (Car): Street parking
Parking (Coach/Bus): As directed by Police
Police Force and Tel No: Metropolitan (020 8556 8855)
Disabled Visitors' Facilities:
Wheelchairs: Windsor Road
Blind: Match commentary supplied on request
Anticipated Development(s): The club is progressing with its plans for the £9 million scheme for the redevelopment of the ground into a 10,500-all-seated stadium. The West Stand and North Terrace have been demolished with the intention of having the new 2,500-seat West Stand in operation ready for the start of the 2005/06 season. Only when this work has been completed will the new North Stand be constructed. This will impact severely on capacity during the 2004/05 season with only the East and South stands being available.

KEY

C Club Offices
S Club Shop
E Entrance(s) for visiting supporters

⬆ North direction (approx)

1. Buckingham Road
2. Oliver Road
3. A112 High Road Leyton
4. To Leyton Tube Station (¼ mile)
5. Brisbane Road
6. Windsor Road
7. To Leyton Midland Road BR station
8. South Stand

Above: 697470; *Right:* 697467

Following a disappointing start to the season, culminating in a 3-0 defeat by Huddersfield Town, manager Paul Brush departed the Orient managerial hot-seat at the end of September. After a period as caretaker manager, Martin Ling took over full-time, with a contract until the end of the 2004/05 season, just before Christmas. Under Ling the team's form improved, although a late season slump saw the club slip down the Third Division table, ultimately to finish in 19th position. The club certainly has the potential to do much better than that but it's hard to escape the conclusion that Orient will perhaps again struggle.

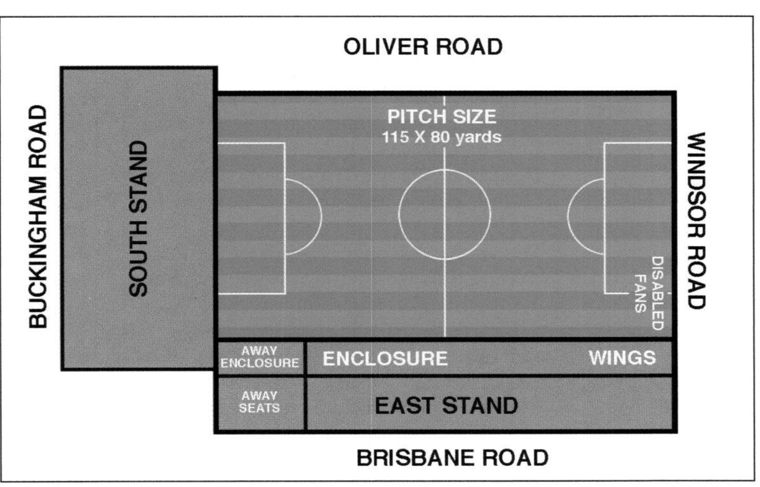

LINCOLN CITY

Sincil Bank, Lincoln, LN5 8LD

Tel No: 01522 880011
Advance Tickets Tel No: 01522 880011
Fax: 01522 880020
Web Site: www.redimps.com
E-Mail: lcfc@redimps.premiumtv.co.uk
League: League Two
Brief History: Founded 1884. Former Ground: John O'Gaunts Ground, moved to Sincil Bank in 1895. Founder-members 2nd Division Football League (1892). Relegated from 4th Division in 1987, promoted from GM Vauxhall Conference in 1988. Record attendance 23,196
(Total) Current Capacity: 11,100 (all seated)
Visiting Supporters' Allocation: 2,000 in Co-op Community Stand (part, remainder for Home fans)
Club Colours: Red and white striped shirts, black shorts
Nearest Railway Station: Lincoln Central
Parking (Car): City centre car parks; limited on-street parking
Parking (Coach/Bus): South Common
Police Force and Tel No: Lincolnshire (01522 529911)
Disabled Visitors' Facilities:
Wheelchairs: The Simons and South (Mundy) Park stands
Blind: No special facility
Anticipated Development(s): Following the replacement of the seats in the Stacey West Stand, Sincil Bank is once again an all-seater stadium.

KEY

C Club Offices
S Club Shop

⬆ North direction (approx)

❶ A46 High Street
❷ Sincil Bank
❸ Sausthorpe Street
❹ Cross Street
❺ Co-op Community Stand (away)
❻ A158 South Park Avenue
❼ Stacey West Stand
❽ Lincoln Central BR Station (1/2 mile)
❾ Family Stand

Above: 697261; *Right:* 697523

In a season overshadowed by concerns over the health of manager Keith Alexander, who spent much of the first half of the season under treatment, the fact that the Imps did as well as they did indicates considerable team spirit. Whilst never good enough to sustain a challenge for automatic promotion, the team secured seventh position, despite a last day defeat at home against nearest rivals Yeovil Town, and thus entry into the Play-Offs. Unfortunately, defeat over the two legs by Huddersfield Town, ensures that League Two football will again be the fare on offer at Sincil Bank in 2004/05. However, the team should again be one of those challenging for a Play-Off berth again at worst.

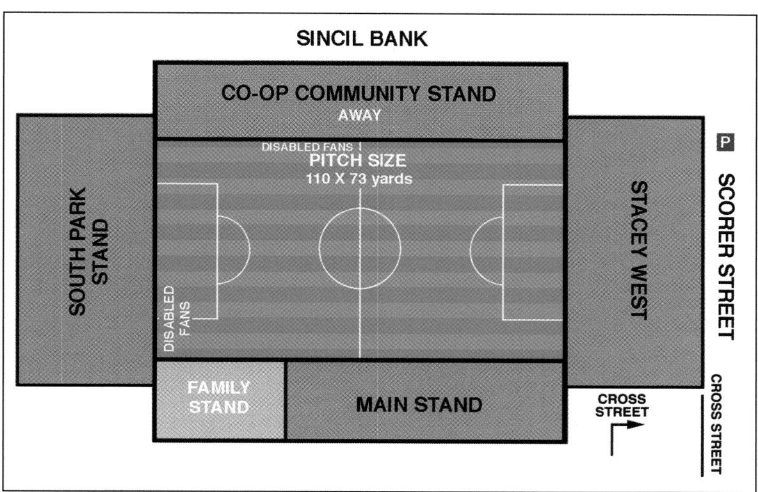

LIVERPOOL

Anfield Road, Liverpool, L4 0TH

Tel No: 0151 263 2361
Advance Tickets Tel No: 0870 153 5353
Ticket Enquiries Fax: 0151 261 1416
Web Site: www.liverpoolfc.tv
Fax: 0151 260 8813
League: F.A. Premier
Brief History: Founded 1892. Anfield Ground formerly Everton F.C. Ground. Joined Football League in 1893. Record attendance 61,905
(Total) Current Capacity: 45,362 (all seated)
Visiting Supporters' Allocation: 1,972 (all seated) in Anfield Road Stand
Club Colours: Red shirts, red shorts
Nearest Railway Station: Kirkdale
Parking (Car): Stanley car park
Parking (Coach/Bus): Priory Road and Pinehurst Avenue
Police Force and Tel No: Merseyside (0151 709 6010)
Disabled Visitors' Facilities:
Wheelchairs: Kop and Main Stands
Blind: Commentary available
Anticipated Development(s): The club is progressing with its plans to relocate to a new 55,000-seat stadium adjacent to Stanley Park, some 200yd from Anfield. It is expected that the new stadium, costing some £80 million, will be complete for the start of the 2006/07 season.

KEY

- **C** Club Offices
- **S** Club Shop

- ⬆ North direction (approx)

1. Car Park
2. Anfield Road
3. A5089 Walton Breck Road
4. Kemlyn Road
5. Kirkdale BR Station (1 mile)
6. Utting Avenue
7. Stanley Park
8. Spion Kop
9. Anfield Road Stand

Above: 695700; *Right:* 695692

A disappointing season for the Anfield faithful saw the club struggle to make an impact domestically and in Europe. Failure to reach the Champions League at the end of 2002/03 meant entry to the UEFA Cup but the campaign ended in defeat by French club Marseilles. In the Premiership, the club eventually finished in fourth position, guaranteeing entry to the first phase of the Champions League, but this success was largely down to the failures of other teams for the most part rather than stunning football from Liverpool. There were rumblings of discontent from the fans and, for the first time Gerard Houllier's position looked less than secure, with pundits commenting that he could be the first manager sacked at Anfield for some 50 years. With the Champions League berth booked, a number of the stars previously reluctant to sign new contracts at Anfield may be persuaded to stay in the short term but, towards the end of the season, a new threat to Houllier emerged with the possible involvement financially in the club of the Prime Minister of Thailand or a local businessman. With the season over, it was announced that Houllier was to step down as manager with Rafael Benitez taking over. Whoever controls the purse strings in 2004/05, it's unlikely that the supporters will accept a further season where the side finishes some 25 points behind the champions. However, without significant investment in the squad in order to enable it to compete with the 'Big Three', it's impossible to see Liverpool being able to achieve better than fourth again.

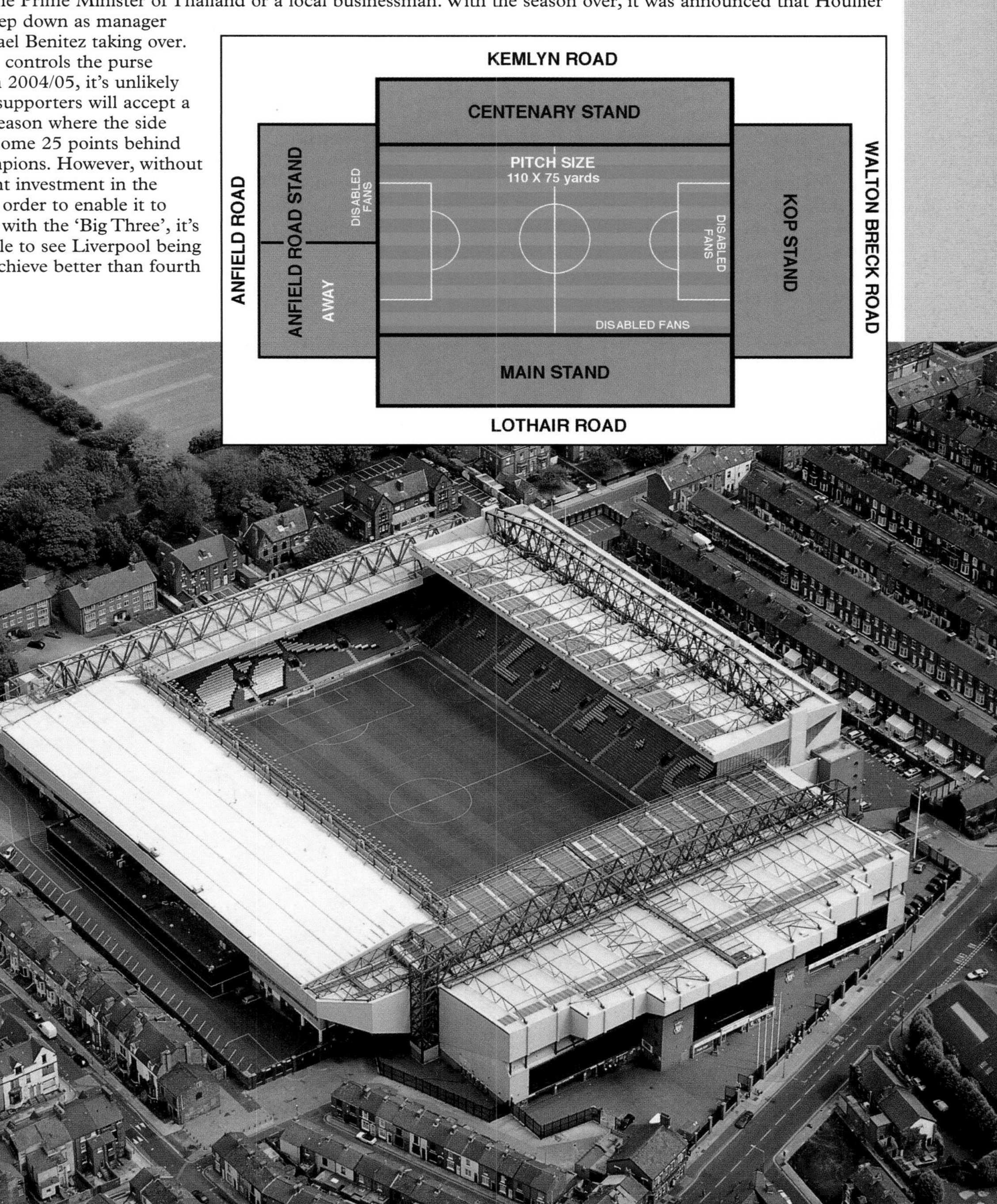

LUTON TOWN

Kenilworth Road Stadium, 1 Maple Road, Luton, LU4 8AW

Tel No: 01582 411622
Advance Tickets Tel No: 01582 416976
Fax: 01582 405070
Web Site: www.lutontown.premiumtv.co.uk
E-Mail: clubsec@lutontown.co.uk
League: League One
Brief History: Founded 1885 from an amalgamation of Wanderers F.C. and Excelsior F.C. Former Grounds: Dallow Lane & Dunstable Road, moved to Kenilworth Road in 1905. Record attendance 30,069
(Total) Current Capacity: 9,970 (all seated)
Visiting Supporters' Allocation: 2,200
Club Colours: Orange and blue shirts, blue shorts
Nearest Railway Station: Luton
Parking (Car): Street parking
Parking (Coach/Bus): Luton bus station
Police Force and Tel No: Bedfordshire (01582 401212)
Disabled Visitors' Facilities:
Wheelchairs: Kenilworth Road and Main stands
Blind: Commentary available
Anticipated Development(s): Towards the end of the season it was announced that the consortium seeking to take the club out of Administration would progress with plans for relocation. The new stadium, to be located close to Junction 10 of the M1, would provide seating for 15,000. The anticipated time-scale is to have the new ground available within three years but nothing is as yet confirmed.

KEY

- **C** Club Offices
- **S** Club Shop
- **E** Entrance(s) for visiting supporters
- **R** Refreshment bars for visiting supporters
- **T** Toilets for visiting supporters

⬆ North direction (approx)

1. To M1 Junction 11
2. Wimborne Road
3. Kenilworth Road
4. Oak Road
5. Dunstable Road
6. Luton BR Station (1 mile)
7. Ticket Office

Above: 695595; *Right:* 695588

Under Mike Newell, the Hatters had a moderately successful campaign in the Second Division, finishing in 10th position after at one stage looking likely to achieve a Play-Off position. One high point was victory at Valley Parade in the FA Cup Third Round over First Division strugglers Bradford City but, given the form of the Bantams, that hardly merited an entry on the Richter scale of cup shocks. Finishing in 10th perhaps represents a good foundation for a club still in Administration at the time of writing — although a new consortium hopes to get the club moving forward again — and the basis of possible further progress in 20045/05.

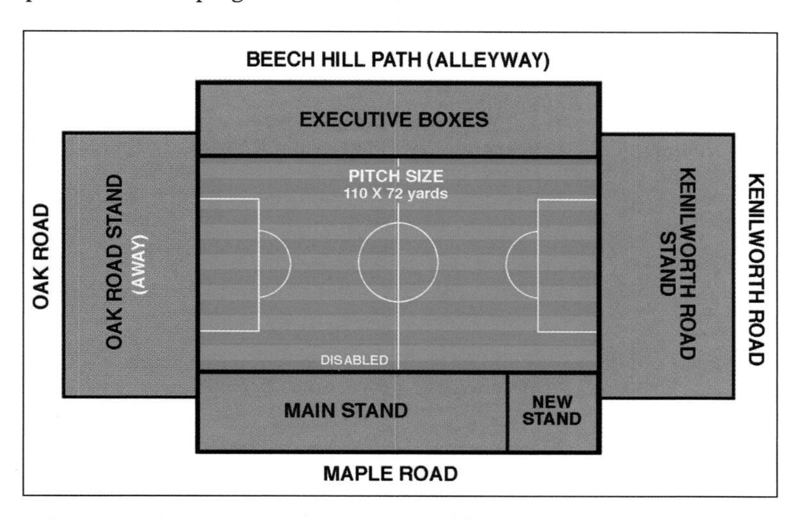

MACCLESFIELD TOWN

Moss Rose Ground, London Road, Macclesfield, SK11 7SP

Tel No: 01625 264686
Advance Tickets Tel No: 01625 264686
Fax: 01625 264692
Web Site: http://www.mtfc.co.uk/
E-Mail: office@mtfc.co.uk
League: League Two
Brief History: Founded 1874. Previous ground: Rostron Field moved to Moss Rose Ground in 1891. Winners of the Vauxhall Conference in 1994/95 and 1997/97. Admitted to Football League for 1997/98 season. Record attendance 10,041
(Total) Current Capacity: 6,307 (2,561 seated)
Visiting Supporters' Allocation: 1,900 (1,500 in Silkman Terrace; 400 seated in Estate Road Stand)
Club Colours: Royal blue, royal blue shorts
Nearest Railway Station: Macclesfield
Parking (Car): No parking at the ground and the nearest off-street car park is in the town centre (25min walk). There is some on-street parking in the vicinity, but this can get crowded.
Parking (Coach/Bus): As directed
Police Force and Tel No: Cheshire (01625 610000)
Disabled Visitors' Facilities:
Wheelchairs: 45 places in Estate Road Stand
Blind: No special facility
Anticipated Development(s): The new Estate Road (Alfred McAlpine) Stand, with its 1,497 seats, was completed towards the end of the season and officially opened on 5 May 2001. This is the first phase of a scheme to redevelop Moss Rose; the next phase will see a seated second tier raised above the existing terrace at the Silkman End. Other recent work has included the provision of permanent toilets at the away end.

KEY

C Club Offices
E Entrance(s) for visiting supporters

⬆ North direction (approx)

❶ A523 London Road
❷ To Town Centre and BR station (1.5 miles)
❸ To Leek
❹ Moss Lane
❺ Star Lane
❻ Silkmans Public House (now closed)
❼ Star Lane End
❽ Silkman End (away section)
❾ Estate Road Stand

Above: 697248; *Right:* 697237

With the Silkmen having won only two of their previous 11 games, Dave Moss was sacked at the end of October following the club's 2-1 home defeat against fellow strugglers Southend United. John Askey was appointed initially as caretaker but in mid-December his appointment was made permanent. However, the club's poor form continued and, with the team in the relegation zone at the end of March, Askey was demoted to assistant. Ex-Port Vale boss, Brian Horton, was confirmed as replacement manager until the end of the season on the following day. Following the final matches of the season, with Town having survived in the Third Division in 20th place seven points off the drop zone, it was confirmed that Horton was to be appointed to the position on a permanent basis. Horton's experience should assist the Silkmen to make a better effort in 2004/05 although it is perhaps too early to see the team as anything more than mid-table material at the present time.

MANCHESTER CITY

The City of Manchester Stadium, Sportcity, Manchester M11 3FF

Tel No: 0161 231 3200
Advance Tickets Tel No: 0870 062 1894
Fax: 0161 438 7999
Web Site: www.mcfc.co.uk
E-mail: mcfc@mcfc.co.uk
League: F.A. Premiership
Brief History: Founded 1880 at West Gorton, changed name to Ardwick (reformed 1887) and to Manchester City in 1894. Former grounds: Clowes Street, Kirkmanshulme Cricket Club, Donkey Common, Pink Bank Lane, Hyde Road and Maine Road (from 1923 until 2003). Moved to the City of Manchester Stadium for the start of the 2003/04 season. Founder-members 2nd Division (1892). Record attendance (at Maine Road) 84,569 (record for a Football League Ground); at City of Manchester Stadium 47,304

(Total) Current Capacity: 48,000
Visiting Supporters' Allocation: 3,000 (South Stand); can be increased to 4,500 if required
Club Colours: Sky blue shirts, white shorts
Nearest Railway Station: Manchester Piccadilly
Parking (Car): As directed
Parking (Coach/Bus): As directed
Police Force and Tel No: Greater Manchester (0161 872 5050)
Disabled Visitors' facilities:
Wheelchairs: tbc
Blind: tbc

KEY

- ⬆ North direction (approx)
- ❶ A662 Ashton New Road
- ❷ Commonwealth Boulevard
- ❸ Stadium Way
- ❹ A6010 Alan Turing Way
- ❺ North Stand
- ❻ South Stand
- ❼ West Stand
- ❽ East Stand
- ❾ National Squash Centre
- ❿ Warm-up track
- ● To Manchester city centre and Piccadilly station (1.5 miles)

Above: 697235; *Right:* 697226

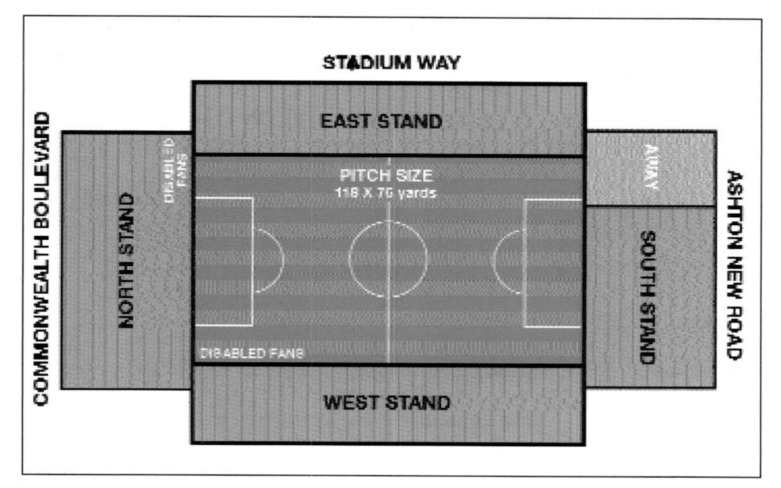

Having gathered a total of points that, in previous years, could have seen the club relegated, the team's first season at the City of Manchester Stadium is one that, perhaps, the faithful would prefer to forget. The fact that there were three teams significantly worse than City was good news for the blue half of Manchester, but to go from vying for a European position one season to relegation candidates the next is less promising, particularly as it would appear that the club will have little to spend in the close season to strengthen the squad. Kevin Keegan, at the time of writing, remains manager and, if he retains the position into the new campaign, it is hard to escape the conclusion that he will face another battle to avoid the drop.

MANCHESTER UNITED

Old Trafford, Sir Matt Busby Way, Manchester, M16 0RA

Tel No: 0161 868 8000
Advance Tickets Tel No: 0870 442 1999
Fax: 0161 868 8804
Web Site: www.manutd.com
E-mail: enquiries@manutd.co.uk
League: F.A. Premier
Brief History: Founded in 1878 as 'Newton Heath L&Y', later Newton Heath, changed to Manchester United in 1902. Former Grounds: North Road, Monsall & Bank Street, Clayton, moved to Old Trafford in 1910 (used Manchester City F.C. Ground 1941-49). Founder-members Second Division (1892). Record attendance 76,962
(Total) Current Capacity: 68,174 (all seated)
Visiting Supporters' Allocation: Approx. 3,000 in corner of South and East Stands
Club Colours: Red shirts, white shorts
Nearest Railway Station: At Ground
Parking (Car): Lancashire Cricket Ground and White City
Parking (Coach/Bus): As directed by Police
Police Force and Tel No: Greater Manchester (0161 872 5050)
Disabled Visitors' Facilities:
Wheelchairs: South East Stand
Blind: Commentary available
Anticipated Development(s): In early March, the club announced that it was investigating the possibility of increasing the ground's capacity from 67,500 to 75,000 through expansion of the ground at its northeast and northwest corners. This work is very much at a preliminary stage and no planning permission has been sought or granted at this stage.

KEY

- **C** Club Offices
- **S** Club Shop
- ⬆ North direction (approx)
- ❶ To A5081 Trafford Park Road to M63 Junction 4 (5 miles)
- ❷ A56 Chester Road
- ❸ Manchester Ship Canal
- ❹ To Old Trafford Cricket Ground
- ❺ To Parking and Warwick Road BR Station
- ❻ Sir Matt Busby Way

Above: 688593; *Right:* 688583

Was 2003/04 finally the season that saw Manchester United's bandwagon finally lose its wheels? Third place in the Premiership and failure in the Champions League once more sees the vultures hovering above Old Trafford suggesting that star players may depart and that Sir Alex Ferguson's position is not as secure as it was 12 months ago, despite victory in the FA Cup. The loss of David Beckham in the summer of 2003 was expected; less expected was the failure to recruit replacement stars, with cash-rich Chelsea amongst clubs beating United for new talent, along with the controversy over Rock of Gibraltar. Whilst United are undoubtedly not the all-powerful threat they once were, they still finished in third place in the Premiership and secured the FA Cup, defeating First Division Millwall 3-0 in the Final. Whilst many of the players are now ageing, in figures such as Ronaldo and Fletcher, Ferguson has some impressive young players to call upon. In terms of the new season, much will depend on the calibre of the players that Ferguson recruits as well as on the players that depart from Old Trafford. United will again undoubtedly be one of the fancied teams for the title and will certainly be there or thereabouts come May next year; it's difficult, however, to see a team in transition threatening the London dominance of the Premiership this time around.

MANSFIELD TOWN

Field Mill Stadium, Quarry Lane, Mansfield, Notts, NG18 5DA

Tel No: 0870 756 3160
Advance Tickets Tel No: 0870 756 3160
Fax: 01623 482495
Web Site: www.mansfieldtown.premiumtv.co.uk
E-mail: stags@stags.plus.com
League: League Two
Brief History: Founded 1910 as Mansfield Wesleyans Boys Brigade, changed to Mansfield Town in 1914. Former Grounds: Pelham Street, Newgate Lane and The Prairie, moved to Field Mill in 1919. Record attendance 24,467
(Total) Current Capacity: 9,990 (all seated)
Visiting Supporters' Allocation: 1,800 (all seated) in South Stand
Club Colours: Amber with blue trim shirts, Blue shorts with amber trim
Nearest Railway Station: Mansfield
Parking (Car): Car park at Ground
Parking (Coach/Bus): Car park at Ground
Police Force and Tel No: Nottinghamshire (01623 420999)
Disabled Visitors' Facilities:
Wheelchairs: Facilities provided in North, West and South (away) stands
Blind: No special facility
Anticipated Development(s): Work on the Main Stand and on the North and Quarry Lane ends was completed in early 2001, leaving the Bishop Street Stand as the only unreconstructed part of Field Mill. Plans exist for this to be rebuilt but the time scale is unconfirmed.

KEY

- **E** Entrance(s) for visiting supporters
- **R** Refreshment bars for visiting supporters
- **T** Toilets for visiting supporters
- ⬆ North direction (approx)

1. Car Park(s)
2. Quarry Lane
3. A60 Nottingham Road to M1 Junction 27
4. Portland Street
5. To A38 and M1 Junction 28
6. To Town Centre
7. Mansfield railway station
8. North Stand
9. Quarry Lane End (South Stand)
10. Bishop Street Stand

● Main (West) Stand

Above: 692632; *Right:* 692627

With Keith Curle in his first full year as manager, the Stags — relegated at the end of 2002/03 — faced Third Division football. Whilst never being strong enough to achieve one of the top three spots, the team did finish a creditable fourth and thus entered the Play-Offs. Victory over the two legs against Northampton Town saw Mansfield head to the Millennium Stadium for a Final against Huddersfield Town. In a tight match, which both teams could have won during both normal and extra time, the game ended 0-0. Unfortunately, Huddersfield's players proved more adept at penalty taking, winning 4-1, with the result that Mansfield would again be playing in League Two in 2004/05. However, there is every possibility that the experience of 2003/04 will assist the club and a serious challenge for either automatic promotion or the Play-Offs is possible.

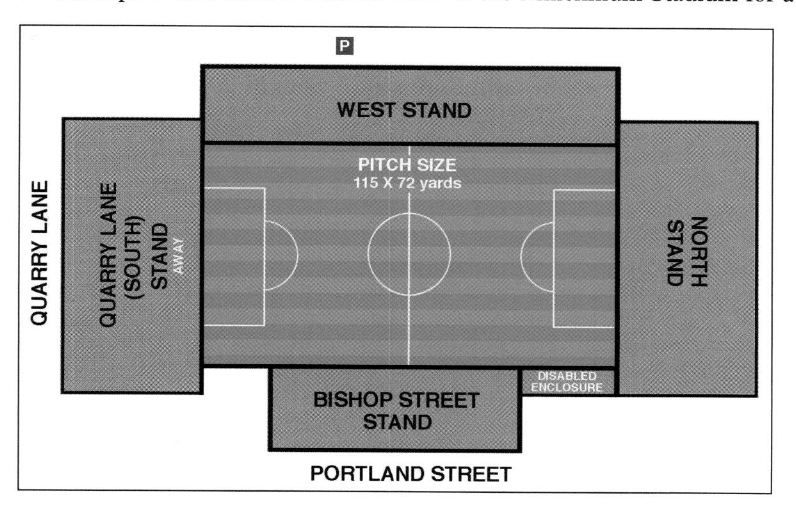

MIDDLESBROUGH

Riverside Stadium, Middlesbrough, Cleveland TS3 6RS

Tel No: 01642 877700
Advance Tickets Tel No: 01642 877745
Fax: 01642 877840
Web Site: www.mfc.co.uk
E-mail: media.dept@mfc.premiumtv.co.uk
League: F.A. Premiership
Brief History: Founded 1876. Former Grounds: Archery Ground (Albert Park), Breckon Hill Road, Linthorpe Road, moved to Ayresome Park in 1903, and to current ground in Summer 1995. F.A. Amateur Cup winners 1894 and 1897 (joined Football League in 1899). Record attendance (Ayresome Park) 53,596, (Riverside Stadium) 35,000
(Total) Current Capacity: 35,100 (all seated)
Visiting Supporters' Allocation: 3,450 (in the South Stand)
Club Colours: Red shirts, red shorts
Nearest Railway Station: Middlesbrough
Parking (Car): All parking at stadium is for permit holders
Parking (Coach/Bus): As directed
Police Force and Tel No: Cleveland (01642 248184)
Disabled Visitors' Facilities:
Wheelchairs: More than 170 places available for disabled fans
Blind: Commentary available
Anticipated Development(s): There remain long term plans for the ground's capacity to be increased to 42,000 through the construction of extra tiers on the North, South and East stands, although there is no confirmed timetable for this work at the current time.

KEY

C Club Offices
S Club Shop

⬆ North direction (approx)

❶ Cargo Fleet Road
❷ To Middlesbrough railway station
❸ To Middlesbrough town centre
❹ Middlesbrough Docks
❺ Shepherdson Way to A66
❻ South Stand

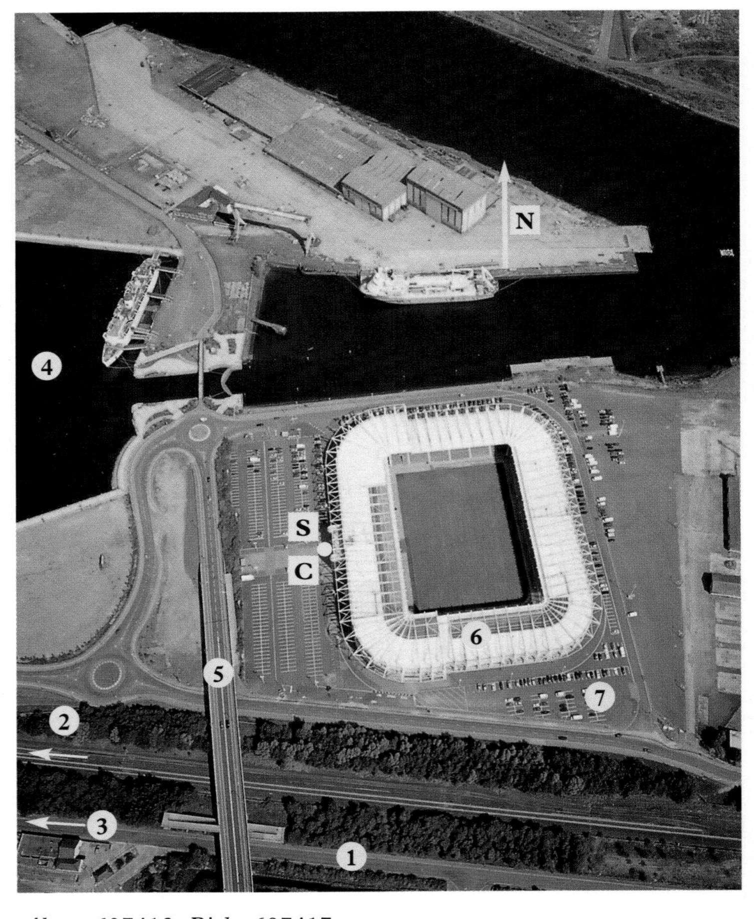

Above: 697413; *Right:* 697417

After 128 years wait, significant silverware finally arrived at Middlesbrough when the team defeated Bolton Wanderers 2-1 in the final of the Carling Cup at the Millennium Stadium at the end of February. Not only did the victory mean that the cleaning staff at the Riverside Stadium acquired an onerous new duty but European football was also guaranteed. In terms of the Premiership, Boro' had a reasonably successful campaign, ultimately finishing in 11th position. As far as the new season is concerned, the team will face the challenge of European football alongside a desire to consolidate further their position in the Premiership by finishing well towards the top. In Steve McClaren, the team possesses one of the more astute English managers but much will depend on whether he can continue to attract good quality players to the Riverside Stadium. In the past, Premiership teams have sometimes struggled to make an impact domestically and in Europe — witness Ipswich Town a couple of years ago — and fans will be hoping that the buzz of a European campaign will not distract the squad from the most important aspect of the season — a strong and sustained challenge in the Premiership.

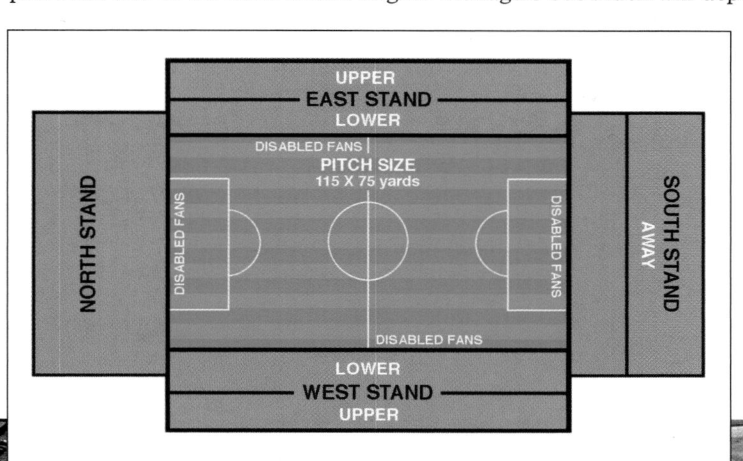

MILLWALL

New Den, Bolina Road, London, SE16 3LN

Tel No: 020 7232 1222
Advance Tickets Tel No: 020 7231 9999
Fax: 020 7231 3663
Web Site: www.millwallfc.premiumtv.co.uk
E-mail: questions@millwallplc.com
League: League Championship
Brief History: Founded 1885 as Millwall Rovers, changed name to Millwall Athletic (1889) and Millwall (1925). Former Grounds: Glengall Road, East Ferry Road (2 separate Grounds), North Greenwich Ground and The Den – Cold Blow Lane – moved to New Den 1993/94 season. Founder-members Third Division (1920). Record attendance (at The Den) 48,672 (at New Den) 20,093

(Total) Current Capacity: 20,150 (all seated)
Visiting Supporters' Allocation: 4,382 in North Stand
Club Colours: Blue shirts, white shorts
Nearest Railway Station: South Bermondsey or Surrey Docks (Tube)
Parking (Car): Juno Way car parking (8 mins walk)
Parking (Coach/Bus): At Ground
Police Force and Tel No: Metropolitan (0207 679 9217)
Disabled Visitors' Facilities:
Wheelchairs: 200 spaces in West Stand Lower Tier
Blind: Commentary available

KEY

- **C** Club Offices
- **S** Club Shop
- **E** Entrance(s) for visiting supporters
- ⬆ North direction (approx)
- ❶ Bolina Road
- ❷ To South Bermondsey station
- ❸ Footpath to station for away fans
- ❹ Zampa Road
- ❺ Stockholm Road
- ❻ North Stand (away)

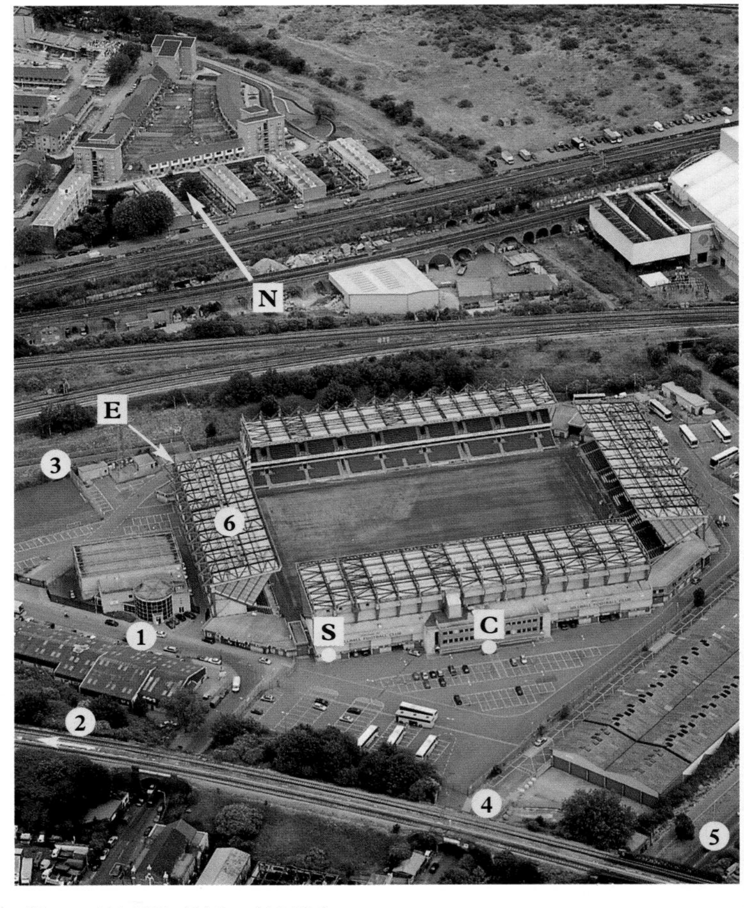

Above: 697379; *Right:* 697384

Following a 1-0 home defeat by Preston in mid-October, Mark McGhee departed as manager, having been at the club for just over three years, during which time he guided the Lions back into the First Division. However, expectations at the club at the start of the season were high and McGhee paid the price for a relatively poor start to the campaign. The club moved quickly to appoint Denis Wise as caretaker player manager, with the experienced Ray Wilkins as his assistant. With the new team achieving a reasonable set of results, Wise was confirmed as the new permanent boss in early November. More importantly, the club's success in the FA Cup — reaching the final for the first time — ensured European football for the team, irrespective of the result as Manchester United were already guaranteed a place in the Champions League. In the event, class overcame spirit and the Lions were tamed 3-0. However, the team, and Wise, will have learnt from their experience and, provided the squad is strengthened, a more serious push towards promotion should be possible in 2004/05. The one downside of the season was that, after the semi-final, the club's league form deteriorated and, once having been close to a Play-Off spot, the team ultimately finished in a disappointing 10th place.

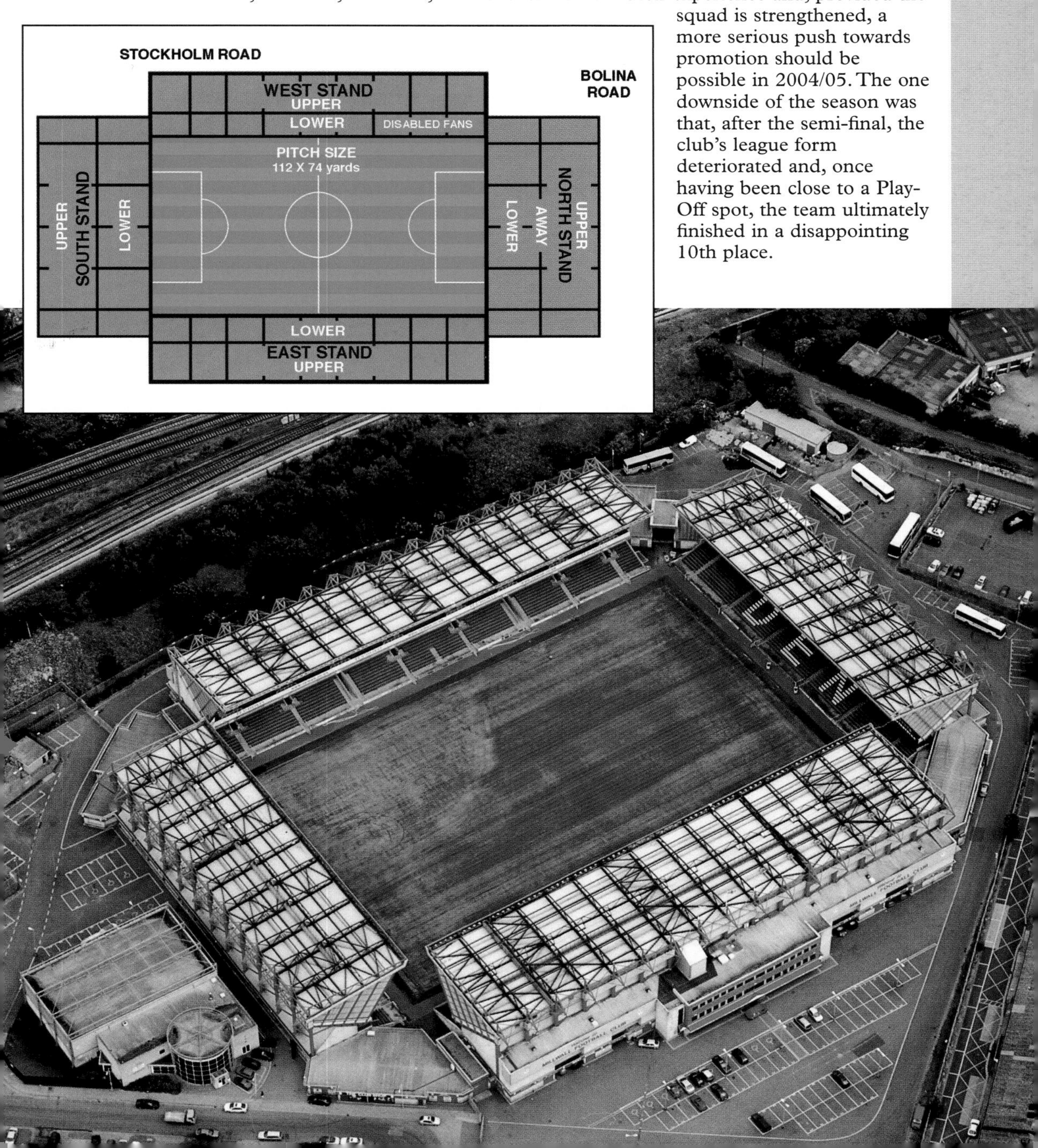

MILTON KEYNES DONS

National Hockey Stadium, Silbury Boulevard, Milton Keynes, MK9 1FA

Tel No: 01908 607090
Advance Tickets Tel No: 01908 607090
Fax: 01908 209449
National Hockey Stadium: 01908 246800
Web Site: www.wimbledon-fc.premiumtv.co.uk
E-Mail: Not confirmed
League: League One
Brief History: Founded 1889 at Wimbledon Old Centrals, changed name to Wimbledon in 1905 and to Milton Keynes Dons in 2004. Former grounds: Wimbledon Common, Pepy's Road, Grand Drive, Merton Hall Road, Malden Wanderers Cricket Ground, Plough Lane and moved to Selhurst Park in 1991. Probable move to National Hockey Stadium 2002. Elected to Football League in 1977. Record attendance (Plough Lane) 18,000; (Selhurst Park) 30,115; (National Hockey Stadium) 8,118
(Total) Current Capacity: 9,000 (all seated)
Visiting Supporters' Allocation: 1,200 (West Stand)
Club Colours: Blue shirts, blue shorts
Nearest Railway Station: Milton Keynes Central
Parking (Car): At ground
Parking (Coach/Bus): As directed
Police Force and Tel No: Thames Valley Police (01865 846000)
Disabled Visitors' Facilities:
Wheelchairs: 48 spaces around the ground
Blind: No special facility at present
Anticipated Development(s): The construction of the two temporary stands, taking the ground's capacity to 9,000, enabled the team to move during the 2003/04 season. The club, now under new ownership, is progressing with plans to construct, in conjunction with a major supermarket chain, a new 28,000 all-seater stadium at Denbigh. The anticipated timescale is that this new facility will be ready for the start of the 2006/07 season although much remains to be confirmed. The club has just announced that it intends to put a cover over the East Stand.

KEY

⬆ North direction (approx)

1. National Hockey Stadium
2. Milton Keynes Central station
3. Grafton Gate
4. A509 Portway
5. A509 Portway to A5 junction
6. Silbury Boulevard
7. To town centre

Above: 696920; *Right:* 696921

The club's first season at its new, temporary, home at the National Hockey Stadium proved to be a disaster on the field with the club's young squad struggling to make an impact following the loss of many experienced professionals as a result of the club's Administration. Almost from the start it appeared that the team was doomed to relegation and, despite the odd good result — such as victory at high-flying Wigan — Stuart Murdoch's team finished last in the First Division and thus Milton Keynes will see League One football in 2004/05. On a more positive note, the club left Administration in mid 2004 and the team will enter League One with a decent squad of youngsters who have been 'blooded' at a higher level. Unfortunately, however, despite leaving Administration, it is hard to see the club as being amongst the most secure in League One and a poor start to the new campaign could see confidence disappear from the team and a further relegation battle loom. The dream of the erstwhile supporters, who left to establish AFC Wimbledon (doing very nicely, thank you, at Kingston), to see their new team play 'Franchise FC' seems to get closer.

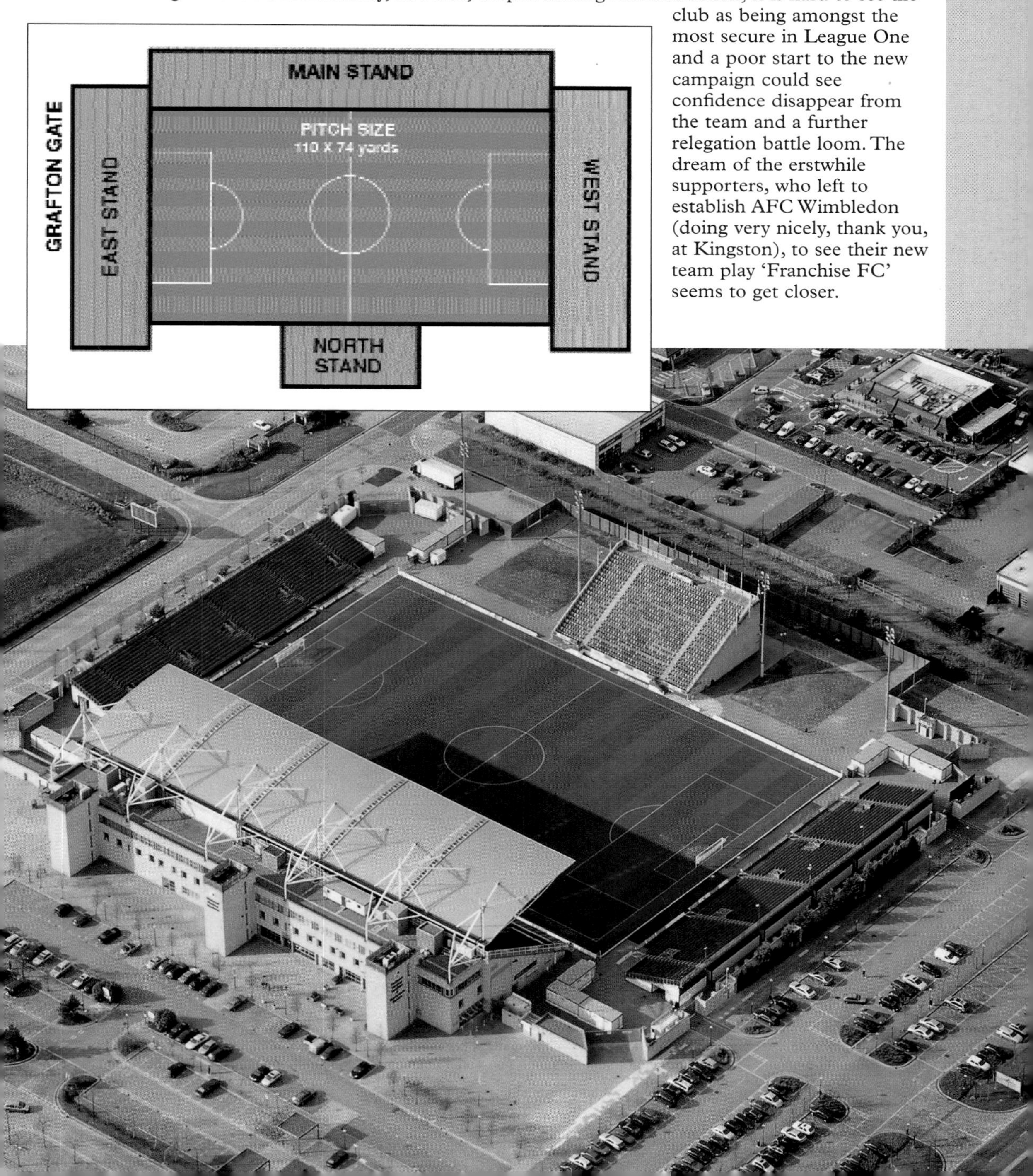

NEWCASTLE UNITED

St. James' Park, Newcastle-upon-Tyne, NE1 4ST

Tel No: 0191 201 8400
Advance Tickets Tel No: 0191 261 1571
Fax: 0191 201 8600
Web Site: www.nufc.premiumtv.co.uk
E-mail: admin@nufc.co.uk
League: F.A. Premier
Brief History: Founded in 1882 as Newcastle East End, changed to Newcastle United in 1892. Former Grounds: Chillingham Road, moved to St. James' Park (former home of defunct Newcastle West End) in 1892. Record attendance 68,386
(Total) Current Capacity: 52,193 (all seated)
Visiting Supporters' Allocation: 3,000 in North West Stand
Club Colours: Black and white striped shirts, black shorts
Nearest Railway Station: Newcastle Central
Parking (Car): Leazes car park and street parking
Parking (Coach/Bus): Leazes car park
Police Force and Tel No: Northumbria (0191 232 3451)
Disabled Visitors' Facilities:
Wheelchairs: 103 spaces available
Blind: Commentary available
Anticipated Development(s): With work now completed on both the enlarged Millburn and Sir John Hall stands, the capacity at St James' Park is now about 52,000. Further redevelopment at the ground is, however, problematic given the lie of the land on the north side, and the club has no immediate plans for further work once the current programme is completed.

KEY

- **C** Club Offices
- **S** Club Shop
- ⬆ North direction (approx)

1. St. James's Park
2. Strawberry Place
3. Gallowgate
4. Away Section
5. To Newcastle Central BR Station (1/2 mile) & A6127(M)
6. Car Park
7. Barrack Road (A189)
8. To A1 and North
9. Corporation Street
10. Percy Road

- ● Metro Station

Above: 694859; *Right:* 694852

Under Bobby Robson the Magpies had something of a curate's egg of a season. Failure to progress beyond the preliminary stages of the Champions League on one hand, counter-balanced by reaching the semi-finals of the UEFA Cup on the other. In the league, the club missed out on the all-important fourth position — and thus entry again into the Champions League — but by finishing fifth will at least ensure that European football will again be a feature of the new season courtesy of the UEFA Cup. Part of the club's failure to maintain a decent challenge for a top-four position was undoubtedly the result of a crippling injury list but it would be foolish to see this as United's only problem; after all, other teams have struggled with injuries at various times and yet battled through. Although Robson's appetite for the game seems undiminished, there must come a point where he would want to hand over to a chosen successor. The club's failure to achieve silverware for almost four decades must be a cause of concern for manager and senior players alike but it's hard to escape the conclusion that, once again, United's best opportunity redeem the situation will be through one of the cup competitions.

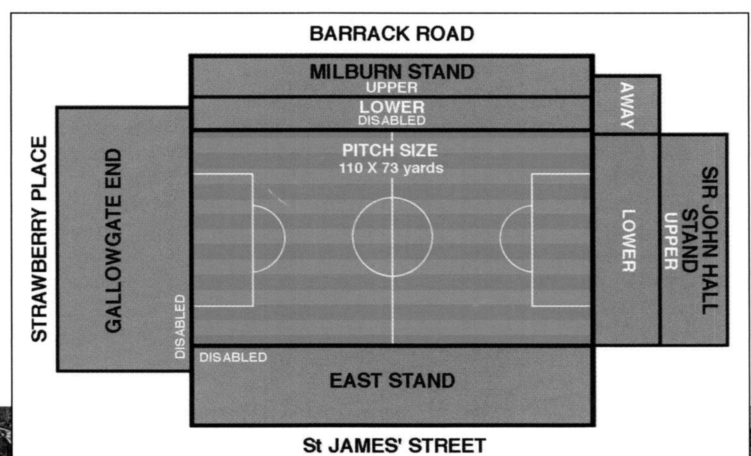

NORTHAMPTON TOWN

Sixfields Stadium, Northampton, NN5 5QA

Tel No: 01604 757773
Advance Tickets Tel No: 01604 588338
Fax: 01604 751613
E-Mail: secretary@ntfc.tv
Web Site: www.ntfc.premiumtv.co.uk
League: League Two
Brief History: Founded 1897. Former, County, Ground was part of Northamptonshire County Cricket Ground. Moved to Sixfields Stadium during early 1994/95 season. Record attendance 24,523 (at County Ground); 7,557 (at Sixfields)
(Total) Current Capacity: 7,653 (all seated)
Visiting Supporters' Allocation: 850 (in South Stand; can be increased to 1,150 if necessary)
Club Colours: Claret with white sleeved shirts, white shorts
Nearest Railway Station: Northampton
Parking (Car): Adjacent to Ground
Parking (Coach/Bus): Adjacent to Ground
Police Force and Tel No: Northants (01604 700700)
Disabled Visitors' Facilities:
Wheelchairs: Available on all four sides
Blind: Available
Anticipated Development(s): The club has plans to increase the capacity of the Sixfields stadium to c16,000 all-seated although there is no timescale for this work.

KEY

- **C** Club Offices
- **S** Club Shop
- **E** Entrance(s) for visiting supporters
- **R** Refreshment bars for visiting supporters
- **T** Toilets for visiting supporters

⬆ North direction (approx)

1. South Stand (away)
2. Athletics Stand
3. Upton Way
4. Car parks
5. A45 towards A43 (Towcester and A5)
6. Weedon Road
7. To Town Centre and station
8. A45 to M1 (Jct 16)

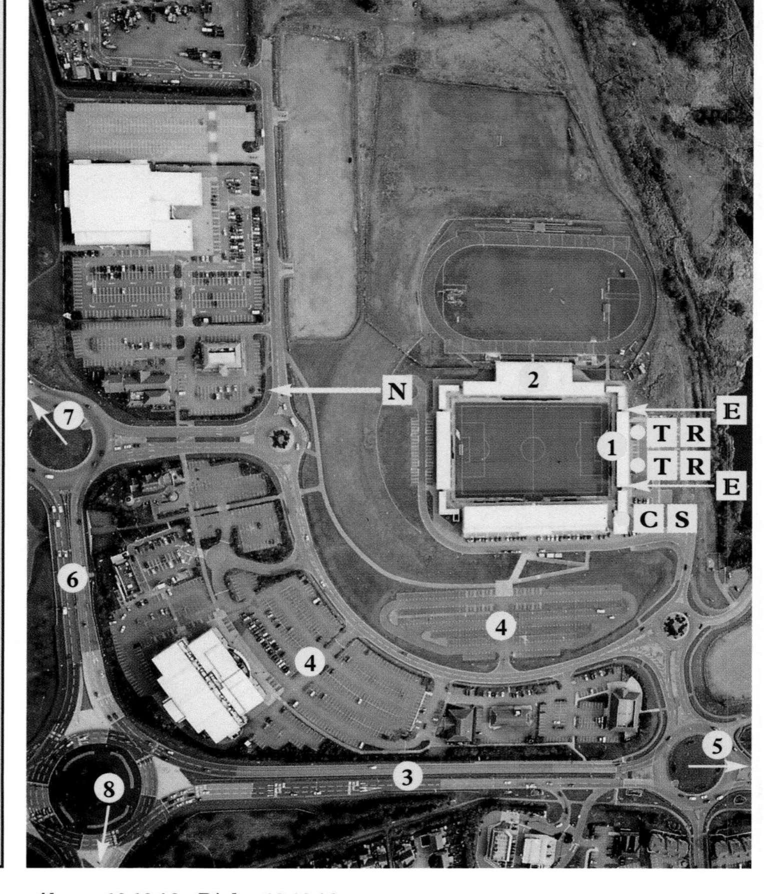

Above: 696943; *Right:* 696943

Following considerable expenditure during the close season, much was expected from Martin Wilkinson's Cobblers following their relegation at the end of 2002/03. However, a poor start to the season, culminating in a 3-0 defeat at Oxford United, saw the team languishing in 16th position and, in late September, Wilkinson was sacked. His assistant, Richard Hill took over as caretaker but Colin Calderwood was appointed in early October to the permanent position. Under Calderwood, the team made a dramatic climb up the table, ultimately finishing in sixth position (having defeated Mansfield Town in the final game of the season). Ironically, Town then faced Mansfield again in the Play-Offs, losing 2-0 at the Sixfields Stadium in the first leg. A dramatic fight-back at field Mill saw Northampton take a 3-0 lead on the night, 3-2 on aggregate, only for the Stags to score a second-half equaliser. With no further score in normal time or in the additional 30min, the game went to penalties where, unfortunately for Northampton fans, Mansfield proved successful. Although Northampton is again faced with League Two football in 2004/05 provided that the team can match its performances of the second half of 2003/04, fans can expect a further push for promotion.

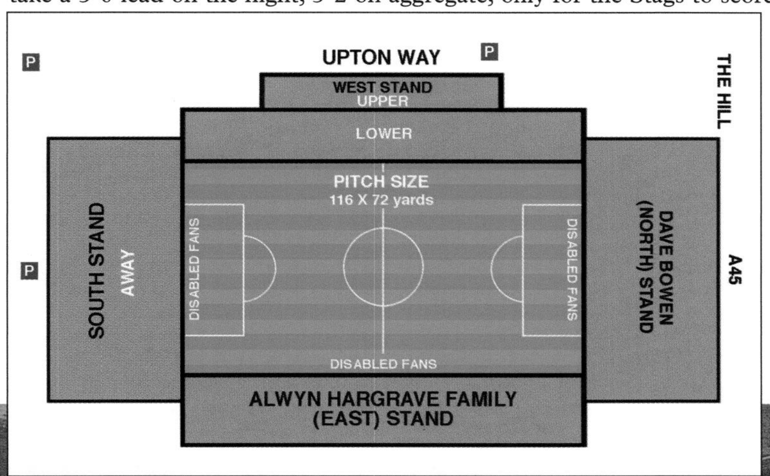

NORWICH CITY

Carrow Road, Norwich, NR1 1JE

Tel No: 01603 760760
Advance Tickets Tel No: 0870 444 1902
Fax: 01603 613886
Web Site: www.canaries.premiumtv.co.uk
E-Mail: reception@ncfc-canaries.co.uk
League: F.A. Premiership
Brief History: Founded 1902. Former grounds: Newmarket Road and the Nest, Rosary Road; moved to Carrow Road in 1935. Founder-members 3rd Division (1920). Record attendance 43,984
(Total) Current Capacity: 24,500
Visiting Supporters' Allocation: 2,000 maximum in South Stand
Club Colours: Yellow with green side panel shirts, green shorts
Nearest Railway Station: Norwich
Parking (Car): City centre car parks
Parking (Coach/Bus): Lower Clarence Road
Police Force and Tel No: Norfolk (01603 768769)
Disabled Visitors' Facilities:
Wheelchairs: tbc
Blind: Commentary available
Anticipated Development(s): The new South (Jarrold) Stand was completed during the 2003/04 season and took Carrow Road's capacity to 24,500. With the team's promotion to the Premiership at the end of the campaign the club has acted quickly to expand the ground's capacity further with the corner in-fill between the South and River End stands being constructed after the end of the season. The new structure is planned to open in two stages, the lower tier in December 2004 and the upper in March 2005. This will provide an additional 1,600 seats and further disabled facilities, taking the total capacity to just over 26,000. The club also has plans, with the pitch having been moved slightly towards the South Stand, to construct a second tier on the City Stand, but there is no confirmation as to a timescale for this work.

KEY

C Club Offices
S Club Shop

⬆ North direction (approx)

1. Carrow Road
2. A47 King Street
3. River Wensum
4. Riverside
5. Car Park
6. Norwich BR Station
7. South Stand
8. Geoffrey Watling (City) Stand
9. Barclay End Stand
10. The Norwich & Peterborough (River End) Stand

Above: 697214; *Right:* 697216

After several years of being close to achieving promotion to the Premiership, including the trauma of losing the Play-Off final two years ago, Nigel Worthington's team finally hit the big time, winning the First Division title in some style. Returning to English football's top flight for the first time in more than decade, the Canaries will discover that much has changed since the team was last in the Premiership and, like all promoted teams, will undoubtedly be one of the pre-season favourites for the drop. Although, in players like Darren Huckerby (whose arrival initially on loan was an undoubted factor in the team's success), the club has some players with Premiership experience, it's unlikely that Delia Smith's book sales over the summer months will be sufficient to raise the many millions required to ensure Premiership survival. Unfortunately, therefore, it's difficult to gainsay the argument for the team's quick return to the League Championship.

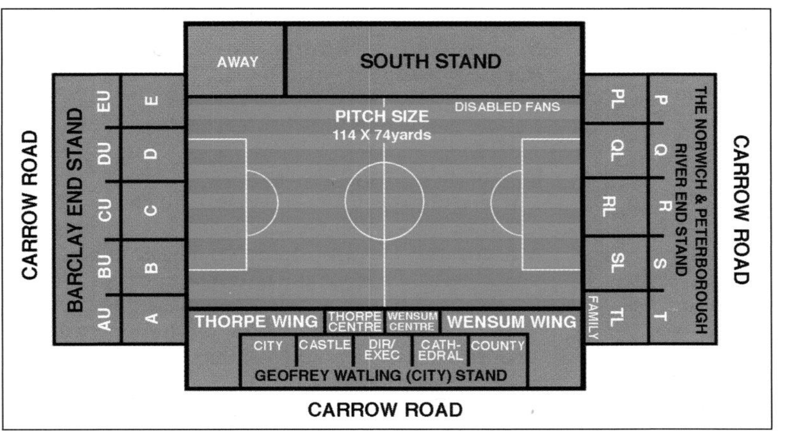

NOTTINGHAM FOREST

City Ground, Nottingham, NG2 5FJ

Tel No: 0115 982 4444
Advance Tickets Tel No: 0871 226 1980
Fax: 0115 982 4455
Web Site: www.nottinghamforest.premiumtv.co.uk
E-Mail: info@nottinghamforest.co.uk
League: League Championship
Brief History: Founded 1865 as Forest Football Club, changed name to Nottingham Forest (c1879). Former Grounds: Forest Recreation Ground, Meadow Cricket Ground, Trent Bridge (Cricket Ground), Parkside, Gregory Ground and Town Ground, moved to City Ground in 1898. Founder-members of Second Division (1892). Record attendance 49,945
(Total) Current Capacity: 30,602 (all seated)
Visiting Supporters' Allocation: Approx 4,750
Club Colours: Red shirts, white shorts
Nearest Railway Station: Nottingham
Parking (Car): East car park and street parking
Parking (Coach/Bus): East car park
Police Force and Tel No: Nottinghamshire (0115 948 1888)
Disabled Visitors' Facilities:
Wheelchairs: Front of Brian Clough Stand
Blind: No special facility
Anticipated Development(s): The club has long-term plans for the redevelopment of the Main Stand, with a view to increasing the ground's capacity to 40,000, but nothing will happen until the club reclaims a position in the Premiership.

KEY

- **C** Club Offices
- **S** Club Shop
- **E** Entrance(s) for visiting supporters

⬆ North direction (approx)

1. Radcliffe Road
2. Lady Bay Bridge Road
3. Trent Bridge
4. Trent Bridge Cricket Ground
5. Notts County F.C.
6. River Trent
7. Nottingham Midland BR Station (1/2 mile)

Above: 692575; *Right:* 692566

Following a 1-0 home defeat by Coventry City, which extended Forest's run of failure to 14 games without a win and left the team rooted in the bottom three, Paul Hart was sacked as manager in early February. The previous season, showing how fickle football can be, Forest had reached the Play-Offs, but 2003/04 was to be different. The club moved quickly to fill the void, appointing the experienced Joe Kinnear almost immediately. The change in fortunes was dramatic, with Kinnear guiding the team away from the drop zone and to safety. Ultimately finishing in 14th position was far better than fans might have expected before Kinnear took over and provided that the squad can maintain the form of the second half of 2003/04 then the new season could be one of considerable promise. An outside bet for the Play-Offs perhaps?

P
UPPER
BRIAN CLOUGH STAND
LOWER
PITCH SIZE
112 X 78 yards
DISABLED FANS
RIVER TRENT
TRENT END STAND
UPPER
LOWER
LOWER
AWAY
BRIDGFORD STAND
UPPER
COLWICK ROAD
MAIN STAND

NOTTS COUNTY

Meadow Lane, Nottingham, NG2 3HJ

Tel No: 0115 952 9000
Advance Tickets Tel No: 0115 955 7210
Fax: 0115 955 3994
Web Site: www.nottscountyfc.premiumtv.co.uk
E-Mail: info@nottscountyfc.co.uk
League: League Two
Brief History: Founded 1862 (oldest club in Football League) as Nottingham, changed to Notts County in c1882. Former Grounds: Notts Cricket Ground (Beeston), Castle Cricket Ground, Trent Bridge Cricket Ground, moved to Meadow Lane in 1910. Founder-members Football League (1888). Record attendance 47,310

(Total) Current Capacity: 19,600 (seated)
Visiting Supporters' Allocation: 5,438 (seated)
Club Colours: Black and white striped shirts, black shorts
Nearest Railway Station: Nottingham Midland
Parking (Car): Mainly street parking
Parking (Coach/Bus): Cattle market
Police Force and Tel No: Nottingham (0115 948 1888)
Disabled Visitors' Facilities:
Wheelchairs: Meadow Lane/Jimmy Sirrel/ Derek Pavis Stands
Blind: No special facility

KEY

E Entrance(s) for visiting supporters

R Refreshment bars for visiting supporters

T Toilets for visiting supporters

⬆ North direction (approx)

1. A6011 Meadow Lane
2. County Road
3. A60 London Road
4. River Trent
5. Nottingham Midland BR Station (1/2 mile)
6. Jimmy Sirrel Stand
7. Kop Stand (away)
8. Derek Pavis Stand
9. Family (Meadow Lane) Stand

Above: 692577; *Right:* 692585

After many months, the club emerged from Administration in December. In early January, following a 5-2 defeat away at fellow strugglers Peterborough United, Billy Dearden resigned as manager with the team rooted in the relegation zone. The club moved quickly to appoint ex-player Gary Mills, previously coach at First Division Coventry, as its new manager. However, the new management team was unable to stop the drift towards relegation and, in 2004/05, League Two football beckons.

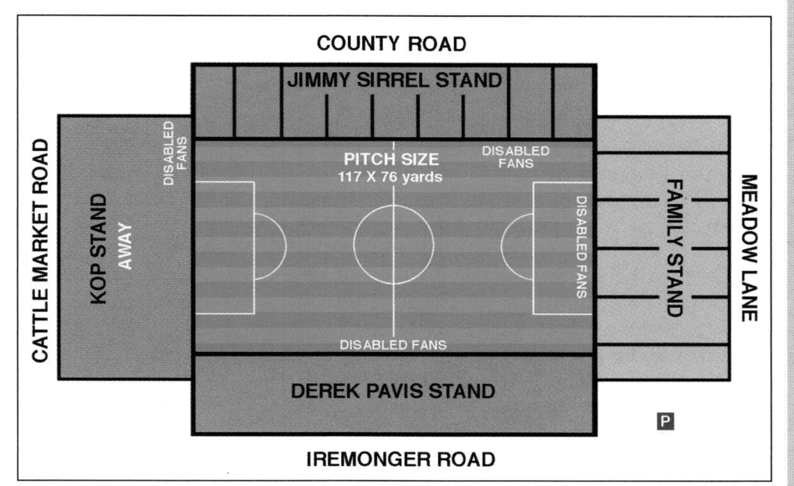

OLDHAM ATHLETIC

Boundary Park, Oldham, OL1 2PA

Tel No: 0870 7532000
Advance Tickets Tel No: 0870 7532000
Fax: 0161 627 5915
Web Site: www.oldhamathletic.co.uk
E-Mail: marketing@oldhamathletic.premiumtv.co.uk
League: League One
Brief History: Founded 1897 as Pine Villa, changed name to Oldham Athletic in 1899. Former Grounds: Berry's Field, Pine Mill, Athletic Ground (later named Boundary Park), Hudson Fold, moved to Boundary Park in 1906. Record attendance 47,671
(Total) Current Capacity: 13,624 (all seated)
Visiting Supporters' Allocation: 1,800 minimum, 4,600 maximum
Club Colours: Blue shirts, blue shorts
Nearest Railway Station: Oldham Werneth
Parking (Car): Lookers Stand car park
Parking (Coach/Bus): At Ground
Other Clubs Sharing Ground: Oldham Roughyeads RLFC
Police Force and Tel No: Greater Manchester (0161 624 0444)
Disabled Visitors' Facilities:
Wheelchairs: Rochdale Road and Seton Stands
Blind: No special facility
Anticipated Development(s): The plans for the construction of a new 15,000-seat ground at Clayton Playing Fields in conjunction with the local RLFC club have been abandoned. As a result, Athletic will now seek to redevelop Boundary Park further, with the first phase being the construction of a new two-tier stand, costing £15 million, to replace the Lookers Stand. There is, however, no confirmed timetable for this work at the current time.

KEY

- **C** Club Offices
- **E** Entrance(s) for visiting supporters
- ⬆ North direction (approx)

1. A663 Broadway
2. Furtherwood Road
3. Chadderton Way
4. To A627(M) and M62
5. To Oldham Werneth BR Station (1½ miles)
6. Car Park
7. Rochdale Road Stand (away)
8. SSL Stand
9. Lookers Stand
10. Pukka Pies Stand

Above: 697199; *Right:* 697195

Just before Christmas, with Oldham just above the drop zone, Iain Dowie resigned as manager, heading for the vacant hot seat at Selhurst Park. He was replaced as joint caretakers by John Sheridan and David Eyres. The club, which had come close to extinction on several occasions, came out of Administration in early February when a new consortium took over. In early March, ex-Rushden manager Brian Talbot took over on a three-year contract with John Sheridan offered the position of first team coach. Under the experienced Talbot, the team was to finish in 15th position. Provided that the team can maintain the progress shown after Talbot's appointment into the new campaign, then 2004/05 ought to see the team improve considerably on the mid-table mediocrity of 2003/04.

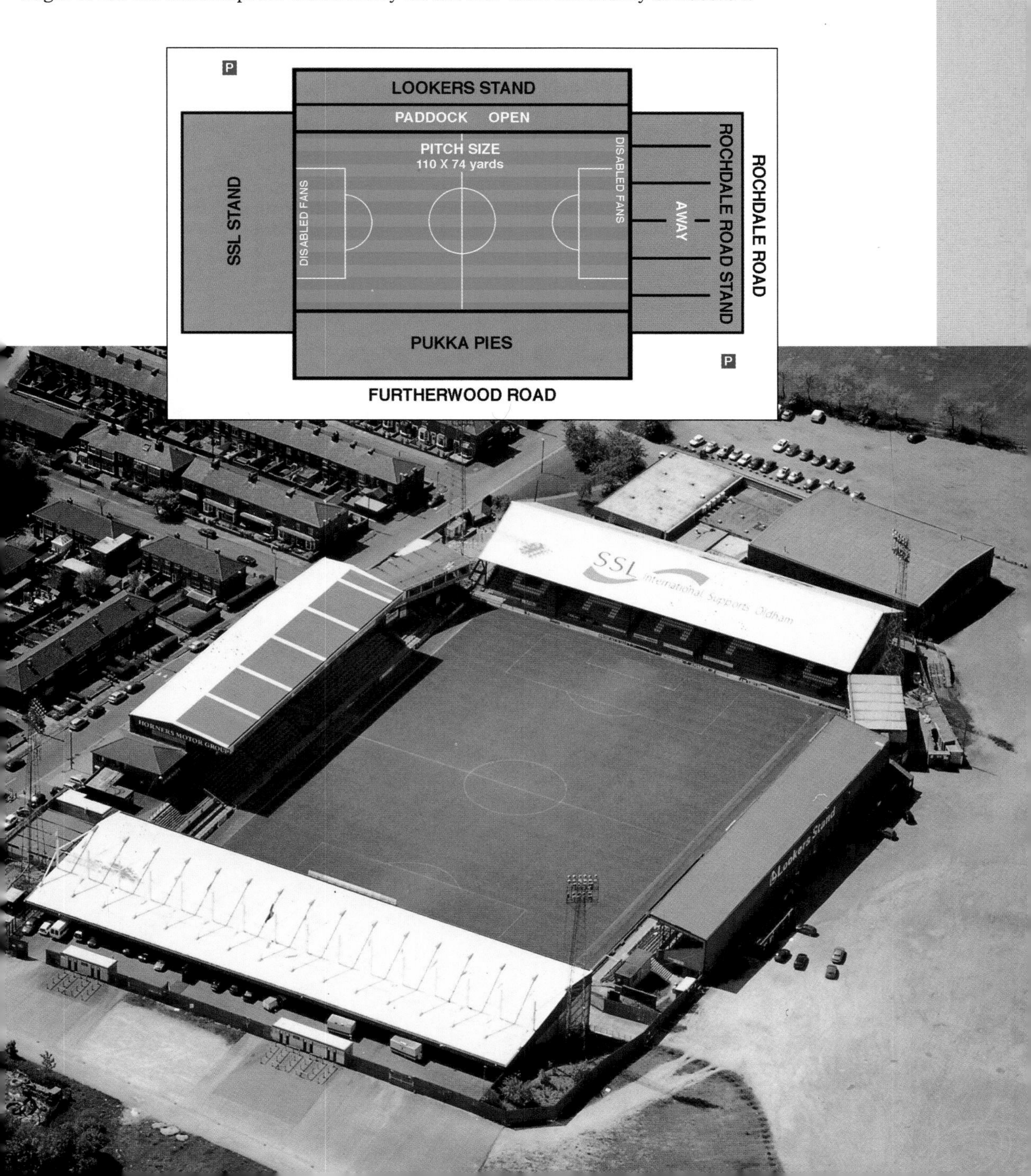

OXFORD UNITED

Kassam Stadium, Grenoble Road, Blackbird Leys, Oxford OX4 4XP

Tel No: 01865 337500
Advance Tickets Tel No: 01865 337533
Fax: 01865 337555
Web Site: www.oufc.premiumtv.co.uk
E-Mail: admin@oufc.co.uk
League: League Two
Brief History: Founded in 1893 as Headington (later Headington United)m changed name to Oxford United in 1960. Former grounds: Britannia Inn Field, Headington Quarry, Wooten's Field, Manor Ground and The Paddocks. The club moved back to the Manor Ground in 1925. Moved — finally — to new ground at Minchery Farm in 2001. Record attendance (at the Manor Ground) 22,730.
(Total) Current Capacity: 12,500
Visiting Supporters' Allocation: c5,000 maximum in North Stand
Club Colours: Yellow with blue trim shirts and navy with yellow trim shorts
Nearest Railway Station: Oxford
Parking (Car): 1,100 spaces at ground
Parking (Coach/Bus): As directed
Police Force and Tel No: Thames Valley (01865 777501)
Disabled Visitors' Facilities:
Wheelchairs: c80 disabled spaces
Blind: No special facility
Anticipated Development(s): Although the club has plans for the construction of the fourth side of the ground there is no confirmed timescale as to when this work will be undertaken.

KEY

C Club Offices
E Entrance(s) for visiting supporters

⬆ North direction (approx)

1. Grenoble Road
2. To A4074
3. Northfield School
4. To Oxford city centre and railway station (four/five miles respectively)
5. Blackbird Leys Estate
6. Knights Road
7. North Stand
8. South Stand
9. East Stand
10. To B480

Above: 692183; *Right:* 692177

Shortly before the postponed game against Mansfield Town in mid-March, and with the team riding high in the promotion race, chairman Firoz Kassam announces that manager Ian Atkins has been suspended. This was the result of an announcement from Bristol Rovers that Atkins was to take over at the Memorial Ground for the start of the 2004/05 season. The club moved rapidly to fill the void, appointing ex-Portsmouth boss Graham Rix as temporary – later confirmed as permanent – manager on the following Monday. However, Atkins' departure saw a disappointing dip in the team's form with the result that the club not only failed to achieve automatic promotion, but it also missed the Play-Offs as well.

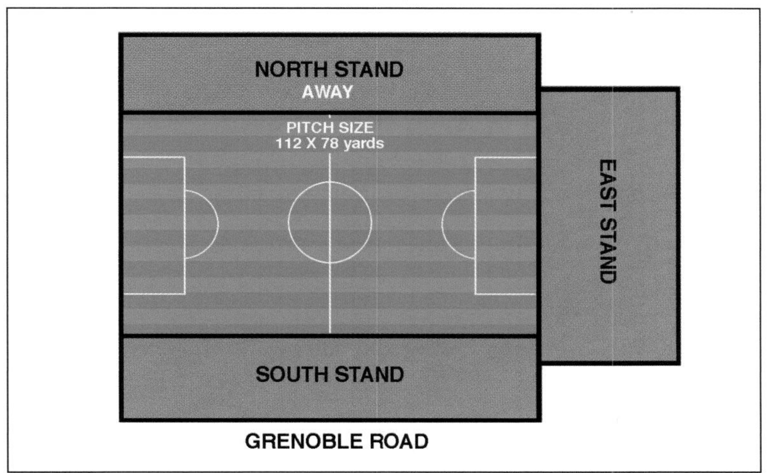

PETERBOROUGH UNITED

London Road, Peterborough, Cambs, PE2 8AL

Tel No: 01733 563947
Advance Tickets Tel No: 0870 550442
Fax: 01733 344140
Web Site: www.theposh.premiumtv.co.uk
E-Mail: info@theposh.com
League: League One
Brief History: Founded in 1934 (no connection with former 'Peterborough and Fletton United' FC). Elected to Football League in 1960. Record attendance 30,096
(Total) Current Capacity: 15,314 (7,669 seated)
Visiting Supporters' Allocation: 3,758 (756 seated)
Club Colours: Blue shirts, white shorts
Nearest Railway Station: Peterborough
Parking (Car): Peterborough
Parking (Coach/Bus): At ground
Police Force and Tel No: Cambridgeshire (01733 563232
Disabled Visitors' Facilities:
Wheelchairs: South Stand
Blind: No special facility
Future Development(s): Following the reroofing of the Moys and London Road ends, long term plans exist for the construction of a new Main Stand — for which plans have been prepared — and other work. However, there is no confirmed timetable for this at present.

KEY

- **C** Club Offices
- **S** Club Shop
- **E** Entrance(s) for visiting supporters
- **R** Refreshment bars for visiting supporters
- **T** Toilets for visiting supporters
- ⬆ North direction (approx)

1. A15 London Road
2. Car Parks
3. Peterborough BR Station (1 mile)
4. Glebe Road
5. A605
6. To A1 (north) (5 miles)
7. River Nene
8. To Whittlesey
9. To A1 (south) (5 miles)
10. Thomas Cook Stand
11. London Road Terrace
12. Moys Terrace (away)
13. Main Stand

Above: 697321; *Right:* 697312

After some eight years at London Road, Barry Fry discovered that he liked Posh so much that he decided to become the owner… At least, that way, he guarantees that no chairman can afford to fire him again. As one of the Second Division strugglers, United were lucky to escape from the relegation battle with their status undamaged — despite defeat on the last day of the season — as other teams proved even worse. Finishing in 18th position and still alive financially were triumphs as far as Fry was concerned but the fact that 18th was only two points off the drop zone is perhaps less encouraging. For 2004/05 the back-room staff at London Road has been strengthened through the recruitment of the experienced Bobby Gould as Head Coach but it's still hard to see Posh as anything other than potential relegation candidates.

PLYMOUTH ARGYLE

Home Park, Plymouth, PL2 3PE

Tel No: 01752 562561
Advance Tickets Tel No: 01752 562562
Fax: 01752 606167
Web-site: www.pafc.premiumtv.co.uk
E-mail: argyle@pafc.co.uk
League: League Championship
Brief History: Founded 1886 as Argyle Athletic Club, changed name to Plymouth Argyle in 1903. Founder-members Third Division (1920). Record attendance 43,596
(Total) Current Capacity: 20,134 (15,684 seated)
Visiting Supporters' Allocation: 1,300 in Barn Park End Stand up to maximum of 2,000
Club Colours: White and green shirts, green shorts
Nearest Railway Station: Plymouth
Parking (Car): Car park adjacent
Parking (Coach/Bus): Central car park
Police Force and Tel No: Devon & Cornwall (0990 777444)
Disabled Visitors' Facilities:
Wheelchairs: Devonport End
Blind: Commentary available
Anticipated Development(s): Work on the three new stands at Home Park progressed well, with work being completed during the 2001/02 season. Plans, however, for the demolition of the existing Main Stand and its replacement have been deferred as a result of the collapse of ITV Digital and there is now no confirmed timescale.

KEY

C Club Offices
S Club Shop

↑ North direction (approx)

1 Outland Road
2 Car Park
3 Devonport Road
4 Central Park
5 Town Centre & Plymouth BR Station (1/2 mile)

Above: 692218; *Right:* 692209

Despite the team riding high at the top of the Second Division and despite the fact that he had signed a new five-year contract in the summer, Paul Sturrock exercised the clause in his contract permitting him to move if a Premiership team was interested in his services and, in early March, he departed to take over at Southampton. Kevin Summerfield was appointed as caretaker. Whilst the club was compensated for the loss of his services, there was a short-term hiatus when the team's form dipped. In the event, however, the Second Division title was secured along with First Division football in 2004/05. Towards the end of April, with promotion already in the bag, it was announced that Bobby Williamson, the manager of Hibernian, was to take over at Home Park. Whilst he arrived too late to have an impact on the 2003/04 season, his role will be pivotal in new season if Argyle are not to make an immediate return to the League One. Although most promoted clubs are always amongst the favourites for automatic relegation, such is the parlous condition financially of a number of existing First Division teams that, like Wigan last year, it may well be that Argyle do more than simply survive at the higher level.

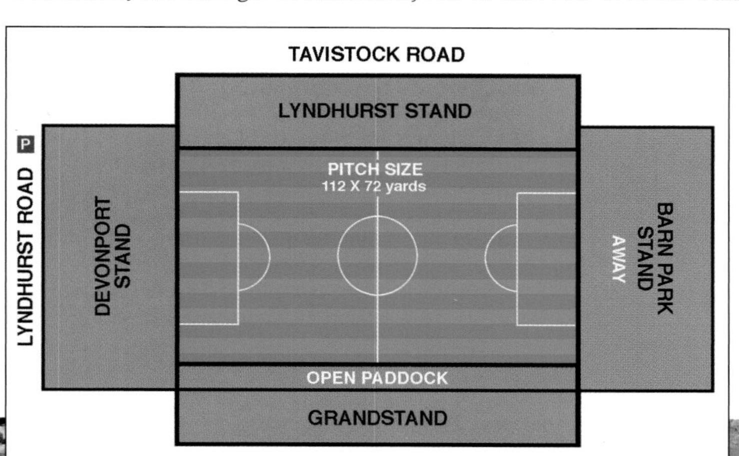

PORTSMOUTH

Fratton Park, 57 Frogmore Road, Portsmouth, Hants, PO4 8RA

Tel No: 02392 731204
Advance Tickets Tel No: 02392 618777
Fax: 02392 734129
Web Site: www.pompeyfc.premiumtv.co.uk
E-Mail: info@pompeyfc.co.uk
League: F.A. Premiership
Brief History: Founded 1898. Founder-members Third Division (1920). Record attendance 51,385
(Total) Current Capacity: 20,101 (all seated)
Visiting Supporters' Allocation: 3,121 (max) in Milton Stand
Club Colours: Blue shirts, white shorts
Nearest Railway Station: Fratton
Parking (Car): Street parking
Parking (Coach/Bus): As directed by Police
Police Force and Tel No: Hampshire (02392 321111)
Disabled Visitors' Facilities:
Wheelchairs: TY Europe Stand
Blind: No special facility
Anticipated Development(s): It was announced at the end of the 2002-03 season that Pompey intended to redevelop the existing Fratton Park site. The work will involve the rotation of the pitch by 90 degrees in order to allow the construction of the new ground. It was intended that the new stadium, with an initial capacity of 28,000 (rising later to 36,000), would be completed by the start of the 2005/06 season at a cost of £26 million.

KEY

- **C** Club Offices
- **S** Club Shop
- **E** Entrance(s) for visiting supporters
- **R** Refreshment bars for visiting supporters
- **T** Toilets for visiting supporters

⬆ North direction (approx)

1. Alverstone Road
2. Carisbrook Road
3. A288 Milton Road
4. A2030 Velder Avenue A27
5. A2030 Goldsmith Avenue
6. Fratton BR station (1/2 mile)
7. TY Europe Stand

Promoted at the end of 2002/03 to the Premiership, Pompey, like most teams making the leap up from the First Division, were considered to be strong candidates for automatic promotion. However, in Harry Redknapp, the club possesses one of the most astute managers in the game and, if anybody was able to keep the team up, he was. And so it proved, with a series of excellent signings providing additional strength to the squad. Although just above the drop-zone for much of the season, the club can look back on some excellent results — such as the draws against Arsenal and the victory over Manchester United at Fratton Park — with pleasure. Whilst, inevitably, the teams promoted from the First Division this season will again be strong favourites for automatic relegation, Pompey can ill-afford to be complacent as, recent experience has shown with Ipswich Town and Bradford City, that sometimes the second season can be more difficult than the first.

PORT VALE

Vale Park, Burslem, Stoke-on-Trent, ST6 1AW

Tel No: 01782 655800
Advance Tickets Tel No: 01782 811707
Fax: 01782 836875
Web Site: www.port-vale.premiumtv.co.uk
E-Mail: pvfc@port-vale.co.uk
League: League One
Brief History: Founded 1876 as Burslem Port Vale, changed name to 'Port Vale' in 1907 (reformed club). Former Grounds: The Meadows Longport, Moorland Road Athletic Ground, Cobridge Athletic Grounds, Recreation Ground Hanley, moved to Vale Park in 1950. Founder-members Second Division (1892). Record attendance 48,749
(Total) Current Capacity: 22,356 (all seated)
Visiting Supporters' Allocation: 4,550 (in Hamil Road [Phones4U] Stand)
Club Colours: White shirts, white shorts
Nearest Railway Station: Longport (two miles)
Parking (Car): Car park at Ground
Parking (Coach/Bus): Hamil Road car park
Police Force and Tel No: Staffordshire (01782 577114)
Disabled Visitors' Facilities:
Wheelchairs: 20 spaces in new Britannic Disabled Stand
Blind: Commentary available
Anticipated Development(s): The club's new owners intend, at some point, to complete the half-built Lorne Street Stand but there is, as yet, no timetable for this work.

KEY

E Entrance(s) for visiting supporters

⬆ North direction (approx)

1. Car Parks
2. Hamil Road
3. Lorne Street
4. To B5051 Moorland Road
5. To Burslem Town Centre
6. Railway Stand
7. Sentinel Stand
8. Hamil Road Stand
9. Lorne Street Stand (under construction)
10. Family Section

Above: 691733; *Right:* 691738

In early February, with the club in seventh place and challenging for a Play-off position it was announced that Brian Horton had vacated the managerial hot-seat by mutual consent. Horton, who had been at the club for five years, had managed the team to its triumph in the LDV Trophy in 2001 and had been at the helm during the period when the club's very existence was in some considerable doubt. The club moved quickly to appoint a replacement, with Youth Team Coach, Martin Foyle, being handed the reins a couple of days later. Under Foyle, the team continued to press for a Play-Off berth but, ultimately were to be denied on goal difference on the last day when, despite a 2-0 victory over Rushden & Diamonds at Nene Park, Hartlepool's 1-1 draw at Swindon guaranteed the Tees-side team the all-important sixth place. Provided that the team can continue to make progress under Foyle then fans can again expect a determined push towards promotion.

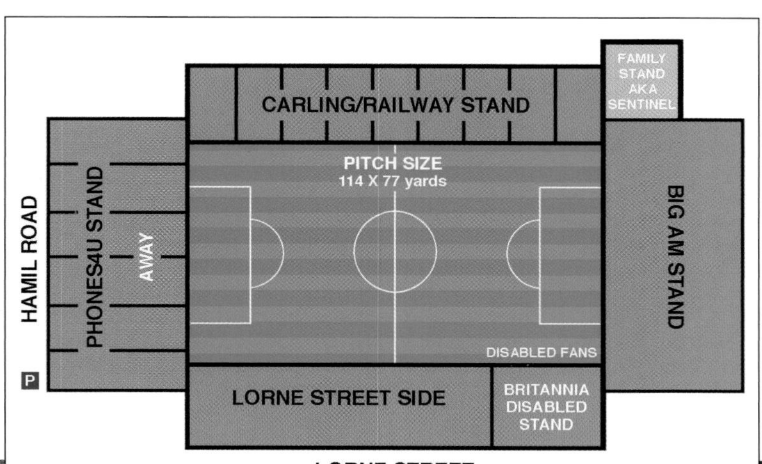

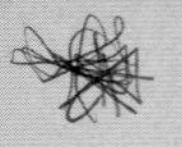

PRESTON NORTH END

Deepdale, Sir Tom Finney Way, Preston, PR1 6RU

Tel No: 0870 442 1964
Advance Tickets Tel No: 0870 4421966
Fax: 01772 693366
Web Site: www.pnefc.premiumtv.co.uk
E-Mail: enquiries@pne.com
League: League Championship
Brief History: Founded 1867 as a Rugby Club, changed to soccer in 1881. Former ground: Moor Park, moved to (later named) Deepdale in 1875. Founder-members Football League (1888). Record attendance 42,684
(Total) Current Capacity: 22,225 (all seated)
Visiting Supporters' Allocation: 6,000 maximum in Bill Shankly Stand
Club Colours: White shirts, blue shorts
Nearest Railway Station: Preston (2 miles)
Parking (Car): West Stand car park
Parking (Coach/Bus): West Stand car park
Police Force and Tel No: Lancashire (01772 203203)
Disabled Visitors' Facilities:
Wheelchairs: Tom Finney Stand and Bill Shankly Stand
Blind: Earphones Commentary
Anticipated Development(s): The completion of the £3 million 6,100-seat Alan Kelly (Town End) Stand means that Deepdale has now been completely rebuilt on three sides. Planning permission has been granted for the construction for the construction of a new two-tier stand to replace the existing Pavilion Stand, taking the ground's capacity to 30,000. However, there is no confirmed timescale for the work at the present time.

KEY

S Club Shop

⬆ North direction (approx)

1. A6033 Deepdale Road
2. Lawthorpe Road
3. Car Park
4. A5085 Blackpool Road
5. Preston BR Station (2 miles)
6. Bill Shankly Stand
7. Tom Finney Stand
8. Town End Stand (under construction

Above: 692526; *Right:* 692522

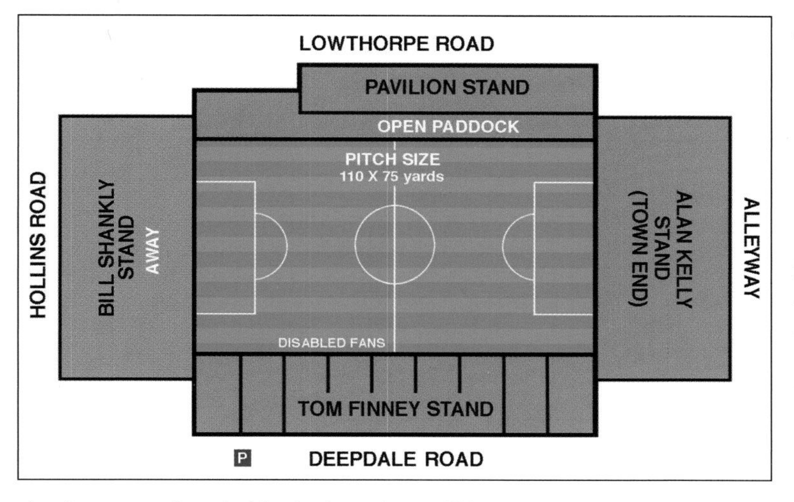

A reasonable start to the season gradually evaporated in the second half and the team eventually finished the 2003/04 campaign in a disappointing 15th position, closer in points terms to the drop zone than to the Play-Offs and lower than the position achieved in 2002/03. The season was ex-Scotland boss Craig Brown's second full year in charge and, with the lack of progress on the field, there is growing unrest amongst the fans. Much will depend on how successful Brown is in terms of strengthening the squad, but the fans — and probably the board — will be expecting Brown to improve significantly in 2004/05. Unfortunately, however, it's hard to escape the conclusion that, once again, the Lilywhites will be one of the teams battling for mid-table mediocrity.

QUEENS PARK RANGERS

Loftus Road Stadium, South Africa Road, London, W12 7PA

Tel No: 020 8743 0262
Advance Tickets Tel No: 0870 112 1967
Fax: 020 8749 0994
Web Site: www.qpr.premiumtv.co.uk
League: League Championship
Brief History: Founded 1885 as 'St. Jude's Institute', amalgamated with Christchurch Rangers to become Queens Park Rangers in 1886. Football League record number of former Grounds and Ground moves (13 different venues, 17 changes), including White City Stadium (twice) final move to Loftus Road in 1963. Founder-members Third Division (1920). Record attendance (at Loftus Road) 35,353
(Total) Current Capacity: 19,148 (all seated)
Visiting Supporters' Allocation: 3,100 (maximum)
Club Colours: Blue and white hooped shirts, white shorts
Nearest Railway Station: Shepherds Bush and White City (both tube)
Parking (Car): White City NCP and street parking
Parking (Coach/Bus): White City NCP
Police Force and Tel No: Metropolitan (020 8741 6212)
Disabled Visitors' Facilities:
Wheelchairs: Ellerslie Road Stand and West Paddock
Blind: Ellerslie Road Stand
Anticipated Development(s): There is vague talk of possible relocation, but nothing has been confirmed. Given the constrained site occupied by Loftus Road, it will be difficult to increase the existing ground's capacity.

KEY

- **C** Club Offices
- **S** Club Shop
- **E** Entrance(s) for visiting supporters
- ⬆ North direction (approx)

1. South Africa Road
2. To White City Tube Station, A219 Wood Lane and A40 Western Avenue
3. A4020 Uxbridge Road
4. To Shepherds Bush Tube Station
5. To Acton Central Station
6. BBC Television Centre
7. Loftus Road
8. Bloemfontein Road

Above: 695957; *Right:* 695948

Under Ian Holloway, QPR were in the thick of the promotion race throughout the campaign and, whilst the championship eluded the west London team, fans will be pleased that the team fought off the dogged challenge of Bristol City to ensure that the second automatic promotion place was guaranteed, although it took results on the last day — with QPR winning at Sheffield Wednesday — to ensure that Bristol City were denied. QPR should have the pedigree and potential to make a decent go of its new League Championship status, although fans should perhaps expect a season of consolidation initially.

SOUTH AFRICA ROAD
SOUTH AFRICA ROAD STAND
SEATED/COVERED PADDOCK
DISABLED FANS
PITCH SIZE
112 X 72 yards
DISABLED FANS
BLOEMFONTEIN ROAD
SCHOOL END
AWAY
LOWER
UPPER
LOFTUS ROAD STAND
LOFTUS ROAD
ELLERSLIE ROAD STAND
ELLERSLIE ROAD

READING

Madejski Stadium, Bennet Road, Reading, RG2 0FL

Tel No: 0118 968 1100
Advance Tickets Tel No: 0118 968 1000
Fax: 0118 968 1101
Web Site: www.readingfc.premiumtv.co.uk
E-Mail: comments@readingfc.co.uk
League: League Championship
Brief History: Founded 1871. Amalgamated with Reading Hornets in 1877 and with Earley in 1889. Former Grounds: Reading Recreation Ground, Reading Cricket Ground, Coley Park, Caversham Cricket Cround and Elm Park (1895-1998); moved to the Madejski Stadium at the start of the 1998/99 season. Founder-members of the Third Division in 1920. Record attendance (at Elm Park) 33,042; (at Madejski Stadium) 22,034
(Total) Current Capacity: 24,200 (all seated)
Visiting Supporters' Allocation: 4,500 (maximum in the Fosters Lager South Stand)
Club Colours: White with blue hoops shirts, white shorts
Nearest Railway Station: Reading (2.5 miles)
Parking (Car): 1,800-space car park at the ground, 700 of these spaces are reserved
Parking (Coach/Bus): As directed
Other Clubs Sharing Ground: London Irish RUFC
Police Force and Tel No: Thames Valley (0118 953 6000)
Disabled Visitors' Facilities:
Wheelchairs: 128 designated spaces on all four sides of the ground
Blind: 12 places for match day commentaries
Anticipated Development(s): The club has plans, if the need arises, to add an additional 5,000-seat section to the East Stand. Ultimately the ground could have a 40,000 capacity, but there is no timescale for this work.

KEY

C Club Offices
S Club Shop

⬆ North direction (approx)

1. North Stand
2. East Stand
3. South Stand (away)
4. West Stand
5. A33 Basingstoke Road
6. A33 to M4 (Jct 11)
7. A33 to Reading Town Centre and station (two miles)
8. Hurst Way
9. Boot End

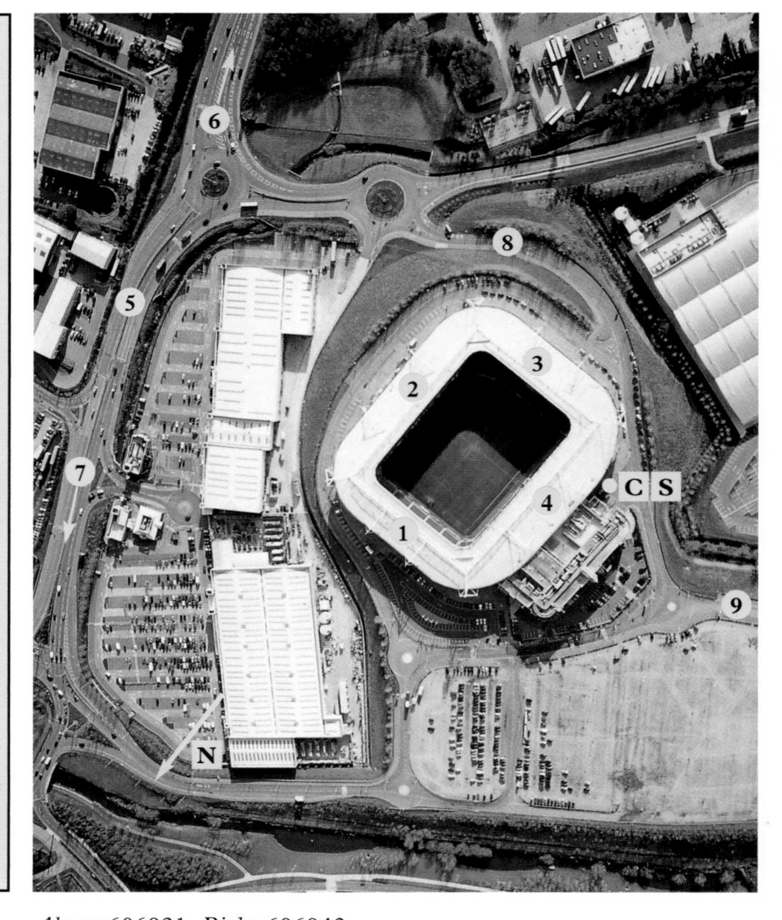

Above: 696931; *Right:* 696942

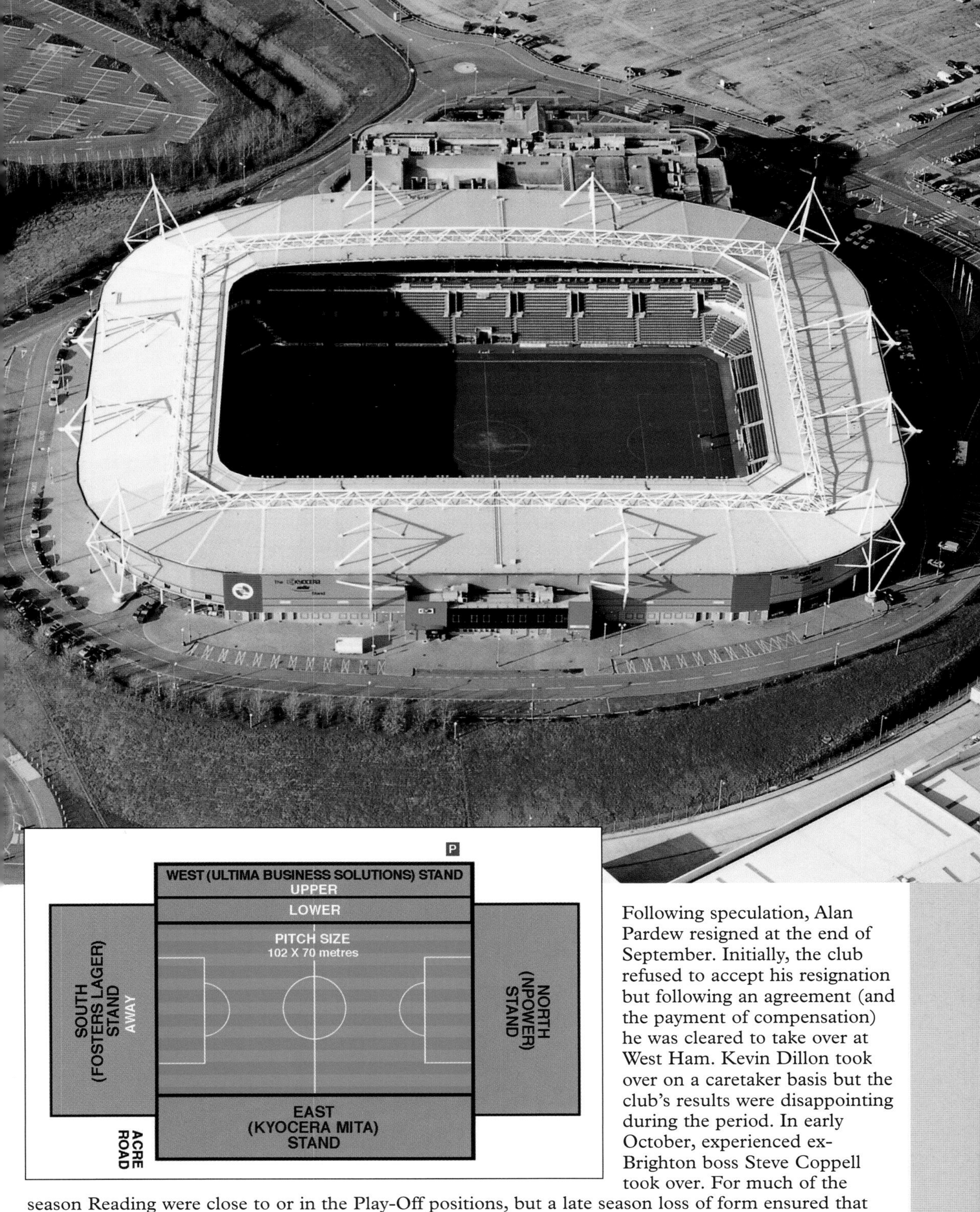

Following speculation, Alan Pardew resigned at the end of September. Initially, the club refused to accept his resignation but following an agreement (and the payment of compensation) he was cleared to take over at West Ham. Kevin Dillon took over on a caretaker basis but the club's results were disappointing during the period. In early October, experienced ex-Brighton boss Steve Coppell took over. For much of the season Reading were close to or in the Play-Off positions, but a late season loss of form ensured that the team missed out — although there remained a slim mathematical chance right up to the final Sunday of the season. Coppell is an astute manager and should be capable of ensuring that Reading again feature in the hunt for the Play-Offs in 2004/05.

ROCHDALE

Willbutts Lane, Spotland Stadium, Rochdale, OL11 5DS

Tel No: 01706 644648
Advance Tickets Tel No: 01706 644648
Fax: 01706 648466
Web-site: www.rochdaleafc.premiumtv.co.uk
E-Mail: office@rochdaleafc.co.uk
League: League Two
Brief History: Founded 1907 from former Rochadale Town F.C. (founded 1900). Founder-members Third Division North (1921). Record attendance 24,231
(Total) Current Capacity: 10,262 (8,342 seated) following completion of Pearl Street Stand
Visiting Supporters' Allocation: 3,650 (seated) in Willbutts Lane (Per-Fit Windows) Stand
Club Colours: Blue shirts, blue shorts
Nearest Railway Station: Rochdale
Parking (Car): Rear of ground
Parking (Coach/Bus): Rear of ground
Other Clubs Sharing Ground: Rochdale Hornets RLFC
Police Force and Tel No: Greater Manchester (0161 872 5050)
Disabled Visitors' Facilities:
Wheelchairs: Main, WMG and Willbutts Lane stands – disabled area
Blind: Commentary available
Anticipated Development(s): None following completion of Willbutts Lane Stand.

KEY

- **C** Club Offices
- **S** Club Shop
- **E** Entrance(s) for visiting supporters

⬆ North direction (approx)

1. Willbutts Lane
2. A627 Edenfield Road
3. Rochdale BR Station (1/2 mile)
4. Sandy Lane
5. To M62
6. To M65 and North
7. Pearl Street Stand
8. Willbutts Lane Stand

Above: 696966; *Right:* 696972

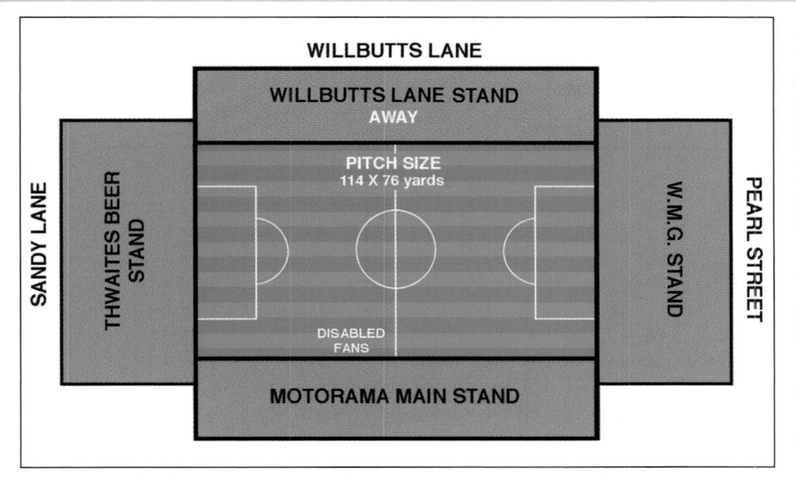

At the end of December, with the club having lost eight of its previous 10 games and sitting only five points off the drop zone, Alan Buckley departed from the Spotland managerial hot-seat by mutual consent. The club moved quickly to appoint ex-boss Steve Parkin, who had been manager previously until November 2001, as new manager on New Year's Eve. Although Parkin kept the team in the Third Division — just — Carlisle United's late burst meant that the team remained only five points above the drop zone in 21st position. With two strong teams coming up from the Conference in 2003/04, Rochdale will probably have a battle to retain its League status again in 2004/05.

ROTHERHAM UNITED

Millmoor Ground, Millmoor Lane, Rotherham, S60 1HR

Tel No: 01709 512434
Advance Tickets Tel No: 0870 224 2076
Fax: 01709 512762
Web Site: www.themillers.premiumtv.co.uk
E-Mail: office@rotherhamunited.net
League: League Championship
Brief History: Founded 1877 (as Thornhill later Thornhill United), changed name to Rotherham County in 1905 and to Rotherham United in 1925 (amalgamated with Rotherham Town – Football League members 1893-97 – in 1925). Former Grounds include: Red House Ground and Clifton Lane Cricket Ground, moved to Millmoor in 1907. Record attendance 25,000
(Total) Current Capacity: 11,486 (6,949 seated)
Visiting Supporters' Allocation: 2,155 (all seated) in Railway End
Club Colours: Red shirts, white shorts
Nearest Railway Station: Rotherham Central
Parking (Car): Kimberworth and Main Street car parks, plus large car park adjacent to ground
Parking (Coach/Bus): As directed by Police
Police Force and Tel No: South Yorkshire (01709 371121)
Disabled Visitors' Facilities:
Wheelchairs: Millmoor Lane
Blind: Commentary available
Anticipated Developments(s): The club announced plans during the 2001/02 season for the rebuilding of Millmoor over a four-year period. The first phase of this work, for which there is no confirmed timescale, involves the construction of a new two-tier 7,000-seat Main Stand costing some £4.25million.

KEY

- **C** Club Offices
- **S** Club Shop
- **E** Entrance(s) for visiting supporters
- **R** Refreshment bars for visiting supporters
- **T** Toilets for visiting supporters

⬆ North direction (approx)

1. Car Park
2. To Rotherham Central BR Station
3. A6109 Masborough Road
4. Millmoor Lane
5. To A6178 and M1 Junction 34

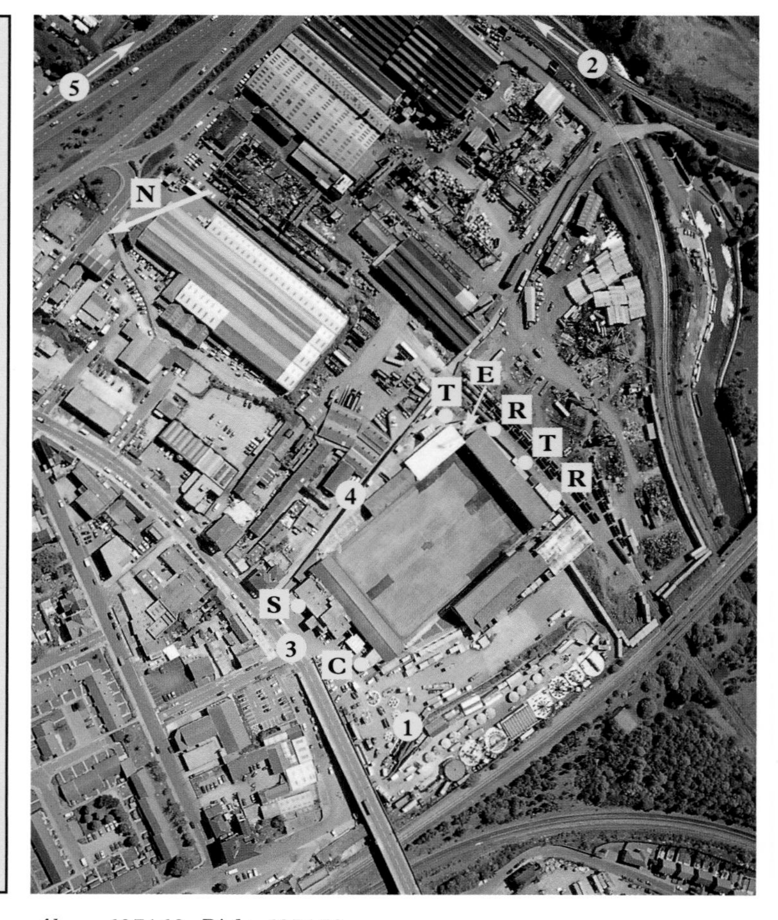

Above: 697162; *Right:* 697152

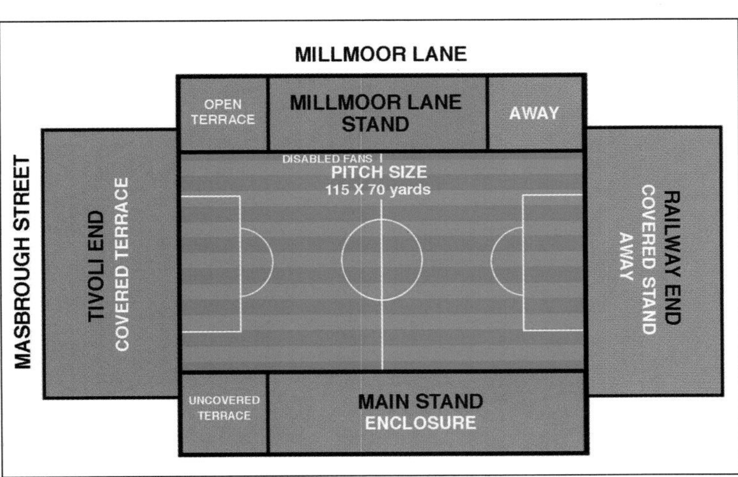

Under Ronnie Moore the Millers again cemented their First Division status, although hopes that the club might sneak into the Play-Offs proved optimistic and, as before, the team was close to being dragged into the relegation battle. The team ultimately finished in 17th position but only three points above relegated Walsall, emphasising how tight the First Division was (apart from the two teams at the bottom and the two promoted to the Premiership — all of whom were in a different class, albeit for different reasons). Under Ronnie Moore, the Millermen have achieved a considerable amount given the resources available but it's hard to escape the conclusion that, in the new season, the club will again regard mid-table safety as a success.

RUSHDEN & DIAMONDS

Nene Park, Diamond Way, Irthlingborough, NN9 5QF

Tel No: 01933 652000
Advance Tickets Tel No: 01933 652936
Fax: 01933 650418
Web Site: www.thediamondsfc.premiumtv.co.uk
E-Mail: dean.howells@airwair.co.uk
League: League Two
Brief History: Rushden & Diamonds represents a merger between two teams — Rushden Town (founded in 1889) and Irthlingborough Diamonds (founded in 1946). The union, engineered by Max Griggs, occurred at the end of the 1991/92 season and from the start the club was based at the Nene Park ground of Irthlingborough Diamonds. Record attendance at Nene Park as a merged team 6,431
(Total) Current Capacity: 6,441 (4,641 seated)
Visiting Supporters' Allocation: 1,000 seats in the north side of the East (Air Wair) Stand (can be increased to 2,372 if needed)
Club Colours: White with red and blue trim shirts; blue shorts
Nearest Railway Station: Wellingborough (six miles)
Parking (Car): 1,000 spaces at ground
Parking (Coach/Bus): As directed by the police
Police Force and Tel No: Northamptonshire (01933 440333)
Disabled Visitors' Facilities:
Wheelchairs: 22 Places in the North Stand allocated to season ticket holders; 12 in the South Stand — limited number available on match by match basis
Blind: No special facility
Anticipated Development(s): None

KEY

⬆ North direction (approx)

❶ A6 Station Road
❷ To Rushden
❸ To Kettering
❹ Station Road (old)
❺ B5348 Station Road to Irthlingborough
❻ Diamond Way
❼ River Nene

Above: 697272; *Right:* 697263

After seven years with the club, during which time he saw the team move from Conference strugglers to Third Division champions and a mid-table position in the Second Division, Brian Talbot resigned as manager in early March as speculation linked him to the vacancy at Oldham Athletic (speculation that proved to be correct). The club moved quickly, appointing Barry Hunter as player-manager until the end of the season. However, Hunter was unable to prevent the team gradually slipping down the table — largely as the result of financial constraints — and, as a result of a home defeat by Port Vale and Chesterfield's victory over Luton in the last games of the season, the team was relegated back to the Third Division after only one season at the higher level. The club should have the potential to make a serious attempt at bouncing straight back, under new boss Ernie Tippett, but the example of other ex-Conference high-fliers (Macclesfield and Cheltenham) who once graced the Second Division only to get relegated indicates this could be a struggle.

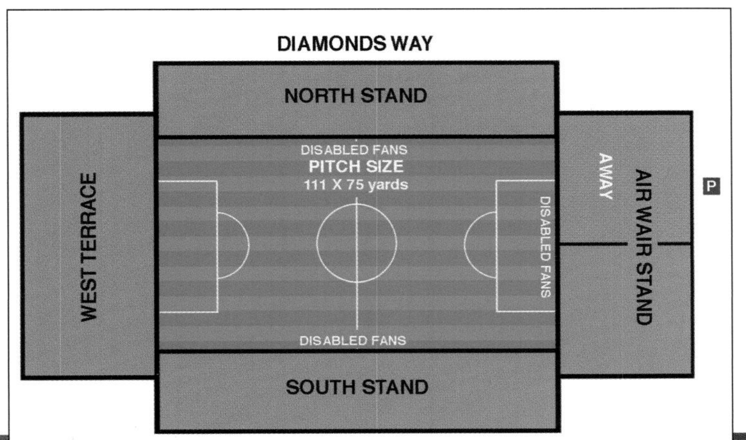

SCUNTHORPE UNITED

Glanford Park, Doncaster Road, Scunthorpe DN15 8TD

Tel No: 01724 848077
Advance Tickets Tel No: 01724 848077
Fax: 01724 857986
Web Site: www.scunthorpe-united.premiumtv.co.uk
E-mail: admin@scunthorpe-united.co.uk
League: League Two
Brief History: Founded 1899 as Scunthorpe United, amalgamated with North Lindsey to become 'Scunthorpe & Lindsey United' in 1912. Changed name to Scunthorpe United in 1956. Former Grounds: Crosby (Lindsey United) and Old Showground, moved to Glanford Park in 1988. Elected to Football League in 1950. Record attendance 8,775 (23,935 at Old Showground)
(Total) Current Capacity: 9,200 (6,400 seated)
Visiting Supporters' Allocation: 1,678 (all seated) in South (Caparo Merchant Bar) Stand
Club Colours: White shirts with claret and blue trim, white shorts
Nearest Railway Station: Scunthorpe
Parking (Car): At ground
Parking (Coach/Bus): At ground
Police Force and Tel No: Humberside (01724 282888)
Disabled Visitors' Facilities:
Wheelchairs: County Chef Stand
Blind: Commentary available
Anticipated Development(s): Although a new stadium – Glanford Park opened in 1988 – there is a possibility that, in the future, the existing Evening Telegraph Stand will be demolished and replaced by a two-tier structure.

KEY

- **C** Club Offices
- **S** Club Shop
- **E** Entrance(s) for visiting supporters
- **R** Refreshment bars for visiting supporters
- **T** Toilets for visiting supporters

⬆ North direction (approx)

1. Car Park
2. Evening Telegraph Stand
3. A18 to Scunthorpe BR Station and Town Centre (1½ miles)
4. M181 and M180 Junction 3

Above: 697516; *Right:* 697507

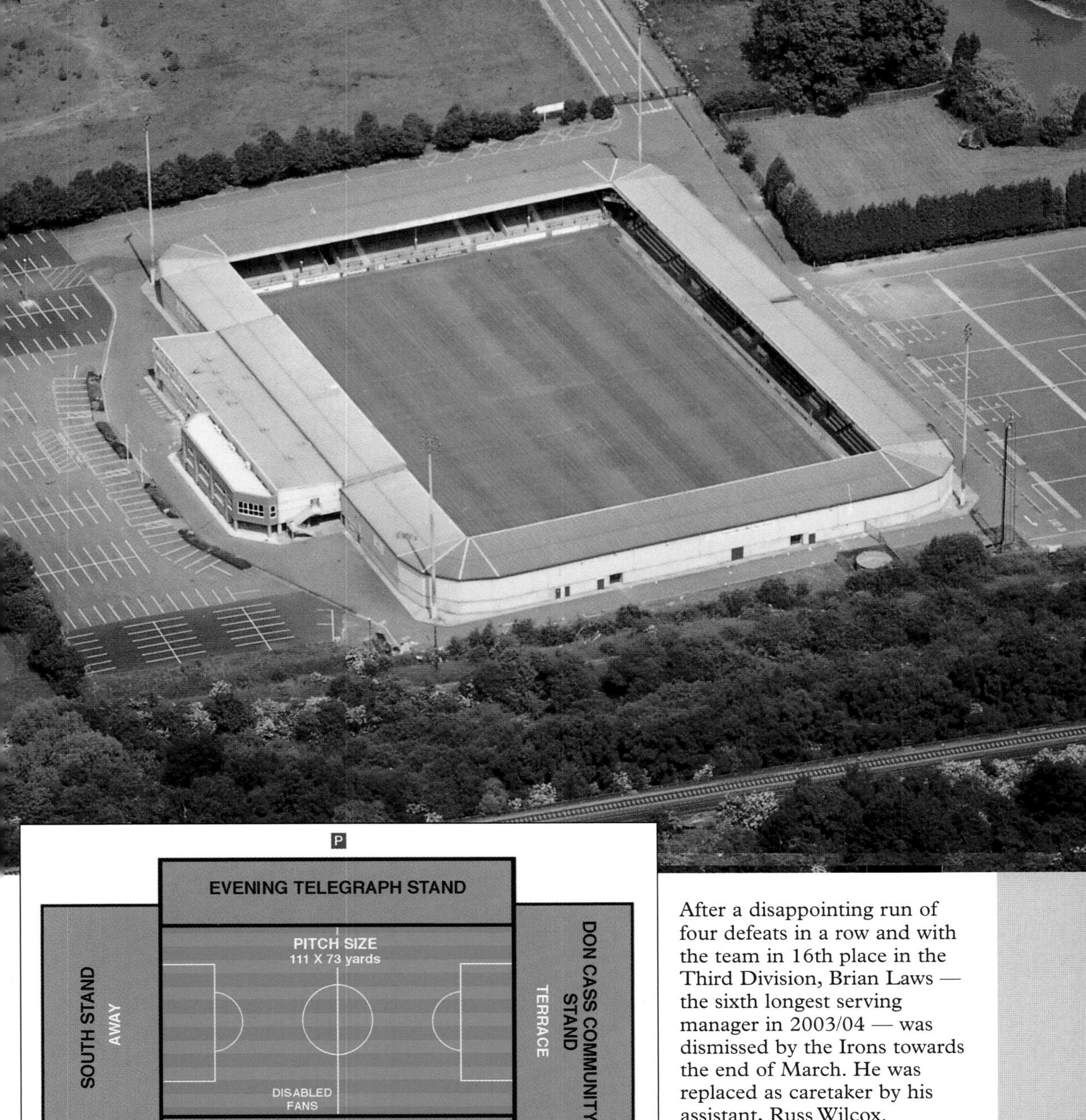

After a disappointing run of four defeats in a row and with the team in 16th place in the Third Division, Brian Laws — the sixth longest serving manager in 2003/04 — was dismissed by the Irons towards the end of March. He was replaced as caretaker by his assistant, Russ Wilcox. However, a continued slump in the team's fortunes and 'palace coup' that saw chairman Chris Holland resign in mid-April as majority shareholder Steve Wharton took control of the club, led to Laws being reinstated with the club just three points above the Third Division drop zone. Laws' re-emergence occurred too late in the campaign to have a dramatic impact on the club's position, although he did ensure that, by finishing 22nd four points above the drop zone, he kept the team above the resurgent Carlisle United and thus ensured League Two football again in 2004/05. Under Laws, Scunthorpe have had a slightly up and down career; from the fans' viewpoint, 2004/05 needs to be one of the up periods as, if the club's fortunes take another dip, Conference football could beckon in 2005/06. The probability is that United will survive but it could again be a mighty close thing.

SHEFFIELD UNITED

Bramall Lane, Sheffield, S2 4SU

Tel No: 0870 787 1960
Advance Tickets Tel No: 0870 787 1799
Fax: 0870 787 3345
Web Site: www.sufc.premiumtv.co.uk
E-Mail: info@sufc.co.uk
League: League Championship
Brief History: Founded 1889. (Sheffield Wednesday occasionally used Bramall Lane c1880.) Founder-members 2nd Division (1892). Record attendance 68,287
(Total) Current Capacity: 30,936 (all seated)
Visiting Supporters' Allocation: 2,700 (seated) can be increased to 5,200 if needed
Club Colours: Red and white striped shirts, black shorts
Nearest Railway Station: Sheffield Midland
Parking (Car): Street parking
Parking (Coach/Bus): As directed by Police
Police Force and Tel No: South Yorkshire (0114 276 8522)
Disabled Visitors' Facilities:
Wheelchairs: South Stand
Blind: Commentary available
Anticipated Development(s): The club is contemplating construction of a corner stand, located between the Laver and Bramall stands, although there is no confirmed timescale for the work.

KEY

- **C** Club Offices
- **S** Club Shop
- **E** Entrance(s) for visiting supporters
- ⬆ North direction (approx)

1. A621 Bramall Lane
2. Shoreham Street
3. Car Park
4. Sheffield Midland BR Station (1/4 mile)
5. John Street
6. Spion Stand
7. John Street Stand
8. St Mary's Road

Above: 697175; *Right:* 697169

Following the success of 2002/03, when the club prospered in both cup competitions as well as the league and having lost in the Play-Off final, much was expected from Neil Warnock's team in 2003/04. In the event the campaign was one of, ultimately, considerable disappointment as the Blades failed to maintain a serious challenge for an automatic promotion place and, as the season wore on, even a Play-Off place looked increasingly unlikely. In the event, it came down to results on the last day and a draw at Preston, combined with results elsewhere, resulted in United finishing in eighth place, two points off the Play-Offs. Thus League Championship football will again be on offer at Bramall Road in 2004/05; whether Warnock survives the full season, however, will depend on the team's form, one suspects, as it's unlikely that fans or board will accept another season of missed promotion opportunities.

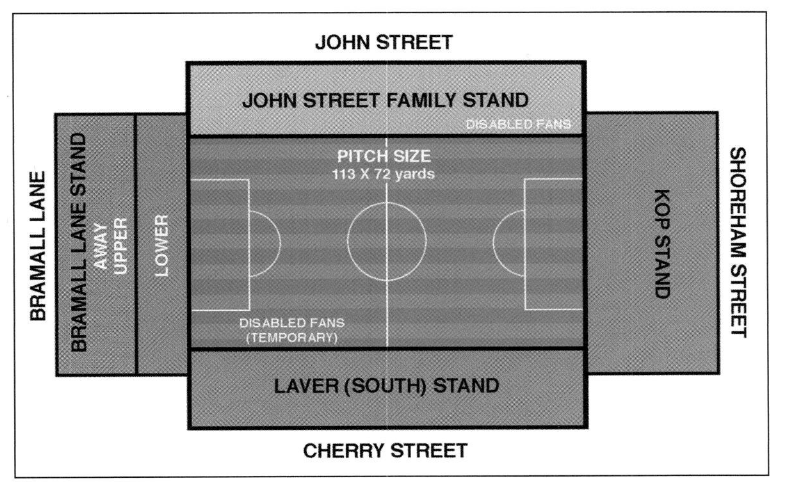

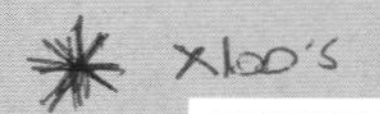

SHEFFIELD WEDNESDAY

Hillsborough, Sheffield, S6 1SW

Tel No: 0114 221 2121
Advance Tickets Tel No: 0114 221 2400
Fax: 0114 221 2122
Web Site: www.swfc.premiumtv.co.uk
E-Mail: enquiries@swfc.co.uk
League: League One
Brief History: Founded 1867 as The Wednesday F.C. (changed to Sheffield Wednesday c1930). Former Grounds: London Road, Wyrtle Road (Heeley), Sheaf House Ground, Encliffe & Olive Grove (Bramall Lane also used occasionally), moved to Hillsborough (then named 'Owlerton' in 1899). Founder-members Second Division (1892). Record attendance 72,841

(Total) Current Capacity: 39,859 (all seated)
Visiting Supporters' Allocation: 3,700 (all seated) in West Stand Upper
Club Colours: Blue and white striped shirts, black shorts
Nearest Railway Station: Sheffield (4 miles)
Parking (Car): Street Parking
Parking (Coach/Bus): Owlerton Stadium
Police Force and Tel No: South Yorkshire (0114 276 8522)
Disabled Visitors' Facilities:
Wheelchairs: North and Lower West Stands
Blind: Commentary available

KEY

- **C** Club Offices
- **E** Entrance(s) for visiting supporters
- ⬆ North direction (approx)

- ❶ Leppings Lane
- ❷ River Don
- ❸ A61 Penistone Road North
- ❹ Sheffield BR Station and City Centre (4 miles)
- ❺ Spion Kop
- ❻ To M1 (North)
- ❼ To M1 (South)
- ❽ West Stand

Above: 697186; *Right:* 697177

Relegated at the end of 2002/03, the Owls were hamstrung through the season by the club's weak financial position. One of a number of ex-Premiership outfits that must rue the debts incurred during their glory days, Wednesday was perhaps more concerned with events at the wrong end of the table. Whilst never being sucked into the relegation battle, unlike fellow ex-First Division outfit Grimsby Town, the Owls ended up in 16th place only three points off the drop zone. Elsewhere, equally disappointing for fans was the fact that the team failed to progress beyond the second round of the FA Cup, losing at home on penalties against Scunthorpe United in the replay. As to the future for Chris Turner and the team, much depends on the future ownership. At the time of writing there is a possibility that ex-Chelsea supreme Ken Bates will mount a take-over and, if he does, fans can expect wholesale change at Hillsborough; if not, then it's hard to escape the conclusion that the Owls may again fail to find their wings in 2004/05 despite the considerable strengthening in the playing squad undertaken during the close season.

SHREWSBURY TOWN

Gay Meadow, Shrewsbury, SY2 6AB

Tel No: 01743 360111
Advance Tickets Tel No: 01743 360111
Fax: 01743 236384
Web-site: www.shrewsburytown.co.uk
E-mail: clubshop@shrewsburytown.co.uk
League: League Two
Brief History: Founded 1886. Former Grounds: Monkmoor Racecourse, Ambler's Field and The Barracks Ground (moved to Gay Meadow 1910). Elected to Football League 1950; relegated to Nationwide Conference at end of 2002/03 and promoted back to the Football League, via the Play-Offs, at the end of 2003/04. Record attendance 18,917
(Total) Current Capacity: 8,000 (2,500 seated)
Visiting Supporters' Allocation: 2,500 (500 seated) in the Station End (standing) and Main Stand (seated)
Club Colours: Blue shirts and blue shorts
Nearest Railway Station: Shrewsbury
Parking (Car): Adjacent car park
Parking(Coach/Bus): Gay Meadow
Police Force and Tel No: West Mercia (01743 232888)
Disabled Visitors' Facilities:
Wheelchairs: Alongside pitch (as directed)
Blind: No special facility
Anticipated Development(s): The club is progressing with its plans to relocate to a new stadium on the Oteley Road. The new stadium, which would cost some £8.5 million and provide seating for some 10,000 fans, however, has yet to receive formal approval and so expect the Shrews to play at Gay Meadow for at least another couple of seasons.

KEY

- **C** Club Offices
- **S** Club Shop
- **E** Entrance(s) for visiting supporters
- **R** Refreshment bars for visiting supporters
- **T** Toilets for visiting supporters

- ⬆ North direction (approx)

- ❶ Entrance road to ground
- ❷ Abbey Foregate
- ❸ River Severn
- ❹ Car Parks
- ❺ Shrewsbury BR Station (1 mile – shortest route)
- ❻ Riverside Terrace
- ❼ English Bridge
- ❽ Wyle Cop
- ❾ Station End (away)
- ❿ Wakeman End
- ⓫ Wakeman/Centre/Station Stand
- ⓬ Old Potts Way (all routes via ring road)

Above: 697458; *Right:* 697454

Following the trauma of 2002/03, when — under Kevin Ratcliffe — Shrewsbury Town conquered Everton in the FA Cup before being defeated by Chelsea and then falling out of the League, 2003/04 was one of considerable progress under new manager Jimmy Quinn. Although never good enough to challenge Chester for automatic promotion — nor Hereford for second — the Shrews ensured a Play-Off position, finishing in third position in the Conference. Victory over Barnet, on penalties, in the Semi-Finals resulted in a tense Play-Off final against Aldershot Town at the Britannia Stadium. With the game ending 1-1 after extra time, the Shrews were ultimately to regain their League status after a year 3-0 on penalties, with Scott Howie proving unbeatable in the shoot-out. Whilst the previous Play-Off victors, Doncaster Rover, romped home with the Third Division championship, it's hard to see Shrewsbury emulating that triumph unless the squad is strengthened significantly. At least for the Gay Meadow faithful, the chant of 'Are you Telford in disguise?' will again acquire pejorative connotations rather than a concern over local rivalry (particularly as that rival suffered financial collapse during the close season). At best, without investment, mid-table beckons.

SOUTHAMPTON

The Friends Provident St Mary's Stadium, Britannia Road, Southampton SO14 5FP

Tel No: 0870 22 00 000
Advance Tickets Tel No: 0870 2200150
Fax: 02380 727727
Web Site: www.saintsfc.co.uk
E-Mail: sfc@saintsfc.co.uk
League: F.A. Premier
Brief History: Founded 1885 as 'Southampton St. Mary's Young Men's Association (changed name to Southampton in 1897). Former Grounds: Northlands Road, Antelope Ground, County Ground, moved to The Dell in 1898 and to St Mary's Stadium in 2001. Founder members Third Division (1920). Record attendance (at The Dell) 31,044 (at St Mary's) 32,151
(Total) Current Capacity: 32,251 (all-seated)
Visiting Supporters' Allocation: c3,200 in North Stand
Club Colours: Red and white shirts, black shorts
Nearest Railway Station: Southampton Central
Parking (Car): Street parking or town centre car parks
Parking (Coach/Bus): As directed by the police
Police Force and Tel No: Hampshire (02380 335444)
Disabled Visitors' Facilities:
Wheelchairs: c200 places
Blind: Commentary available
Anticipated Development(s): Following completion of the new stadium the club has no further plans at present.

KEY

- **C** Club Offices
- **S** Club Shop
- **E** Entrance(s) for visiting supporters
- ⬆ North direction (approx)

1. A3024 Northam Road
2. B3028 Britannia Road
3. River Itchen
4. To M27 (five miles)
5. To Southampton Central station and town centre
6. Marine Parade
7. To A3025 (and Itchen toll bridge)
8. Belvedere Road
9. North Stand

Above: 692503; *Right:* 692500

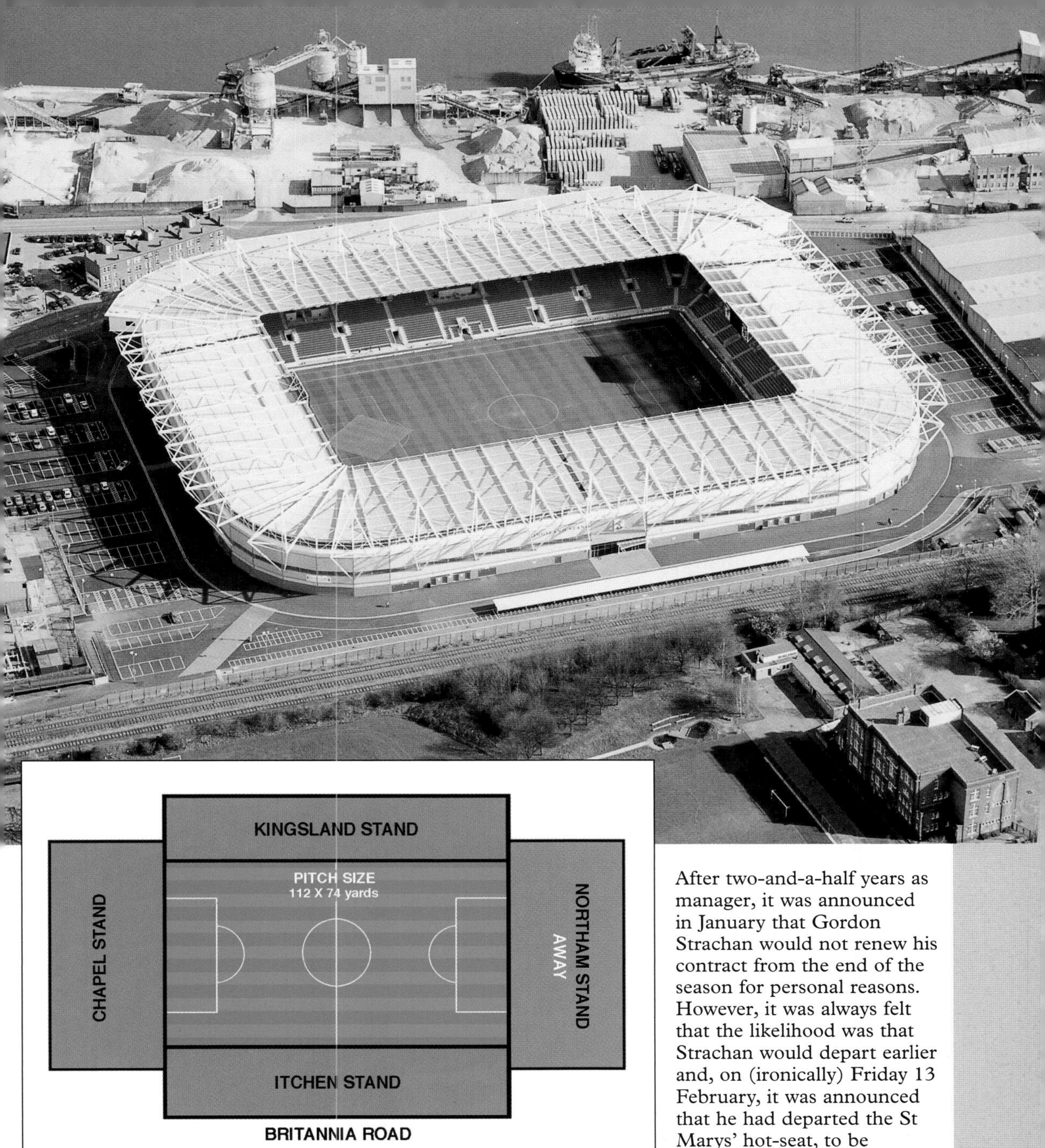

After two-and-a-half years as manager, it was announced in January that Gordon Strachan would not renew his contract from the end of the season for personal reasons. However, it was always felt that the likelihood was that Strachan would depart earlier and, on (ironically) Friday 13 February, it was announced that he had departed the St Marys' hot-seat, to be replaced temporarily by Steve Wigley. Whilst it was thought that Wigley would remain in charge until the end of the season, in the event the club moved to appoint Plymouth boss Paul Sturrock to the job permanently in early March. At Plymouth (and before that in Scotland), Sturrock had proved himself an astute manager and, with Southampton already secure in the Premiership for another season, he took the opportunity to assess closely the squad that he inherited. Gone are the days that the Saints were always to be regarded as favourites for the drop, but like so many Premiership teams, it's now difficult to see the club achieving anything further than a position in mid-table — always likely to beat the lower teams but not being strong enough to mount a sustained challenge for a European spot. As in 2002/03, the team's best opportunity for glory may well come in one of the cup competitions.

SOUTHEND UNITED

Roots Hall Ground, Victoria Avenue, Southend-on-Sea, SS2 6NQ

Tel No: 0870 174 2000
Advance Tickets Tel No: 0870 174 2001
Fax: 01702 304124
Web Site: www.southendunited.premiumtv.co.uk
E-mail: info@southendunited.co.uk
League: League Two
Brief History: Founded 1906. Former Grounds: Roots Hall, Kursaal, the Stadium Grainger Road, moved to Roots Hall (new Ground) 1955. Founder-members Third Division (1920). Record attendance 31,033
(Total) Current Capacity: 12,392 (all seated)
Visiting Supporters' Allocation: 2,700 (maximum) (all seated) in North Stand and North West Enclosure
Club Colours: Blue shirts, blue shorts
Nearest Railway Station: Prittlewell
Parking (Car): Street parking
Parking (Coach/Bus): Car park at Ground
Police Force and Tel No: Essex (01702 431212)
Disabled Visitors' Facilities:
Wheelchairs: West Stand
Blind: Commentary available
Anticipated Development(s): In early May 2004 it was announced that the local council had backed plans for the construction of the proposed new 16,000-seat stadium. The club is now awaiting final planning permission for the construction of the new ground. At this stage, there is no timescale, but it would certainly appear that after some years of uncertainty that Roots Hall is now living on borrowed time.

KEY

- **C** Club Offices
- **E** Entrance(s) for visiting supporters
- **R** Refreshment bars for visiting supporters
- **T** Toilets for visiting supporters
- ⬆ North direction (approx)

- ❶ Director's Car Park
- ❷ Prittlewell BR Station (1/4 mile)
- ❸ A127 Victoria Aveneue
- ❹ Fairfax Drive
- ❺ Southend centre (1/2 mile)
- ❻ North Stand

Above: 697297; *Right:* 697286

With the club in 22nd position in the Third Division, following a 1-0 defeat by Northampton, Steve Wignall was sacked as manager in early November. Serial ex-boss Dave Webb took over on a caretaker basis although his reign was to be shortlived and Steve Tilson was to be appointed as caretaker manager later in the month. In March it was that Tilson, assisted by ex-Orient boss Paul Brush, would remain in charge until the end of the season. Ultimately, the club was to finish in 17th position, nine points above relegated Carlisle, thus ensuring League Two football again at Roots Hall in 2004/05. Away from the league, the team suffered an embarrassing 1-0 home defeat by non-league Scarborough in FA Cup Third Round replay, but reached the final of the LDV Trophy and thus a trip to the Millennium Stadium. Unfortunately, however, Blackpool were to prove triumphant in that competition, winning 2-0.

STOCKPORT COUNTY

Edgeley Park, Hardcastle Road, Edgeley, Stockport, SK3 9DD

Tel No: 0161 286 8888
Advance Tickets Tel No: 0161 286 8888
Fax: 0161 286 8900
Web Site: www.stockportcounty.premiumtv.co.uk
E-Mail: steve.bellis@stockportcounty.com
League: League One
Brief History: Founded 1883 as Heaton Norris Rovers, changed name to Stockport County in 1890. Former Grounds: Heaton Norris Recreation Ground, Heaton Norris Wanderers Cricket Ground, Chorlton's Farm, Ash Inn Ground, Wilkes Field (Belmont Street) and Nursery Inn (Green Lane), moved to Edgeley Park in 1902. Record attendance 27,833
(Total) Current Capacity: 11,541 (all seated)
Visiting Supporters' Allocation: 800 (all seated) in Vernon Stand (can be increased by 1,300 all-seated on open Railway End if needed)
Club Colours: Blue with white stripe shirts, blue shorts
Nearest Railway Station: Stockport
Parking (Car): Street Parking
Parking (Coach/Bus): As directed by Police
Other Clubs Sharing Ground: Sale Sharks RUFC
Police Force and Tel No: Greater Manchester (0161 872 5050)
Disabled Visitors' Facilities:
Wheelchairs: Main and Cheadle stands
Blind: Headsets available
Anticipated Development(s): Although the club is still planning for the reconstruction of the Railway End, with the intention of constructing a new 5,500-seat capacity stand on the site, there is no time scale for this work (which had originally been planned for 1999/2000). Theoretically, the next phase after the Railway End would be an upgrade to the Vernon BS Stand, with the intention of making the ground's capacity 20,000.

KEY

- **C** Club Offices
- **E** Entrance(s) for visiting supporters
- ↑ North direction (approx)

1. Mercian Way
2. Hardcastle Road
3. Stockport BR station (1/4 mile)
4. Railway End
5. Main Stand
6. Cheadle Stand
7. Vernon BS Stand

Above: 695712; *Right:* 695706

Although County had started reasonably well, a new regime at Edgeley Park saw Carlton Palmer dismissed as manager at the end of September. Although John Hollins took over as temporary manager, the club appointed ex-Northern Ireland (and Macclesfield) boss Sammy McIlroy in mid-October. As the campaign developed, however, the club was dragged towards the relegation battle and a last day defeat at home by Barnsley meant that the team ultimately finished in 19th position only two points above relegated Grimsby Town. Another dark day in the team's season was defeat 2-1 away at non-league Stevenage in the First Round of the FA Cup. McIlroy has plenty of experience of management at this level and, therefore, ought to be able to engineer an improvement in 2004/05 in his first full season at the club.

STOKE CITY

Britannia Stadium, Stanley Matthews Way, Stoke-on-Trent ST4 4EG

Tel No: 01782 592222
Advance Tickets Tel No: 01782 592206
Fax: 01782 592221
Web Site: www.stokecityfc.premiumtv.co.uk
E-Mail: info@stokecityfc.com
League: League Championship
Brief History: Founded 1863 as Stoke F.C., amalgamated with Stoke Victoria in 1878, changed to Stoke City in 1925. Former Grounds: Sweetings Field, Victoria Ground (1878-1997), moved to new ground for start of 1997/98 season. Record attendance (at Victoria Ground): 51,380; at Britannia Stadium 28,218
(Total) Current Capacity: 28,383 (all-seater)
Visiting Supporters' Allocation: 4,800 (in the South Stand)
Club Colours: Red and white striped shirts, white shorts
Nearest Railway Station: Stoke-on-Trent
Parking (Car): The 650 parking spaces at the ground are for officials and guests only. The 1,600 spaces in the South car park are pre-booked only, with the majority held by season ticket holders. There is some on-street parking, but with a 10-15min walk.
Parking (Coach/Bus): As directed
Police Force and Tel No: Staffordshire (01782 744644)
Disabled Visitors' Facilities:
Wheelchairs: 164 places for disabled spectators
Blind: Commentaries available
Anticipated Development(s): There are long-term plans to increase the ground's to 30,000 by the construction of a corner stand between the John Smith Stand and the Boothen End but there is no timescale for this work.

KEY

⬆ North direction (approx)

1. Victoria Ground (site of)
2. Stoke BR station
3. A500 Queensway
4. North Stand
5. West Stand
6. East Stand
7. South Stand (away)
8. A50 to Uttoxeter
9. To M6 northbound
10. To M6 southbound

Following their escape from relegation at the end of 2002/03, many expected Stoke City to feature amongst the candidates for relegation at the end of 2003/04. In the event, however, under the management of Tony Pulis, the team prospered and achieved a top-half finish. Whilst still well off the Play-Off zone, the team's performance in 2003/04 will encourage fans in the belief that the team can continue to make progress in the new season and, perhaps, get to the fringes of the race for the Play-Offs.

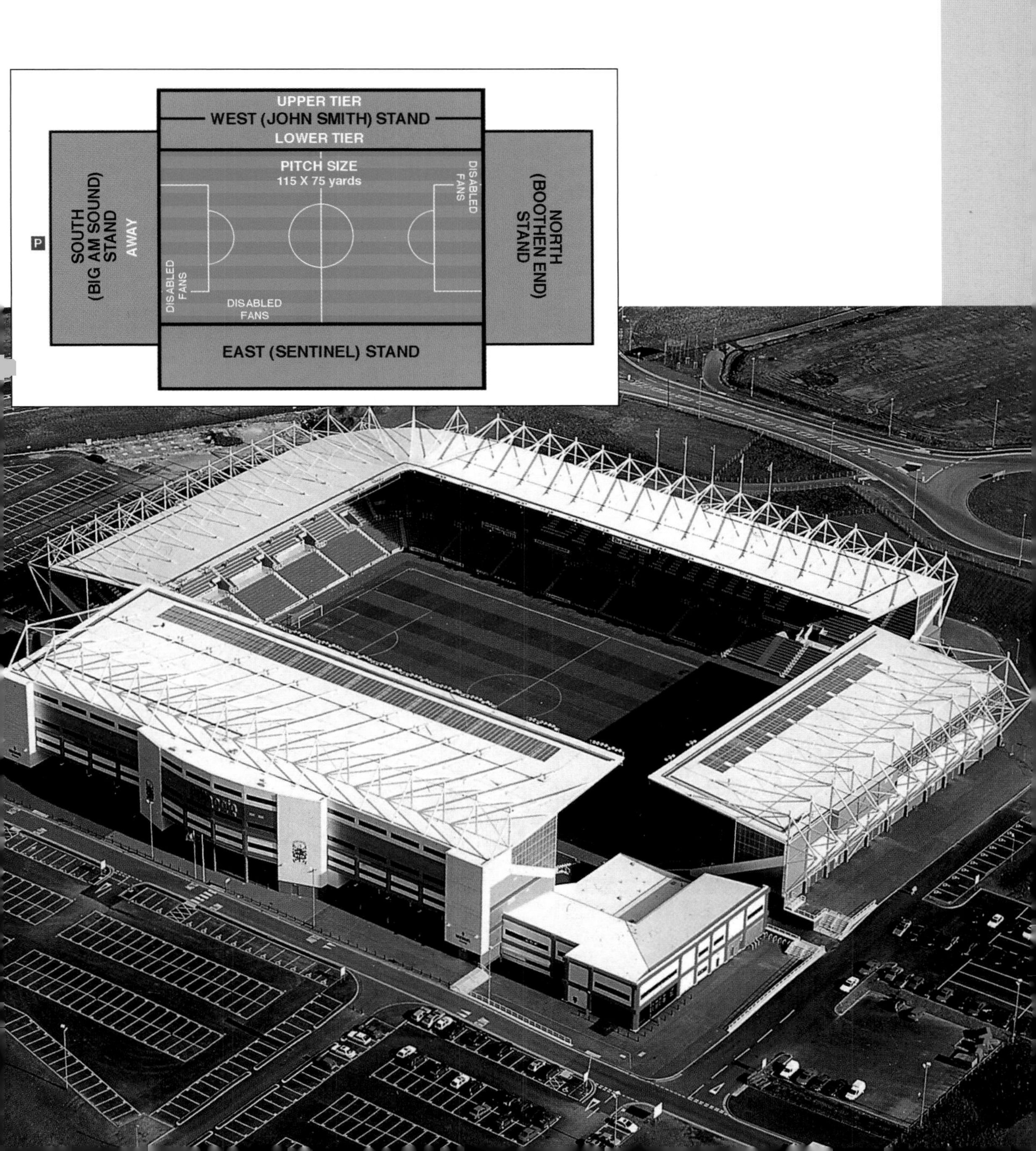

SUNDERLAND

Stadium of Light, Sunderland, SR5 1SU

Tel No: 0191 551 5000
Advance Tickets Tel No: 0191 551 5151
Fax: 0191 551 5123
Web Site: www.safc.com
E-Mail: communications@safc.com
League: League Championship
Brief History: Founded 1879 as 'Sunderland & District Teachers Association', changed to 'Sunderland Association' in 1880 and shortly after to 'Sunderland'. Former Grounds: Blue House Field, Groves Field (Ashbrooke), Horatio Street, Abbs Field, Newcastle Road and Roker Park (1898-1997); moved to Stadium of Light for the start of the 1997/98 season. Record crowd (at Roker Park): 75,118; at Stadium of Light (48,353)
(Total) Current Capacity: 48,353 all-seater
Visiting Supporters' Allocation: 3,000 (South Stand)
Club Colours: Red and white striped shirts, black shorts
Nearest Railway Station: Stadium of Light (Tyne & Wear Metro
Parking (Car): Car park at ground reserved for season ticket holders. Limited on-street parking (but the police may decide to introduce restrictions). Otherwise off-street parking in city centre
Parking (Coach/Bus): As directed
Police Force and Tel No: Tyne & Wear (0191 510 2020)
Disabled Visitors' Facilities:
Wheelchairs: 180 spots
Blind: Commentary available
Anticipated Development(s):

KEY

- **C** Club Offices
- **S** Club Shop
- **E** Entrance(s) for visiting supporters
- ⬆ North direction (approx)
- ❶ River Wear
- ❷ North (McEwans) Stand
- ❸ South (Metro FM) Stand (away)
- ❹ To Sunderland BR station (0.5 mile)
- ❺ Southwick Road
- ❻ Stadium Way
- ❼ Millennium Way
- ❽ Hay Street
- ❾ To Wearmouth Bridge (via A1018 North Bridge Street) to City Centre

Above: 688659; *Right:* 688650

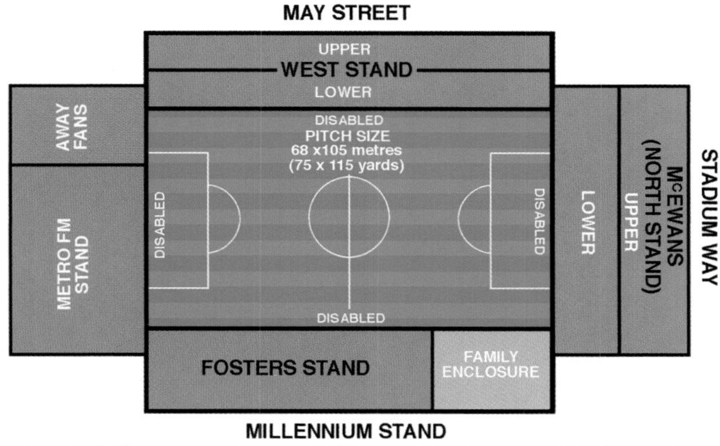

Following the trauma of relegation at the end of 2002/03, the Sunderland faithful were expecting the Black Cats to make an immediate return to the Premiership under Mick McCarthy. McCarthy's reign towards the end of 2002/03 had shown 100% — defeats that was — and it must have been a relief for fans when the team returned to winning ways in the First Division. The club, however, was never close enough to the top to mount a consistent assault on the automatic promotion places but ultimately did achieve third place and, thus, the Play-Offs. However, facing Crystal Palace in the Play-Offs, the Black Cats were ultimately to lose on penalties at the Stadium of Light, the two legs having finished 4-4 on aggregate after extra time. Thus Sunderland face a further season of League Championship football in 2004/05 with the realisation that the Premiership parachute ends at the end of the season, failure to achieve promotion could cost the club a great deal (and presumably see McCarthy's reign end). Despite this premise, it's difficult to see Sunderland as again achieving more than the Play-Offs at best.

SWANSEA CITY

Vetch Field, Swansea SA1 3SU

Tel No: 01792 633400
Advance Tickets Tel No: 01792 633425
Fax: 01792 646120
Web Site: www.swanseacity.premiumtv.co.uk
E-mail: dawn@swanseacityfc.co.uk
League: League Two
Brief History: Founded 1900 as Swansea Town, changed to Swansea City in 1970. Former Grounds: various, including Recreation Ground. Moved to Vetch Field in 1912. Founder-members Third Division (1920). Record attendance 32,796
(Total) Current Capacity: 11,477 (3,414 seated)
Visiting Supporters' Allocation: 1,541 (on the West Terrace)
Club Colours: White shirts, white shorts
Nearest Railway Station: Swansea High Street
Parking (Car): Kingsway car park and adjacent Clarence Terrace (supervised car park)
Parking (Coach/Bus): As directed by Police
Police Force and Tel No: South Wales (01792 456999)
Disabled Visitors' Facilities:
Wheelchairs: Glamorgan Street
Blind: No special facility
Anticipated Development(s): Work is proceeding apace with the construction of the new stadium at Morfa with the intention that it will be available from the start of the 2005/06 season. The new ground is being funded largely by Swansea City Council and will be shared between City and the local Rugby union team. The new stadium will provide a 20,000 all-seated capacity.

KEY

- **C** Club Offices
- **S** Club Shop
- **E** Entrance(s) for visiting supporters
- **R** Refreshment bars for visiting supporters
- **T** Toilets for visiting supporters

⬆ North direction (approx)

1. Glamorgan Street
2. William Street
3. Richardson Street
4. A4067 Oystermouth Road (8 miles to M4 Junction 42)
5. Swansea High Street BR Station (1/2 mile)
6. Supervised Car Park
7. North Bank

Above: 615398; *Right:* 615403

In the middle of March, following a loss of form which had seen the team drop out of contention for the Play-Offs, Brian Flynn, who had secured the club's Third Division status at the end of the 2002/03 season and who had signed a new contract in the summer of 2003, departed from the Vetch with his assistant Kevin Reeves. The club acted quickly, appointing Alan Curtis and Richard Evans into caretaker roles. In early April, the club appointed ex-Welsh international Kenny Jackett as new full-time manager with a contract until the end of the 2005/06 season, making him the Swans' sixth manager in just over 30 months. On the pitch, the team ultimately finished in tenth position, which sounds reasonable until one realises that there was a 12 point gap between the Swans and ninth placed Oxford United. However, if the squad can maintain the progress of 2003/04 then a Play-Off position is a distinct possibility in the new season.

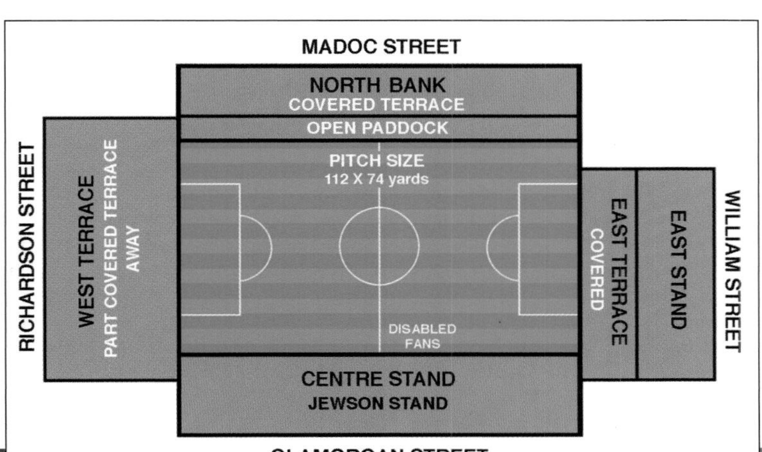

SWINDON TOWN

County Ground, County Road, Swindon, SN1 2ED

Tel No: 0870 443 1969
Advance Tickets Tel No: 0870 443 1894
Fax: 01793 333703
Web Site: www.swindontownfc.premiumtv.co.uk
E-Mail: enquiries@swindontownfc.co.uk
League: League One
Brief History: Founded 1881. Former Grounds: Quarry Ground, Globe Road, Croft Ground, County Ground (adjacent to current Ground and now Cricket Ground), moved to current County Ground in 1896. Founder-members Third Division (1920). Record attendance 32,000
(Total) Current Capacity: 15,700 (all seated)
Visiting Supporters' Allocation: 3,342 (all seated) in Arkell's Stand and Stratton Bank (open)
Club Colours: Red shirts, white shorts
Nearest Railway Station: Swindon
Parking (Car): Town Centre
Parking (Coach/Bus): Adjacent car park
Police Force and Tel No: Wiltshire (01793 528111)
Disabled Visitors' Facilities:
Wheelchairs: In front of Arkell's Stand
Blind: Commentary available
Anticipated Development(s): Towards the end of March, club chairman Willie Carson announced at a press conference that the club was planning to relocate to a brand-new 22,000-seat stadium at Shaw Tip, to the west of the town. If all goes according to plan, the new stadium, to be built by the same company (St Mowden Properties) behind Stoke City's Britannia Stadium, would be available for the start of the 2007/08 season.

KEY

- **C** Club Offices
- **S** Club Shop
- **E** Entrance(s) for visiting supporters
- **R** Refreshment bars for visiting supporters
- **T** Toilets for visiting supporters

- ⬆ North direction (approx)

1. Shrivenham Road
2. County Ground
3. A345 Queens Drive (M4 Junction 15 – 3½ miles)
4. Swindon BR Station (½ mile)
5. Town End
6. Car Park
7. County Cricket Ground
8. Nationwide Stand
9. Arkell's Stand

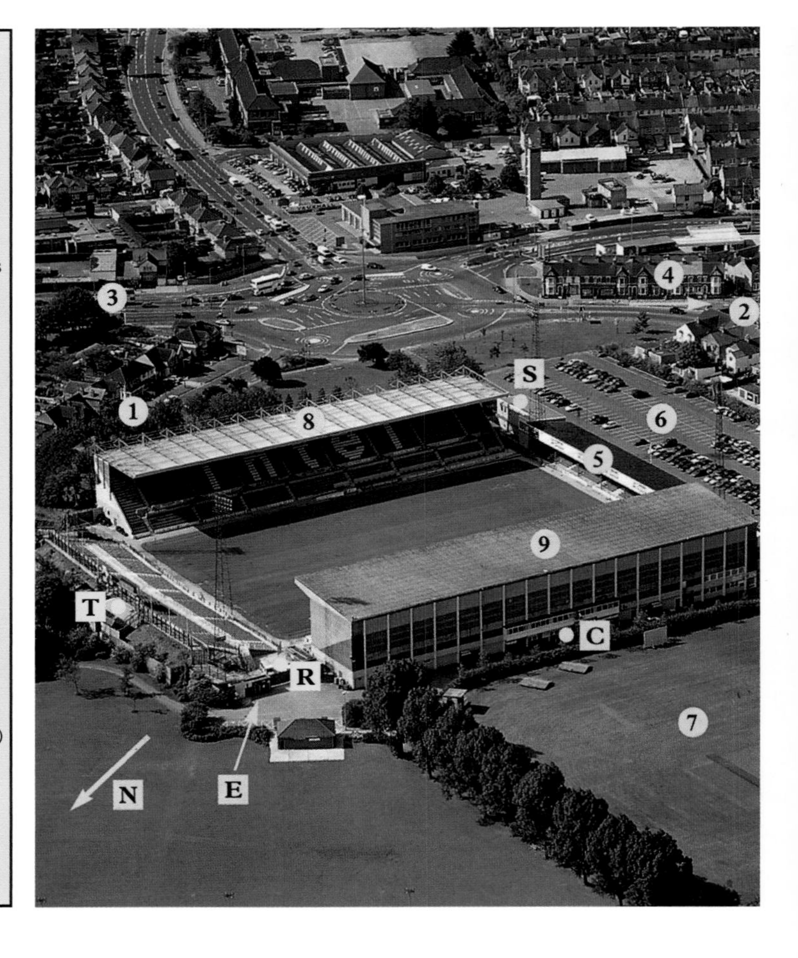

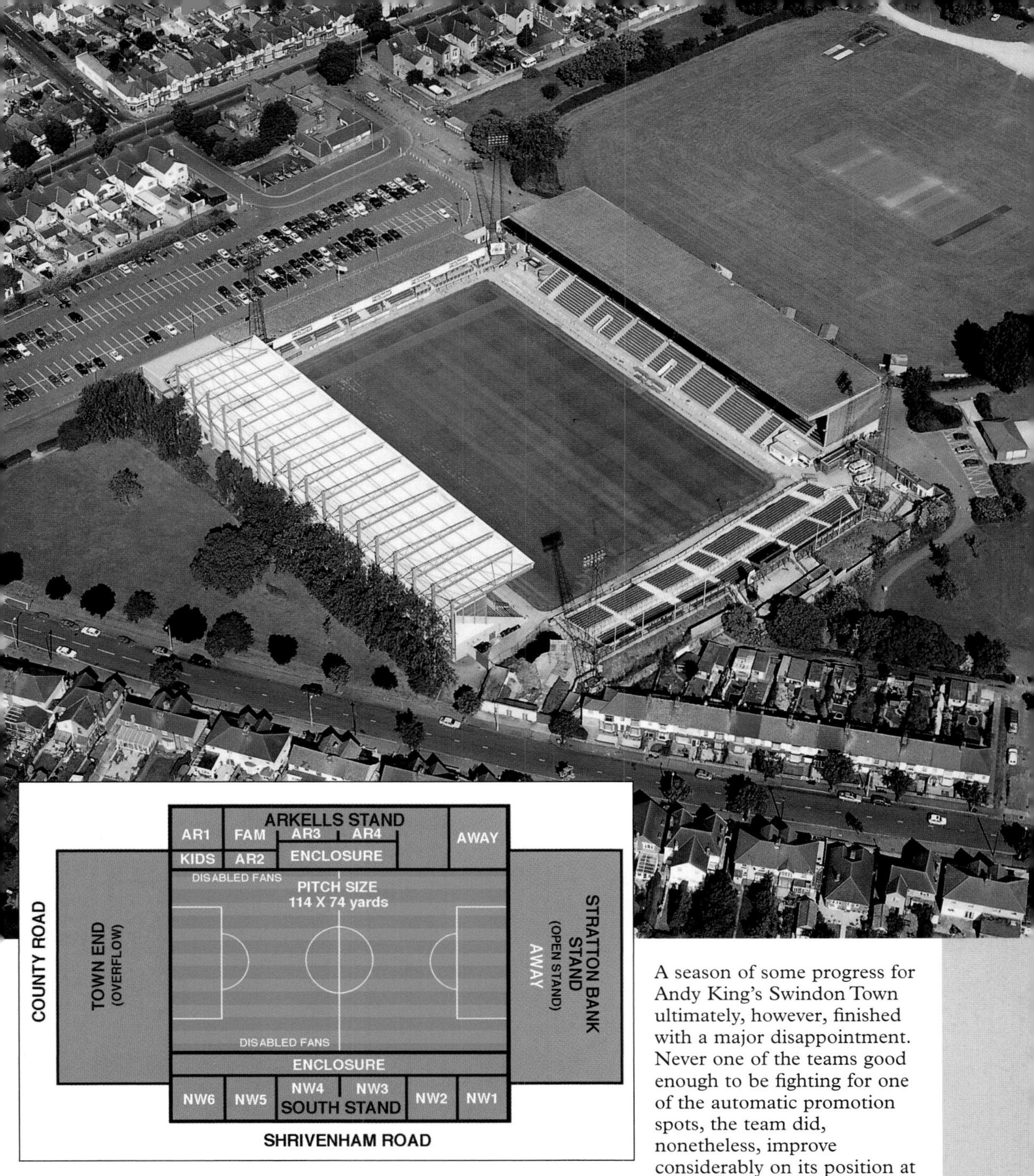

A season of some progress for Andy King's Swindon Town ultimately, however, finished with a major disappointment. Never one of the teams good enough to be fighting for one of the automatic promotion spots, the team did, nonetheless, improve considerably on its position at the end of 2002/03. Finishing in fifth place, Town faced Brighton in the Play-Offs. However, having lost at home 1-0 in the first leg, all seemed to be over as time disappeared at the Withdean Stadium. A late equaliser saw Town take the tie into extra time when, for the first time in the two-legs, Town took the lead. It was a lead that the Robins retained until 15sec from the end of the second period when a very late equaliser saw the tie settled by penalties. Unfortunately, Brighton proved more adept from the spot, thus booking their place in the Final and condemning Swindon to another season of League One fare. However, if the club can maintain its forward momentum, there is every chance that the team will again feature in the promotion hunt in 2004/05.

TORQUAY UNITED

Plainmoor Ground, Torquay, TQ1 3PS

Tel No: 01803 328666
Advance Tickets Tel No: 01803 328666
Fax: 01803 323976
Web Site: www.torquayunited.premiumtv.co.uk
E-Mail: gullsfc@freeuk.com
League: League One
Brief History: Founded 1898, as Torquay United, amalgamated with Ellacombe in 1910, changed name to Torquay Town. Amalgamated with Babbacombe in 1921, changed name to Torquay United. Former Grounds: Teignmouth Road, Torquay Recreation Ground, Cricketfield Road & Torquay Cricket Ground, moved to Plainmoor (Ellacombe Ground) in 1910. Record attendance 21,908
(Total) Current Capacity: 6,283 (2,446 seated)
Visiting Supporters' Allocation: 1,004 (196 seated)
Club Colours: Yellow with white stripe shirts, yellow shorts
Nearest Railway Station: Torquay (2 miles)
Parking (Car): Street parking
Parking (Coach/Bus): Lymington Road coach station
Police Force and Tel No: Devon & Cornwall (01803 214491)
Disabled Visitors' Facilities:
Wheelchairs: Ellacombe End
Blind: Commentary available
Anticipated Development(s): There are proposals for a joint project with a local school for the rebuilding of the Main Stand. This would give United a 2,500-seat stand but there is no confirmed timescale.

KEY

- **C** Club Offices
- **S** Club Shop
- **E** Entrance(s) for visiting supporters
- **R** Refreshment bars for visiting supporters
- **T** Toilets for visiting supporters

⬆ North direction (approx)

1. Warbro Road
2. B3202 Marychurch Road
3. Marnham Road
4. Torquay BR Station (2 miles)
5. To A38
6. Babbacombe End

Above: 692266; *Right:* 692257

A season of considerable progress on the field saw Leroy Rosenior's team grab automatic promotion at the last. With Huddersfield Town occupying the third promotion spot going into the last round of games, United needed to beat Southend United at Roots Hall and rely on Cheltenham denying Town a win. Torquay set up a tense 2-1 victory in Essex but, with Cheltenham down to 10 men and drawing 1-1 with Huddersfield, a late goal in Gloucestershire would have sent the Yorkshiremen through. In the event, results went United's way and, for only the third time in the club's history, promotion was achieved. League One football beckons for United in 2004/05 but, like most teams promoted from the Third Division, the club will struggle to survive. As far as 2003/04 is concerned, the only negative was perhaps the 2-1 defeat by Conference side Burton Albion in the First Round of the FA Cup.

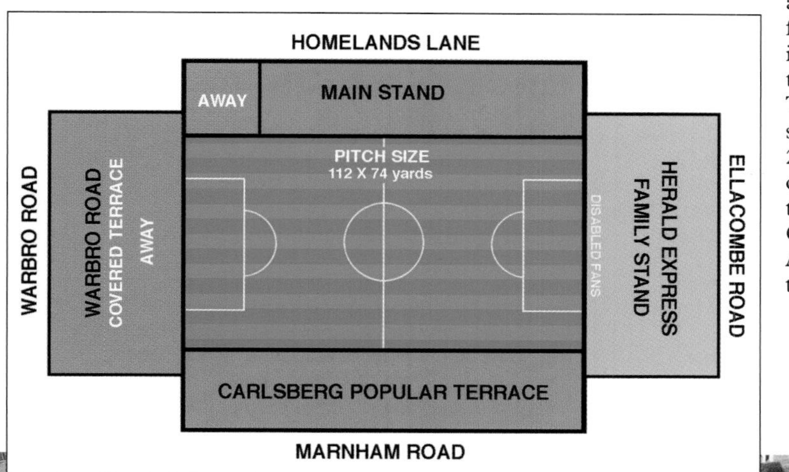

TOTTENHAM HOTSPUR

Bill Nicholson Way, 748 High Road, Tottenham, London N17 0AP

Tel No: 0208 365 5000
Ticket Line: 0870 420 5000
Fax: 020 8365 5005
Web Site: www.spurs.co.uk
E-Mail: e-mail@spurs.co.uk
League: F.A. Premier
Brief History: Founded 1882 as 'Hotspur', changed name to Tottenham Hotspur in 1885. Former Grounds: Tottenham Marshes and Northumberland Park, moved to White Hart Lane in 1899. F.A. Cup winner 1901 (as a non-League club). Record attendance 75,038
(Total) Current Capacity: 36,257 (all seated)
Visiting Supporters' Allocation: 3,000 (in South Stands)
Club Colours: White shirts, navy blue shorts
Nearest Railway Station: White Hart Lane plus Seven Sisters and Manor House (tube)
Parking (Car): Street parking (min 1/4 mile from ground)
Parking (Coach/Bus): Northumberland Park coach park
Police Force and Tel No: Metropolitan (0208 801 3443)
Disabled Visitors' Facilities:
Wheelchairs: North and South Stands (by prior arrangement)
Blind: Commentary available
Anticipated Development(s): The local council gave permission in October 2001 for the construction of a third tier on the East Stand taking capacity to 44,000, although there is no schedule for the work and it depends on other local regeneration work. Despite the potential that this increase offers, the club is still interested ultimately in relocation.

KEY

C Club Offices
S Club Shop
E Entrance(s) for visiting supporters
R Refreshment bars for visiting supporters
T Toilets for visiting supporters

⬆ North direction (approx)

1. Park Lane
2. A1010 High Road
3. White Hart Lane BR station
4. Paxton Road
5. Worcester Avenue
6. West Stand
7. South Stand

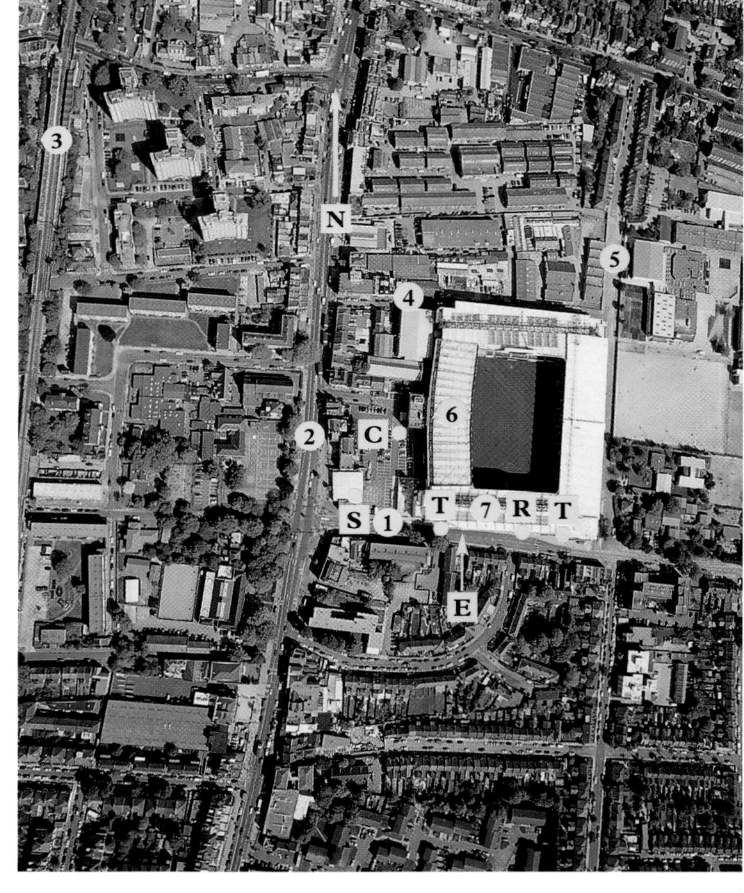

Above: 695627; *Right:* 695621

Following the club's worst ever start in the Premiership, Glenn Hoddle was shown the exit door at White Hart Lane at the end of September as the first managerial casualty of the season in the Premiership. Ironically, his last game in charge was the home defeat against Southampton, the club he walked out on when he took over at Spurs in early 2001. Initially, David Pleat was appointed to take over as caretaker with the club seeking a new appointment. In the event, Pleat remained in control until the end of what proved to be a highly disappointing season, with the club placed perilously close to the drop zone. In early June it was announced that the team's new manager would be Jacques Santini, the former French national manager, who was to take over once Euro 2004 was completed. Whilst there are players of undoubted skill and enterprise at White Hart Lane, it's hard to escape the conclusion that any manager, however experienced, will struggle to raise Spurs' game to rival that of the Premiership's 'Big Hitters'. Even more galling for Tottenham fans was the fact that arch rivals Arsenal won the Championship at White Hart Lane as a result of the 2-2 draw.

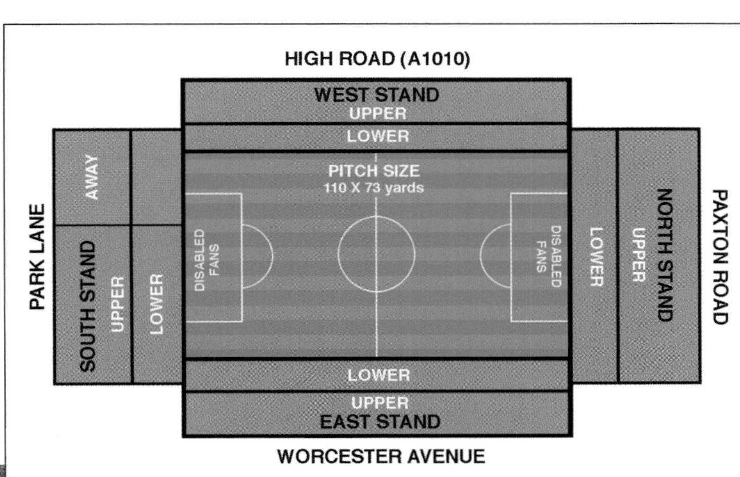

TRANMERE ROVERS

Prenton Park, Prenton Road West, Birkenhead, CH42 9PY

Tel No: 0151 609 3333
Advance Tickets Tel No: 0151 609 3322
Fax: 0151 609 0606
Web Site: www.tranmererovers.premiumtv.co.uk
League: League One
Brief History: Founded 1884 as Belmont F.C., changed name to Tranmere Rovers in 1885 (not connected to earlier 'Tranmere Rovers'). Former grounds: Steele's Field and Ravenshaw's Field (also known as Old Prenton Park, ground of Tranmere Rugby Club), moved to (new) Prenton Park in 1911. Founder-members 3rd Division North (1921). Record attendance 24,424

(Total) Current Capacity: 16,587 (all seated)
Visiting Supporters' Allocation: 2,500 (all-seated) in Cow Shed Stand
Club Colours: White shirts, white shorts
Nearest Railway Station: Hamilton Square or Rock Ferry
Parking (Car): Car park at Ground
Parking (Coach/Bus): Car park at Ground
Police Force and Tel No: Merseyside (0151 709 6010)
Disabled Visitors' Facilities:
Wheelchairs: Main Stand
Blind: Commentary available

KEY

- **C** Club Offices
- **S** Club Shop
- **E** Entrance(s) for visiting supporters
- ⬆ North direction (approx)

1. Car Park
2. Prenton Road West
3. Borough Road
4. M53 Junction 4 (B5151) – 3 miles
5. Birkenhead (1 mile)
6. Cow Shed Stand
7. Kop Shed

Above: 692608; *Right:* 692605

Although taking the club towards the Play-Offs at the end of 2002/03, a disappointing start to the 2003/04 season saw Ray Mathias depart from Prenton Park at the end of September to be replaced by the experienced Brian Little. As doughty cup fighters in previous seasons, it came as no surprise that the team again prospered in the FA Cup, defeating Premiership outfit Bolton Wanderers in a Third Round replay at the Reebox stadium, before finally losing a Quarter Final replay at home against eventual finalists Millwall. In the league, Little brought a resurgence on the field, which took the team ultimately to eighth position, six points off the Play-Off zone. Given Little's experience, there is every chance that Rovers will feature again in the chase for a Play-Off spot at worst.

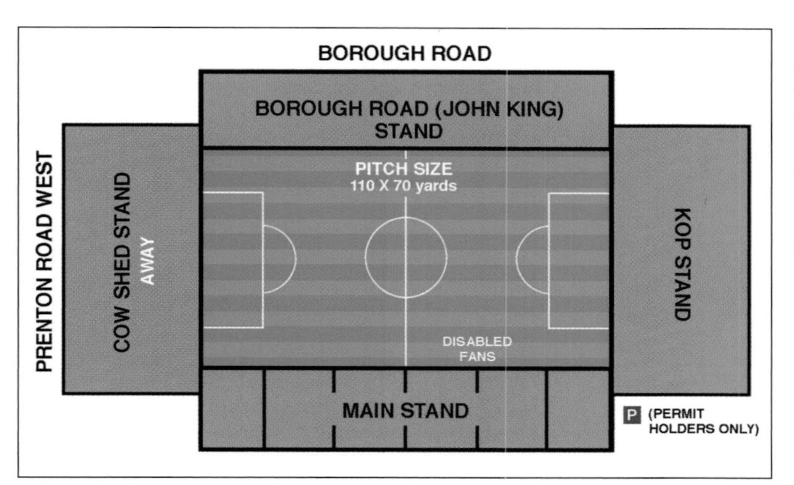

WALSALL

Bescot Stadium, Bescot Crescent, Walsall, West Midlands, WS1 4SA

Tel No: 0870 442 0442
Advance Tickets Tel No: 0870 442 0111
Fax: 01922 613202
Web Site: www.saddlers.premiumtv.co.uk/
E-Mail: info@walsallfc.co.uk
League: League One
Brief History: Founded 1888 as Walsall Town Swifts (amalgamation of Walsall Town – founded 1884 – and Walsall Swifts – founded 1885), changed name to Walsall in 1895. Former Grounds: The Chuckery, West Bromwich Road (twice), Hilary Street (later named Fellows Park, twice), moved to Bescot Stadium in 1990. Founder-members Second Division (1892). Record attendance 10,628 (25,343 at Fellows Park)
(Total) Current Capacity: 11,300 (all seated) (prior to redevelopment)
Visiting Supporters' Allocation: 2,000 maximum in William Sharp Stand
Club Colours: Red shirts, red shorts
Nearest Railway Station: Bescot
Parking (Car): Car park at Ground
Parking (Coach/Bus): Car park at Ground
Police Force and Tel No: West Midlands (01922 638111)
Disabled Visitors' Facilities:
Wheelchairs: Bank's Stand
Blind: No special facility
Anticipated Development(s): The club is seeking to rebuild the William Sharp Stand to add a further 2,500 to the ground's capacity, taking it to 13,500 on completion. The new stand will be partly funded through the provision of advertising hoardings facing the adjacent M6.

KEY

C Club Offices
S Club Shop
E Entrance(s) for visiting supporters

⬆ North direction (approx)

❶ Motorway M6
❷ M6 Junction 9
❸ Bescot BR Station
❹ Car Parks
❺ Bescot Crescent
❻ Gilbert Alsop Stand
❼ William Sharp Stand

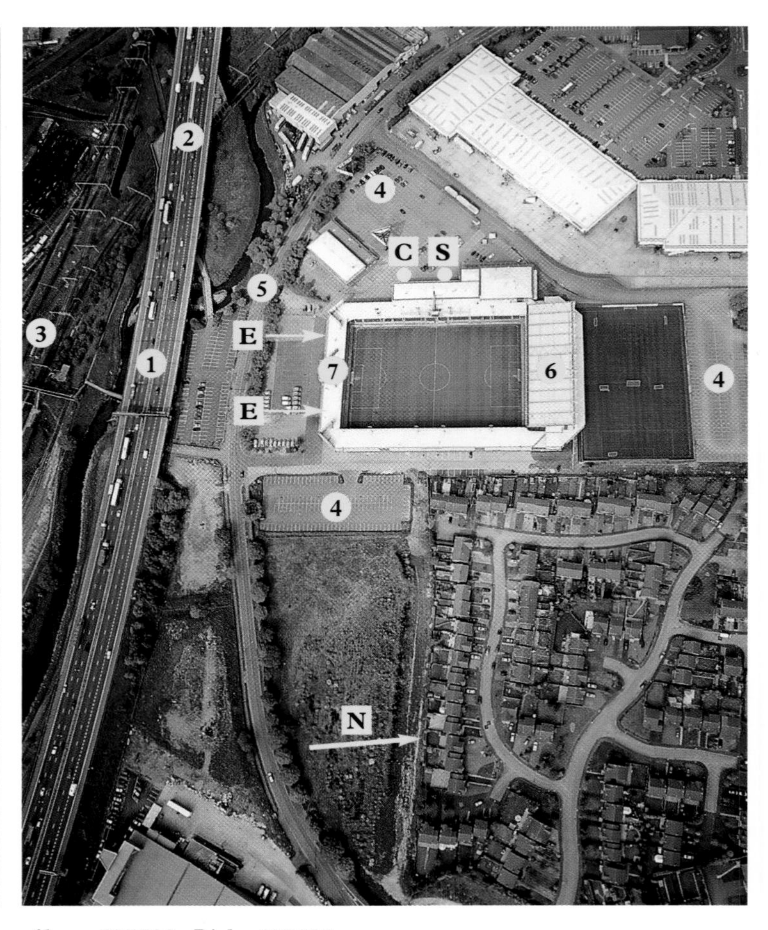

Above: 695539; *Right:* 695531

In mid-April it was revealed that manager Colin Lee, despite having pledged his long-term future in the autumn of 2003, had been having talks with Plymouth Argyle over the managerial vacancy at Home Park. As a result, chairman Jeff Bonser decided to terminate Lee's contract at the Bescot Stadium with the team battling to avoid the drop back to the Second Division. Paul Merson and Simon Osborn took temporary charge of the team, as the Saddlers faced a tricky away fixture at promotion-chasing Norwich City. However, despite a 3-2 victory against Rotherham in the final game of the season, Gillingham's 0-0 draw at Stoke City ensured that the Saddlers would be playing League One football in 2004/05. Shortly after the end of the campaign, it was announced that Merson would be in control for the new campaign; last time Walsall were relegated they made an immediate return to the First Division. However, that was with an experienced manager; it will be interesting to see if a tyro can have the same impact. In all probability, a Play-Off place is the best that the Bescot faithful can expect.

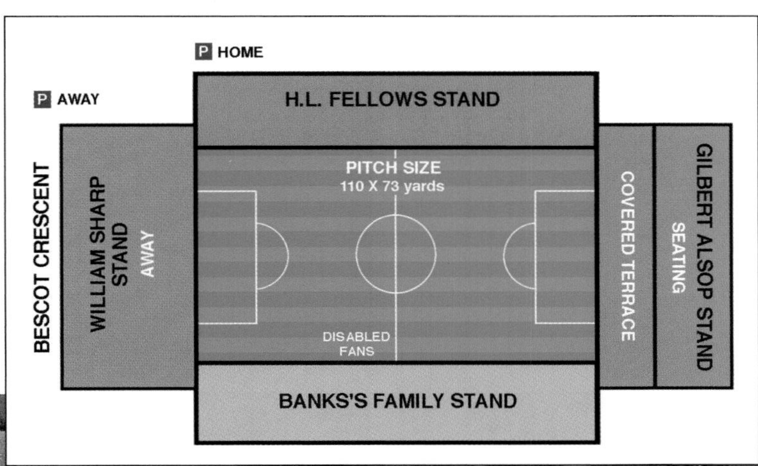

WATFORD

Vicarage Road Stadium, Vicarage Road, Watford, WD18 0ER

Tel No: 01923 496000
Advance Tickets Tel No: 01923 496010
Fax: 01923 496001
Web Site: www.watfordfc.premiumtv.co.uk
E-Mail: yourvoice@watfordfc.com
League: 1st Division
Brief History: Founded 1898 as an amalgamation of West Herts (founded 1891) and Watford St. Mary's (founded early 1890s). Former Grounds: Wiggenhall Road (Watford St. Mary's) and West Herts Sports Ground, moved to Vicarage Road in 1922. Founder-members Third Division (1920). Record attendance 34,099
(Total) Current Capacity: 20,250 (all seated)
Visiting Supporters' Allocation: 4,500 in Vicarage Road (North) Stand
Club Colours: Yellow shirts, red shorts
Nearest Railway Station: Watford High Street or Watford Junction
Parking (Car): Nearby multi-storey car park in town centre (10 mins walk)
Parking (Coach/Bus): Cardiff Road car park
Other Clubs Sharing Ground: Saracens RUFC
Police Force and Tel No: Hertfordshire (01923 472000)
Disabled Visitors' Facilities:
Wheelchairs: Corner East Stand and South Stand (special enclosure for approx. 24 wheelchairs), plus enclosure in North East Corner
Blind: Commentary available in the East Stand (20 seats, free of charge)
Anticipated Development(s): The club's plans for the reconstruction of the East Stand are still in abeyance. However, as a result of safety concerns, part of the existing structure was closed during the close season, reducing the ground's capacity. This necessitated relocating some 600 season ticket holders as well as the board and press box. The plans for the new stand, for which there remains no definite timescale, anticipate the construction of a new 4,500-seat structure, taking Watford's capacity to 23,000.

KEY

C Club Offices
S Club Shop

⬆ North direction (approx)

❶ Vicarage Road
❷ Occupation Road
❸ Rous Stand
❹ Town Centre (1/2 mile) – Car Parks, High Street BR Station
❺ Vicarage Road Stand (away)
❻ East Stand
❼ Rookery End

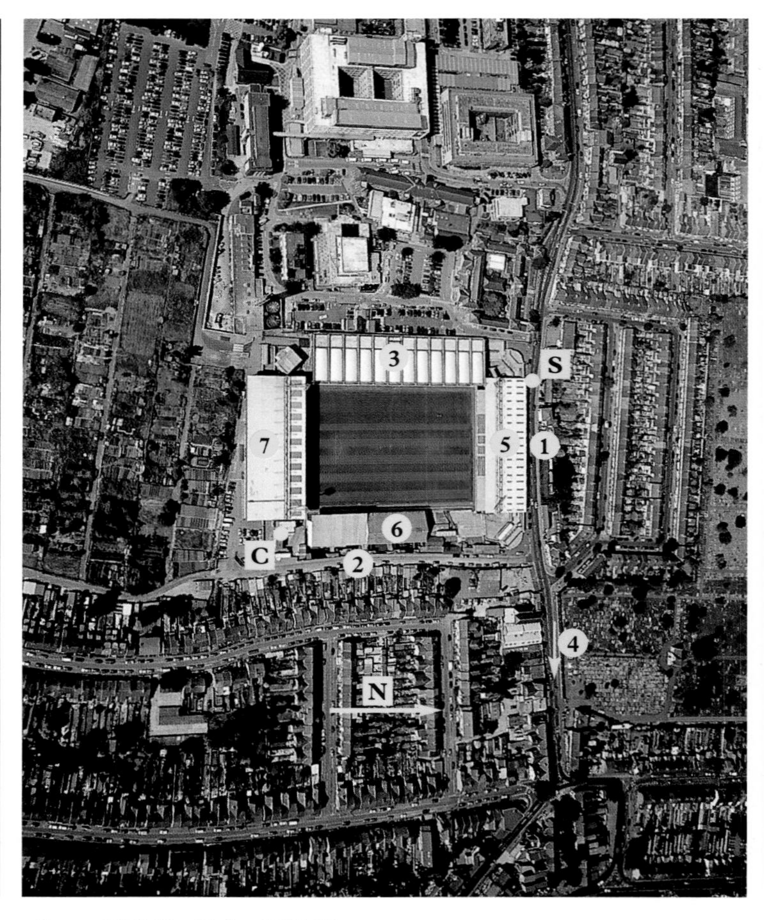

Above: 695969; *Right:* 695965

Hovering just above the drop zone for much of the season, a late run of form saw Ray Lewington's team pull away from the bottom three and thus secure a further season of League Championship football at Vicarage Road. Like other ex-Premiership teams, however, Watford has struggled financially and, with stronger teams coming up from the Second Division, there must be concerns amongst fans that the team will again struggle in 2004/05 with relegation a serious possibility particularly as Lewington has been forced, as a result of the club's financial position, to reduce significantly the wage bill (and thus the size) of his squad.

H
ROUS STAND
UPPER
LOWER
PITCH SIZE
115 X 75 yards
ALLOTMENTS
ROOKERY STAND
DISABLED FANS
NORTH VICARAGE ROAD STAND
AWAY
VICARAGE ROAD (A4145)
DISABLED FANS
FAMILY AREA
A
EAST STAND
E
B C D
OCCUPATION ROAD

WEST BROMWICH ALBION

The Hawthorns, Halfords Lane, West Bromwich, West Midlands, B71 4LF

Tel No: 0121 525 8888
Advance Tickets Tel No: 0121 525 8888
Fax: 0121 524 3462
Web Site: www.wba.premiumtv.co.uk
E-Mail: enquiries@wbafc.co.uk
League: F.A. Premiership
Brief History: Founded 1879. Former Grounds: Coopers Hill, Dartmouth Park, Four Acres, Stoney Lane, moved to the Hawthorns in 1900. Founder-members of Football League (1888). Record attendance 64,815
(Total) Current Capacity: 28,000 (all seated)
Visiting Supporters' Allocation: 3,000
Club Colours: Navy blue and white striped shirts, white shorts
Nearest Railway Station: The Hawthorns
Parking (Car): Halfords Lane and Rainbow Stand car parks
Parking (Coach/Bus): Rainbow Stand car park
Police Force and Tel No: West Midlands (0121 554 3414)
Disabled Visitors' Facilities:
Wheelchairs: Apollo 2000 and Smethwick Road End
Blind: Facility available
Anticipated Development(s): There is speculation that the club will seek to increase capacity to 30,000 by rebuilding the area between the Apollo and East stands, but nothing is confirmed.

KEY

- **C** Club Offices
- **S** Club Shop
- **E** Entrance(s) for visiting supporters

- ⬆ North direction (approx)

1. A41 Birmingham Road
2. To M5 Junction 1
3. Birmingham Centre (4 miles)
4. Halfords Lane
5. Main Stand
6. Smethwick End
7. Rolfe Street, Smethwick BR Station (1½ miles)
8. To The Hawthorns BR Station
9. East (Rainbow) Stand

Above: 692739; *Right:* 692731

Having kept faith with Gary Megson following the team's relegation from the Premiership at the end of the 2002/03 season, the Baggies were rewarded with an immediate return to the top flight as the team secured the second automatic promotion spot behind Norwich City. The fact that the team relegated from the Premiership was strengthened rather than weakened, as is so often the case with relegated teams, meant that the club was able to ride above many of the other aspiring teams in the top half of the First Division table. Unfortunately, whilst, unlike Norwich, Albion has had recent experience of the Premiership and, therefore, may be better prepared for the new campaign, without significant strengthening of the squad in the close season, it's hard to escape the conclusion that a swift return to the League Championship beckons.

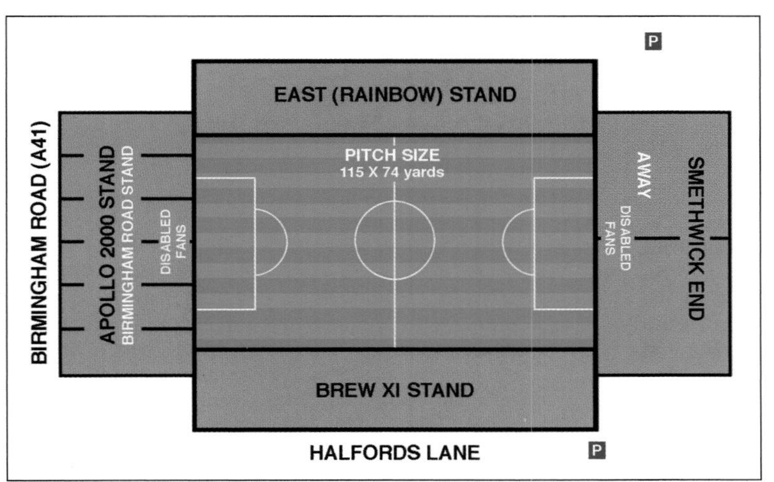

WEST HAM UNITED

Boleyn Ground, Green Street, Upton Park, London, E13 9AZ

Tel No: 020 8548 2748
Advance Tickets Tel No: 0870 112 2700
Fax: 020 8548 2758
Web Site: http://www.whufc.co.uk
E-Mail: yourcomments@westhamunited.co.uk
League: League Championship
Brief History: Founded 1895 as Thames Ironworks, changed name to West Ham United in 1900. Former Grounds: Hermit Road, Browning Road, The Memorial Ground, moved to Boleyn Ground in 1904. Record attendance 42,322
(Total) Current Capacity: 35,647 (all seated)
Visiting Supporters' Allocation: 3,700 maximum
Club Colours: Claret and blue shirts, white shorts
Nearest Railway Station: Barking BR, Upton Park (tube)
Parking (Car): Street parking
Parking (Coach/Bus): As directed by Police
Police Force and Tel No: Metropolitan (020 8593 8232)
Disabled Visitors' Facilities:
Wheelchairs: West Lower, Bobby Moore and Centenary Stands
Blind: Commentaries available
Anticipated Development(s): The new 15,247-seat Dr Martens Stand opened in November 2001. The next phase of the ground's redevelopment will see the reconstruction of the East Stand. Although the club had plans to reconstruct the East Stand and extend both the Bobby Moore and Centenary stands, with a view to increasing the ground's capacity to 40,00, this work had been deferred as a result of relegation and the loss of income that playing in the First Division results in.

KEY

E Entrance(s) for visiting supporters

⬆ North direction (approx)

1. A124 Barking Road
2. Green Street
3. North Stand
4. Upton Park Tube Station (1/4 mile)
5. Barking BR Station (1 mile)
6. Bobby Moore Stand
7. East Stand
8. West Stand

Above: 692171; *Right:* 692169

As one of the pre-season favourites for promotion, West Ham expected to make a better start to their First Division campaign. However, after only three games, with the team struggling — and after an embarrassing defeat at Rotherham when the Hammers' squad refused to use the away dressing room at Millmoor — Glenn Roeder was sacked in late August. Trevor Brooking, protesting that he would only do the job on a temporary basis, took over as caretaker. Following much controversy, ex-Reading boss Alan Pardew was appointed. Under Pardew's guidance, the team was in the chase for a Play-Off position for much of the season, ultimately finishing in fourth position. Victory over Ipswich in the two legs of the Semi-Final saw the Hammers take on Crystal Palace at the Millennium Stadium; unfortunately, however, for the Upton Park faithful, it was the Eagles that proved victorious, thereby consigning West Ham to a further season of League Championship toil. With the Premiership parachute coming to an end at the close of 2004/05, pressure will be on Pardew both to reduce his existing squad and also to make a further sustained challenge for promotion. The League Championship is probably the hardest to escape from and in 2004/05, it will be probably harder than usual. Perhaps the Play-Offs are the best that the team can look forward to.

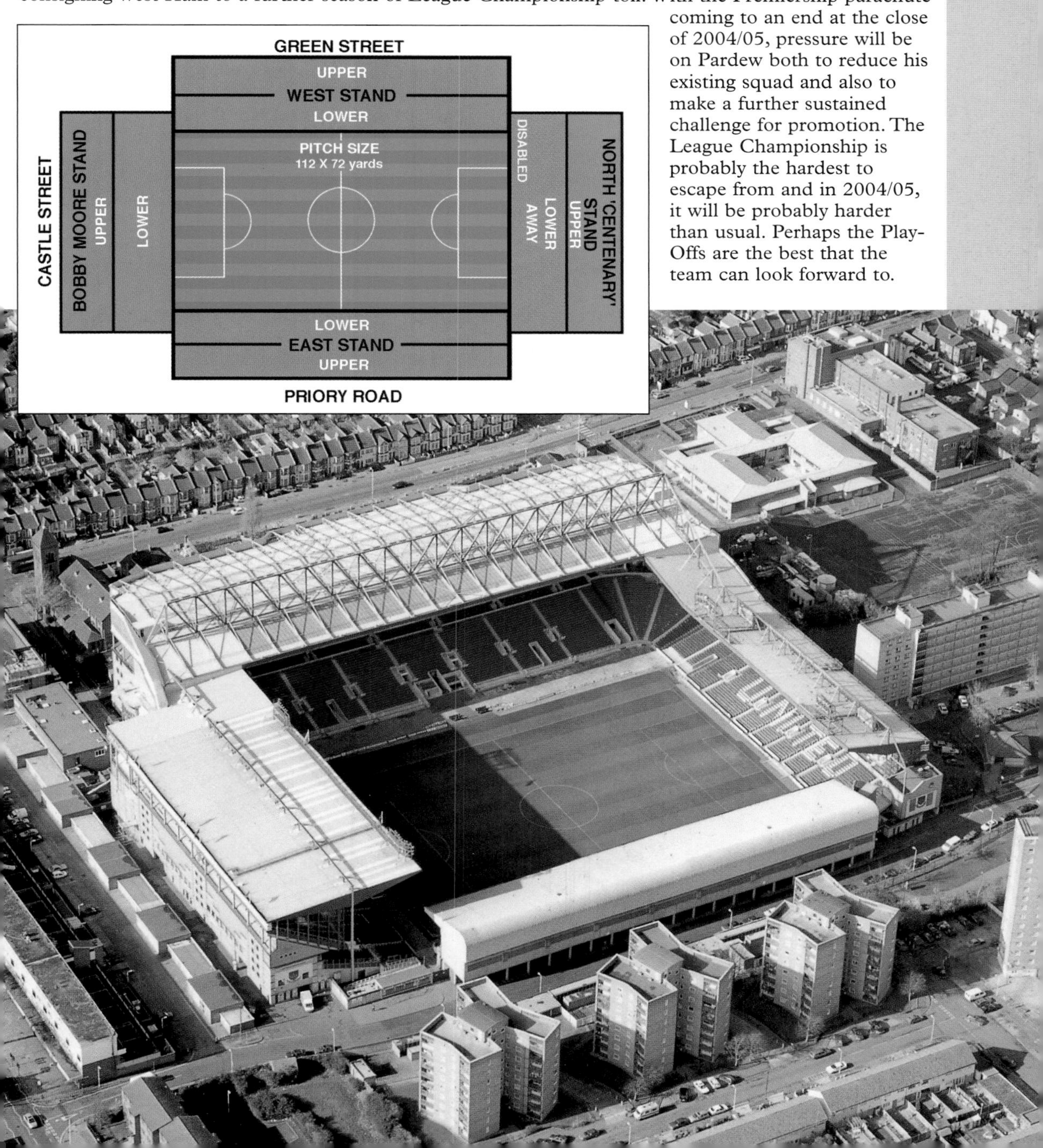

WIGAN ATHLETIC

JJB Stadium, Loire Drive, Robin Park, Wigan, Lancashire WN5 0UH

Tel No: 01942 774000
Advance Tickets Tel No: 0870 112 2552
Fax: 01942 770477
Web Site: www.wiganlatics.premiumtv.co.uk
E-Mail: s.hayton@jjbstadium.co.uk
League: League Championship
Brief History: Founded 1932. Springfield Park used by former Wigan Borough (Football League 1921-1931) but unrelated to current club. Elected to Football League in 1978 (the last club to be elected rather than promoted). Moved to JJB Stadium for start of 1999/2000 season. Record attendance at Springfield Park 27,500; at JJB Stadium 20,669
(Total) Current Capacity: 25,000 (all-seated)
Visiting Supporters' Allocation: 8,178 (maximum) in East Stand (all-seated)
Club Colours: White and blue shirts, blue shorts
Nearest Railway Stations: Wigan Wallgate/Wigan North Western (both about 1.5 miles away)
Parking (Car): 2,500 spaces at the ground
Parking (Coach/Bus): As directed
Other Clubs Sharing Ground: Wigan Warriors RLFC
Police Force and Tel No: Greater Manchester (0161 872 5050)
Disabled Visitors' Facilities
Wheelchairs: 100 spaces
Blind: No special facility although it is hoped to have a system in place shortly
Anticipated Development(s): None following completion of the ground.

KEY

C Club Offices
E Entrance(s) for visiting supporters

⬆ North direction (approx)

1. Loire Drive
2. Anjoy Boulevard
3. Car Parks
4. Robin Park Arena
5. River Douglas
6. Leeds-Liverpool Canal
7. To A577/A49 and Wigan town centre plus Wigan (Wallgate) and Wigan (North Western) station
8. East Stand
9. South Stand
10. North Stand
11. West Stand

Above: 685070; *Right:* 685060

Under Paul Jewell, Wigan were one of the surprise teams of the First Division in 2003/04. For much of the season, the team seemed to be challenging for one of the automatic promotion spots and then for a Play-Off place at worst. However, a late season loss of form — including defeat by lowly Wimbledon — resulted in the team just missing out on the Play-Offs; the cruellest blow of a long season being Brian Deane's equaliser in the last minute of the final game of the season against West Ham when victory would have seen Wigan overhaul Crystal Palace and enter the Play-Offs. With Dave Whelan seemingly happy to carry on bankrolling the team with a view to getting Premiership football, it's likely that Wigan will again feature as one of the teams to beat in 2004/05, particularly if Jewell can continue to recruit quality players to the JJB Stadium. Having just missed out in 2003/04, the team must be one of the fancied clubs to hit the Play-offs at worst in 2004/05.

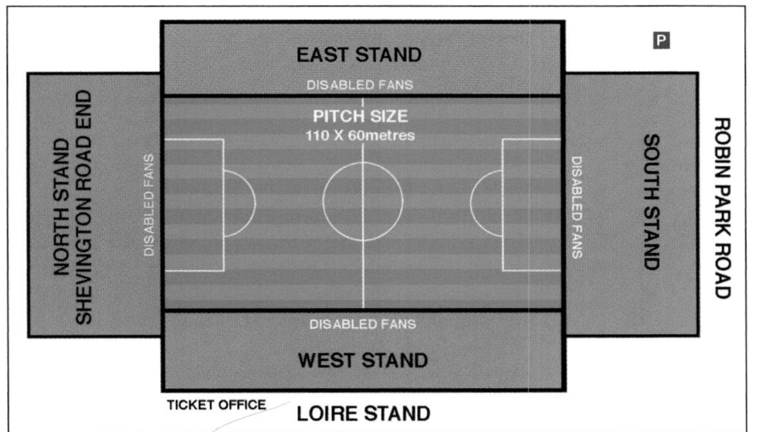

WOLVERHAMPTON WANDERERS

Molineux Ground, Waterloo Road, Wolverhampton, WV1 4QR

Tel No: 0870 442 0123
Advance Tickets Tel No: 0870 442 0123
Fax: 01902 687006
Web Site: www.wolves.premiumtv.co.uk
E-Mail: info@wolves.co.uk
League: League Championship
Brief History: Founded 1877 as St. Lukes, combined with Goldthorn Hill to become Wolverhampton Wanderers in 1884. Former Grounds: Old Windmill Field, John Harper's Field and Dudley Road, moved to Molineux in 1889. Founder-members Football League (1888). Record attendance 61,315
(Total) Current Capacity: 29,400 (all seated)
Visiting Supporters' Allocation: 3,200 in lower tier of Steve Bull Stand
Club Colours: Gold shirts, black shorts
Nearest Railway Station: Wolverhampton
Parking (Car): West Park and adjacent North Bank
Parking (Coach/Bus): As directed by Police
Police Force and Tel No: West Midlands (01902 649000)
Disabled Visitors' Facilities:
Wheelchairs: 104 places on two sides
Blind: Commentary (by prior arrangement)
Anticipated Developments: The club installed some 900 seats on a temporary stand between the Billy Wright and Jack Harris stands for the season in the Premiership. The club has plans to expand the capacity of Molineux to more than 40,000 by adding second tiers to the Stan Cullis and Jack Harris stands and completely rebuilding the Steve Bull Stand. There is no timescale for the work but it is unlikely to proceed until the club regains (and retains) a place in the Premiership.

KEY

- **C** Club Offices
- **S** Club Shop
- **E** Entrance(s) for visiting supporters
- **R** Refreshment bars for visiting supporters
- **T** Toilets for visiting supporters
- ⬆ North direction (approx)

1. Stan Cullis Stand
2. John Ireland Stand
3. Billy Wright Stand
4. Ring Road – St. Peters
5. Waterloo Road
6. A449 Stafford Street
7. BR Station (1/2 mile)
8. Jack Harris Stand
9. Molineux Street
10. Molineux Way
11. Temporary additional seating

Above: 696908; *Right:* 696013

Inevitably perceived as almost certain candidates for relegation following promotion at the end of 2002/03, Wolves did little to alter this perception early in the season when the club struggled to make the leap in standards. With the club holding the dreaded 20th position in the Premiership at Christmas — remember no team in this position has ever survived come May — form in the New Year was better. Results, such as a 1-0 defeat of Manchester United, held out hope for Dave Jones and the team, but, ultimately, too many defeats against teams in the lower half of the table consigned Wolves back to the League Championship. Like WBA the previous year, Wolves did not invest too heavily in Premiership survival and so will be in a reasonable position to make another attempt at promotion in 2004/05. The only doubt about the club's position must in the long-term commitment of Sir Jack Hayward, who has already intimated that he wishes to reduce his role.

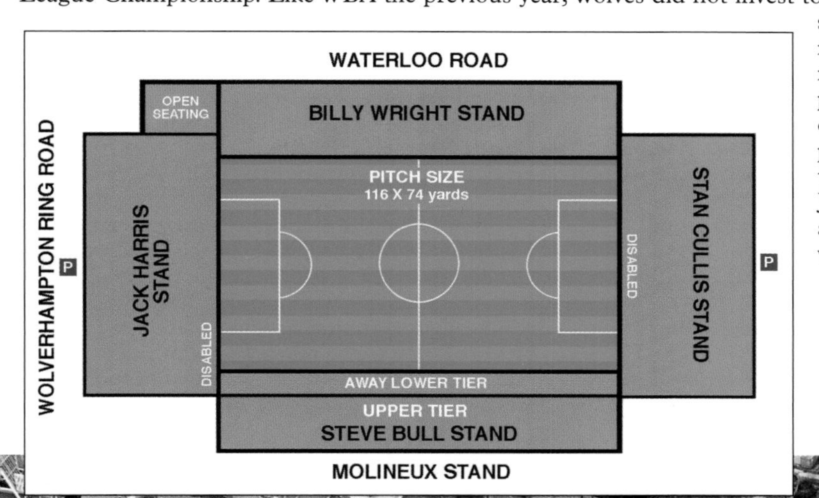

WREXHAM

Racecourse Ground, Mold Road, Wrexham, Clwyd LL11 2AH

Tel No: 01978 262129
Advance Tickets Tel No: 01978 366388
Web Site: www.wrexhamafc.premiumtv.co.uk
E-Mail: geraint@wrexhamfc.co.uk
Fax: 01978 357821
League: League One
Brief History: Founded 1873 (oldest Football Club in Wales). Former Ground: Acton Park, permanent move to Racecourse Ground c.1900. Founder-members Third Division North (1921). Record attendance 34,445
(Total) Current Capacity: 15,500 (11,500 seated)
Visiting Supporters' Allocation: 3,100 (maximum; all seated)
Club Colours: Red shirts, white shorts
Nearest Railway Station: Wrexham General
Parking (Car): (Nearby) Town car parks
Parking (Coach/Bus): As directed by Police
Police Force and Tel No: Wrexham Division (01978 290222)
Disabled Visitors' Facilities:
Wheelchairs: Pryce Griffiths Stand
Blind: No special facility
Anticipated Development(s): The club's new managing director announced after the end of the season that the club was investigating the possibility of redevelopment at the Racecourse Ground in order to maximise the potential from the site. This work would include rebuilding the ground having rotated the pitch by 90°. There is, at present, no confirmed timescale for this work and detailed proposals are awaited.

KEY

- **C** Club Offices
- **S** Club Shop
- **E** Entrance(s) for visiting supporters
- **R** Refreshment bars for visiting supporters
- **T** Toilets for visiting supporters

↑ North direction (approx)

1. Wrexham General Station
2. A541 – Mold Road
3. Wrexham Town Centre
4. Pryce Griffiths Stand
5. Kop Town End
6. To Wrexham Central Station

Above: 685071; *Right:* 685072

Following promotion at the end of 2002/03, the new season was always going to be one of ultimately consolidation for Denis Smith's Wrexham side and, in that, finishing in 14th position was probably a reasonable result. With the team's League One status now consolidated and with a number of much weaker teams joining the division in 2004/05 (from both directions), the new season could be an excellent opportunity for the team to make a serious push towards the Play-Offs.

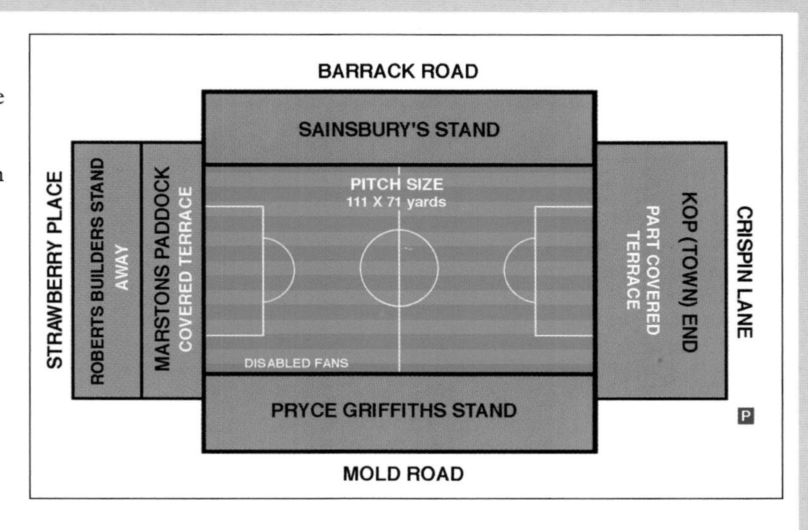

WYCOMBE WANDERERS

Causeway Stadium, Hillbottom Road, Sands, High Wycombe, Bucks HP12 4HJ

Tel No: 01494 472100
Advance Tickets Tel No: 01494 441118
Fax: 01494 527633
Web Site: wycombewanderers.premiumtv.co.uk
E-Mail: wwfc@wycombewanderers.co.uk
League: League Two
Brief History: Founded 1884. Former Grounds: The Rye, Spring Meadows, Loakes Park, moved to Adams Park 1990. Promoted to Football League 1993. Record attendance 15,678 (Loakes Park); 9,921 (Adams Park)
(Total) Current Capacity: 10,000 (8,250 seated)
Visiting Supporters' Allocation: c2,000 in the Roger Vere Stand
Club Colours: Sky blue with navy blue quartered shirts, blue shorts
Nearest Railway Station: High Wycombe (2 1/2 miles)
Parking (Car): At Ground and Street parking
Parking (Coach/Bus): At Ground
Other Clubs Sharing Ground: London Wasps RUFC
Police Force and Tel No: Thames Valley (01494 465888)
Disabled Visitors' Facilities:
Wheelchairs: Special shelter – Main Stand, Hillbottom Road end
Blind: Commentary available
Anticipated Development(s): With the completion of the new 2,000-seat Roger Vere Stand there is no further work currently planned.

KEY

C Club Offices
S Club Shop
E Entrance(s) for visiting supporters

North direction (approx)

1 Car Park
2 Hillbottom Road (Industrial Estate)
3 M40 Junction 4 (approx 2 miles)
4 Wycombe Town Centre (approx 2 1/2 miles)
5 Woodlands Stand
6 Roger Vere Stand (away)

Above: 692830; *Right:* 692818

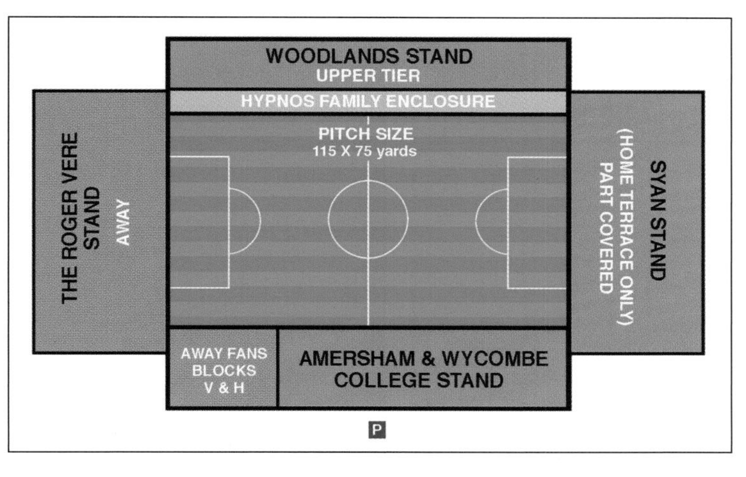

After a disappointing 2002/03 Lawrie Sanchez's position at Wycombe was always under threat and, following seven defeats in the first 11 games of the 2003/04 campaign, Sanchez was dismissed at the end of September after four and a half years at the club. The club moved quickly to appoint John Gorman, assistant to Glenn Hoddle at Spurs before both left, as caretaker. In early November the club announced that ex-Arsenal and England captain Tony Adams had been tempted to start his managerial career at Wycombe and that Gorman would remain as his assistant for a time. However, the latter left shortly after Adams' appointment. Unfortunately, Adams' arrival did not result in a dramatic improvement in form and League Two football beckons for the club in 2004/05.

YEOVIL TOWN

Huish Park, Lufton Way, Yeovil, Somerset BA22 8YF

Tel No: 01935 423662
Advance Tickets Tel No: 01935 423662
Fax: 01935 473956
Web Site: www.ytfc.net
E-Mail: webmaster@ytfc.net
League League Two
Brief History: Founded as Yeovil Casuals in 1895 and merged with Petters United in 1920. Moved to old ground (Huish) in 1920 and relocated to Huish Park in 1990. Founder members of Alliance Premier League in 1979 but relegated in 1985. Returned to Premier League in 1988 but again relegated in 1996. Promoted to the now retitled Conference in 1997 and promoted to the Nationwide League in 2003. Record Attendance: (at Huish) 16,318 (at Huish Park) 9,348

(Total) Current Capacity: 9,400 (5,212 seated)
Visiting Supporters' Allocation: 1,700 on Copse Road Terrace (open) plus c400 seats in Bartlett Stand.
Club Colours: Green shirts, white shorts
Nearest Railway Station: Yeovil Junction or Yeovil Pen Mill
Parking (Car): Car park near to stadium for 800 cars
Parking (Coach/Bus): As directed
Police Force and Tel No: Avon & Somerset (01935 415291)
Disabled Visitors' Facilities:
Wheelchairs: Up to 20 dedicated located in the Bartlett Stand
Blind: No special facility

KEY

- ⬆ North direction (approx)
- ❶ Western Avenue
- ❷ Copse Road
- ❸ Lufton Way
- ❹ Artillery Road
- ❺ Main Stand
- ❻ Bartlett Stand
- ❼ Westland Stand
- ❽ Copse Road Terrace (away)
- ❾ Memorial Road
- ❿ Mead Avenue
- ● To town centre (one mile) and stations (two to four miles)

Above: 695579; *Right:* 695573

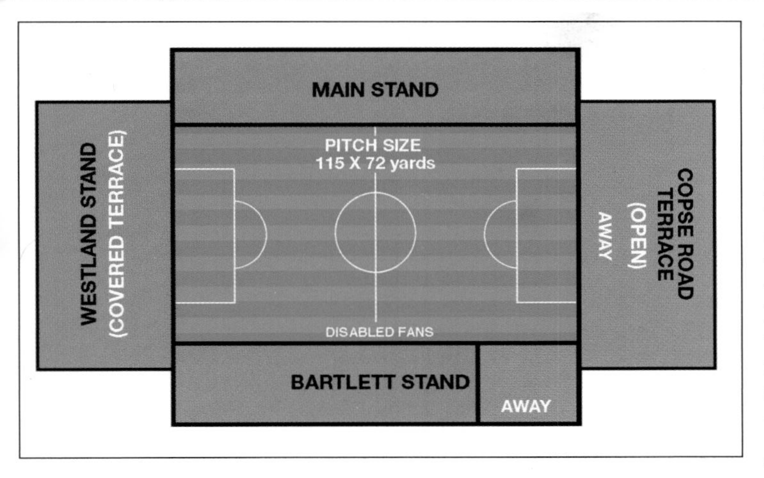

For much of the team's first season in the Football League it looked likely, if not probable, that Yeovil would be guaranteed a Play-Off position. Whilst never emulating Doncaster Rovers, whose rise to the top of the table was impressive, the Glovers seemed to be destined to achieve a Play-Off spot at worst. However, a late season loss of form meant that, ultimately, it came down to results on the last day of the season. Whilst the Glovers defeated rivals Lincoln City 3-2 at Sincil Bank, Northampton Town were also victorious, winning at Mansfield Town, with the result that Yeovil finished in eighth position losing out on goal difference to Lincoln City. Provided that Gary Johnson's squad can get over the disappointment of the last day than there is every possibility that the new season should again see the team threaten to achieve the Play-Offs at worst.

WEMBLEY

Wembley Stadium, Wembley HA9 0DW

Tel No: tbc
Advance Tickets Tel No: tbc
Fax: tbc
Brief History: Inaugurated for FA Cup Final of 1923, venue for many major national and international matches including the World Cup Final of 1966. Also traditionally used for other major sporting events and as a venue for rock concerts and other entertainments. Last used prior to redevelopment as a football ground versus Germany in October 2001. Ground subsequently demolished during late 2002.
(Total) Current Capacity: tbc
Nearest Railway Station: Wembley Complex (National Rail), Wembley Central (National Rail and London Underground), Wembley Park (London Underground)
Parking (Car): Limited parking at ground and nearby
Parking (Coach Bus): As advised by police
Police Force: Metropolitan
Disabled Facilities
Wheelchairs: tbc
Blind: tbc
Anticipated Development(s): After several years of dithering and following the final game played at the 'old' Wembley, demolition of the old ground was completed in late 2002 and work started on the construction of the new stadium. This is scheduled for completion in 2006.

Above: 697407